# A Staff Guide to Addressing Disruptive and Dangerous Behavior on Campus

There is an increasing population of students coming to college who challenge and frustrate staff. Students struggle with complex mental health problems, environmental stress, anger difficulties, and the potential for explosively acting out with threats or violence. This practical guide provides college and university staff with direction when working with these students in a variety of college environments, including community colleges, four-year institutions, and online learning environments. Coverage includes how to identify and assess students who are at risk, calm and de-escalate a crisis, motivate and inspire change, and how to manage and maintain change in a positive direction over time. Grounded in theory and research, this book offers practical and tangible advice and guidance to make it easier to assist students in need.

**Brian Van Brunt** is Senior Vice President for Professional Program Development at the National Center for Higher Education Risk Management (NCHERM), USA.

**Amy Murphy** is Assistant Professor of Student Development and Leadership in Higher Education at Angelo State University and formerly the Dean of Students at Texas Tech University, USA.

# A Staff Guide to Addressing Disruptive and Dangerous Behavior on Campus

Brian Van Brunt and
Amy Murphy

Routledge
Taylor & Francis Group

NEW YORK AND LONDON

First published 2018
by Routledge
711 Third Avenue, New York, NY 10017

and by Routledge
2 Park Square, Milton Park, Abingdon, Oxon, OX14 4RN

*Routledge is an imprint of the Taylor & Francis Group, an informa business*

*Library of Congress Cataloging-in-Publication Data*
A catalog record for this book has been requested

ISBN: 978-1-138-63193-9 (hbk)
ISBN: 978-1-138-63194-6 (pbk)
ISBN: 978-1-315-20853-4 (ebk)

Typeset in Perpetua
by HWA Text and Data Management, London

To mom and dad. For showing me what strength looks like and how to use it with kindness and grace.

– A.M.

To Jason Ebbeling. You were a friend and mentor. The world is darker without you in it. I miss your Cali ways and pirate poker skills. Rest well, my friend.

– B.VB.

"I'm sick of sitting 'round here trying to write this book..."
— Bruce Springsteen, *Dancing in the Dark*

"Fabulous secret powers were revealed to me the day I held aloft my magic sword..."
— He-Man and the Masters of the Universe

# Contents

# Tables

# Preface

If you have been in the field of higher education for more than a few months, it's likely you have begun to collect stories of disruptive and dangerous student scenarios you have encountered. The students we care about so much have been known to be the source of endless frustration and annoyance for even the most seasoned staff.

The words we use to describe these students don't change much across the country. Taken together, they read like a spectrum of escalation: entitled, frustrating, annoying, demanding, disrespectful, inconsiderate, aggressive, threatening, and violent. These challenges often leave staff feeling strained and tired, questioning how best to approach these situations, and feeling stressed and overwhelmed.

Bringing together our experiences as Director of Counseling, Dean of Students, and teaching faculty, we hope to share with you some guidance and advice to better address student behavior that pushes our buttons and challenges our sense of equanimity. The book is written for the variety of staff who work with students across the campus community, from administrative supervisors to front office staff, from residential life to academic advising. While the advice and guidance is similar in many ways across the different departments, we wanted to make sure to include clear examples and practical advice for each department and position.

The structure of the book is straightforward. The first half outlines foundations and theory related to addressing student behavior. The second half contains practical advice and case studies to put the foundations and theory into practice. Chapter 1 outlines the difference between disruptive and dangerous behavior with clear examples and case studies. Chapter 2 helps the reader better understand the multi-faceted challenges colleges face working with a deep variety of students from different generations, with mental health challenges, and across a variety of campus settings including brick and mortar schools and those with a stronger online presence.

It is helpful to see Chapters 3, 4 and 5 in context of each other. They offer a detailed review of three important phases to bring about change. These are handling the initial crisis, offering support to inspire change, and managing the ongoing behavior.

Chapter 3 addresses the initial phase of crisis where a student often presents with aggression and potential violence. There is a discussion of identifying signs of imminent danger, understanding how a student may escalate, and the importance of developing a calm, cool, and collected stance to address the behavior. There is also a discussion of how student development theory helps those intervening in a crisis to have a deeper understanding of the motivation and context of the crisis.

Chapter 4 describes for the reader how to best motivate and inspire change with students after the initial crisis has been managed or addressed. We review the importance of forming relationships through the building of rapport, how to maintain roles and boundaries with those we are trying to help, and a practical review of how techniques such as motivational intervening, change theory, and Rational Emotive Behavioral Therapy (REBT) can be useful to assist those who are struggling with change. The chapter concludes by highlighting the importance of referral and working together as part of a larger community.

Chapter 5 addresses the larger issue that all student behavior does not resolve once the initial crisis is resolved and inspirational advice and guidance is given. Many times, the student behavior remains and the student becomes a "frequent flyer" to a given department. The chapter reviews the approaches outlined in positive psychology, how to achieve longer term happiness and success, addressing anger, and making a plan and sticking to it. We review the importance of staying solution focused and how to be trauma-informed when working with longer term problems. The chapter concludes with a discussion of how staff can care for themselves when working with challenging students.

Behavioral Intervention Teams (BITs) exist on most campuses to help identify potential violence and develop ways to intervene. Chapter 6 discusses current trends in BITs as well as reviewing concepts related to threat assessment and dangerousness. Staff are expected to understand their role as the eyes and ears of the BIT and assist with the threat assessment process.

The second half of the book offers six chapters outlining specific advice for different departments around campus. Each chapter contains a brief overview of the central concepts unique to the departments being discussed followed by five to six case studies. Each case study offers a central narrative, review of the key concepts related to calming the initial crisis, motivating and inspiring change, and managing the ongoing behavior. Discussion questions are provided to allow the reader to explore the case studies in more depth.

Chapter 7 offers advice and guidance to residential life staff who are working with difficult and challenging students. The case studies include issues related to dating violence, roommate conflicts, eating disorders, anger, and aggression, suicide, and racial tensions. Chapter 8 focuses on academic advisors and the challenges they face in the quick-paced, time pressured world of offering support and advice to students related to their academic challenges. Case studies include issues of confusion over course of study, arguing with faculty, isolation and depression, veteran challenges, and relationship problems.

Chapter 9 provides insight for front office staff on how to meet the challenges of working with disruptive and dangerous students who show up to their departments demanding resolution to their problems. Case studies include addressing a financial aid crisis, graduation concerns, mental health crisis, overuse of services, demanding and entitled behavior, and aggression and threat. Chapter 10 offers a discussion for case management staff seeking to address behavioral concerns in their work. The chapter opens with an exploration of case management concepts and why this growing division is so essential to a campus. Case studies include recovering from a trauma, working with an international student, addressing aggressive behavior, and working with mental health challenges and social isolation.

Student activities staff are given advice and guidance in Chapter 11. This broad term addresses staff who may be working with student organizations, fraternities, and sororities, campus programming boards, athletic teams, multicultural and diversity programs, orientation programs, or recreational sports. Case examples include addressing inappropriate group behaviors, how to intervene with bullying, responding to a sexual assault, helping with depression, discussing racial comments, and addressing conflict among group members. Chapter 12 offers advice for a wide range of departments including: admissions and orientation staff, marketing and public relations, custodians, food service, parking, grounds staff, and campus administrators. Cases are written to reflect the various departments. The chapter concludes with an overview of how to train supervisors and staff in these departments on the topics offered in the book.

Chapter 13 concludes the book with a discussion between the authors on the central concepts taught throughout. This humorous, personal exploration seeks to bring the concepts home to the reader in a more personable and entertaining manner. The chapter includes some reflections on the most important aspects of crisis de-escalation, tailoring interventions to students, self-care, emerging competency areas for staff to manage disruptive and dangerous students, addressing microaggressions and BIT, and threat assessment.

Joe Allen, a friend and colleague of the authors, shares some important thoughts about customer service in the Afterword. Joe discusses the difference between the gold and platinum rules, understanding the context of the crisis, factors that contribute to escalation, and the importance of effort and focus in our interventions.

In Appendix A, the authors include a detailed series of forty-five additional training case scenarios for Resident Advisors in a Behind-Closed-Doors training fashion. Appendix B contains a planning worksheet helpful for staff looking for ways to set goals with students.

# PART I

# FOUNDATIONS AND THEORY

# Chapter 1

# Introduction

## Defining Disruptive and Dangerous Behavior

> I carried a watermelon.
>
> Frances "Baby" Houseman, *Dirty Dancing*

The work we do each day helping and assisting students is important work. Whether we offer academic support, resolve a roommate conflict, assist a student navigating financial aid forms, give advice on whether to add or drop a course, or simply carry a watermelon, it is important work. And while the work is rewarding, it can also be demanding, draining, and difficult.

Sometimes we need some help.

This book helps the reader better handle some of the most difficult and demanding student behaviors they experience. It was written as a follow-up to the 2014 book *A Faculty Guide to Addressing Disruptive and Dangerous Behavior.* During our training engagements throughout the country, faculty found the concepts related to classroom management extremely useful in managing crisis events as well as knowing when to refer students to Behavioral Intervention Teams (BITs) for follow-up and further management.

We thought a staff version would be equally well received. As we traveled, staff asked for a book written from their perspective. While we made some initial arguments that the faculty book concepts applied equally to staff scenarios, there was something to be said about writing a book specifically for the staff audience who also struggle with challenging student behavior.

To this end, join us as we discuss effective ways to address some of the disruptive and dangerous behavior we see on campus and look at novel ways to address the problems facing new higher education staff professionals.

## PROBLEMS AROUND CAMPUS

Imagine Jose, a twenty-eight-year-old student overwhelmed by financial stress at home and the academic rigors of attending a two-year technical college. He is behind in several of his classes and becomes enraged that the tutoring and academic support center doesn't have an appointment open to read and proofread his paper before it is due tomorrow. He yells at the office staff and storms out of the office making a veiled threat that "this school better start taking me seriously or they will see what a bad hombre really looks like." The staff of the academic support center are worried about this threat and aren't sure what they should do now that Jose has left the building.

Think of Lina, an eighteen-year-old college first generation college student, living on a large four-year campus far from her rural home. She becomes increasingly isolated and depressed and is worried she made the wrong choice trying to come away to college. She spends her days tearful and homesick, starts missing classes, and her roommate shares with the Resident Advisor that Lina has started talking about "feeling trapped and like she should just end it all."

Consider Carlos, a thirty-four-year-old war veteran returning to college after several active duty tours in Afghanistan. He does well in his classroom environments but is someone who likes order and consistency in his work and time. He begins to become increasingly anxious that his military paperwork and financial aid forms haven't been processed correctly and shows up several times a day to ask the financial aid and veterans affairs office to check their records. The behavior is confusing to the staff and, beyond checking their records, they aren't quite sure how to help Carlos.

Three different students, all with different problems, all from different walks of life. Some staff may have the training and experience to notice the mental health difficulties, financial stress, and family expectations that contribute to the scenarios. Some may understand the cultural or generational differences that can exacerbate the incident into a crisis.

The key to being effective in these situations is for staff to better appreciate the motivating situational and environmental stressors and difficulties that today's students face on campus and be better prepared to de-escalate the current crisis, motivate and inspire the student to change their behavior, and manage ongoing behaviors. Chapter 2 will provide a more detailed overview of the foundational differences students have in terms of their experience and the effects of differences in generations, non-traditional students, veterans, culture, sexual orientation, mental health, and physical disabilities. These lay the groundwork for better understanding the worldview and unique challenges our students bring with them into our offices and departments.

While we make a case for recognizing the different stressors and mental health challenges facing today's college students, there is also the challenge of appreciating the different departments, training, and resources staff have at their disposal. Student affairs staff with master-degree training in counseling and student development theory may be better prepared than a student worker providing tutoring services. A campus library staff with amazing resources and training may be better prepared to address students in crisis than the lone staff member at a community college library with no training budget. Resident advisors with training and resources and the ability to meet face to face with students may have a better follow-up than disability advisors at an online school with high caseloads and limited training resources.

## WE ARE A PRODUCT OF OUR OWN SUCCESS

Before we start a dive into managing the disruptive and dangerous behaviors you encounter, allow us a brief soapbox moment. There is a tendency to see under-prepared college students as largely a failure of the admission department, overprotective parenting, or a general societal breakdown to prepare a new generation for academic study. While there is certainly some truth to these assertions, another way to look at the students who are crossing our doorways would be to see them as individuals striving to become better, wanting to better themselves, and reach for something valuable, albeit perhaps in uninformed, frustrating, and/or annoying ways.

We have raised a generation of students with early access to mental health care. They have had access to Individualized Educational Plans (IEPs) in ways that other generations could only have dreamed of having as supports during their K-12 study. Children and teenagers have access to better therapeutic care, medications, supportive therapy, and educational resources. They have had the support they need to reach for something other generations could never have dreamed of reaching for—namely college and university study.

Perhaps, a helpful starting place for working with students who push our buttons and challenge our very sanity and mental well-being is to acknowledge that we are working with a generation that has had extraordinary access to support and resources that has helped them, to no small degree, step into a path toward a college or university degree. Before learning ways to be more successful in our interventions, perhaps there is a value in seeing the students we are working with as truly striving to become something better.

And in this striving, it doesn't always look pretty. It annoys us. It looks entitled and arrogant. It seems selfish and lacking a nobler sense of altruism or purpose. It can feel threatening, disrespectful, and rude. But if we choose to see students from this striving lens, then perhaps we are more willing to emulate those qualities and ideals—helping, caring, understanding, kindness, empathy—that are precisely the kind of behaviors we want them to learn.

Students learn by example. And perhaps it is too early in the book to make such an assertion, but we'll take the chance nonetheless. When we are faced with a disruptive or dangerous student, see the crisis as an opportunity for us to demonstrate our skills. Our patience and grace, our kindness and empathic understanding. When we start here, we teach this parallel process to our students. We emulate what we want them to become.

## DISRUPTIVE OR DANGEROUS?

An important question to grapple with throughout the book is centered on this idea of separating disruptive versus dangerous behavior. In the previous book, *A Faculty Guide* (Van Brunt and Lewis, 2014), the authors provided a list of behaviors that helped the reader sort out what we would consider disruptive or dangerous in the classroom. We have included a similar list for staff here.

### DISRUPTIVE BEHAVIORS IN PERSON

- Taking/making calls, texting, using smartphones for social media, etc., while waiting in line in front of you or while they are supposed to be engaging with you.
- Frequent interruption while talking and asking of non-relevant, off-topic questions.
- Inappropriate or overly revealing clothing, including extremely sexually provocative clothes, pajamas, or sleepwear.
- Crosstalk or carrying on side conversations while you are trying to speak. May be to a friend or on a phone.
- Interruptions in conversation, frequent use of the restroom, smoke breaks, etc.
- Poor personal hygiene that makes it difficult to continue a conversation.
- Lack of focus or paying attention to conversation. Excessive sighs or eye rolls.
- Use of alcohol or other substances in your presence. Attending a meeting while under the influence of a substance.
- Entitled or disrespectful talk to staff or other students.
- Arguing points of contention or asking for special treatment after the staff requests the student to stop.
- Eating or consuming beverages in meetings without permission (or against the office norms).
- Showing up to meetings in inappropriate or strange clothing (dressed in military gear, Halloween costumes when it is not Halloween, etc.).
- Reading magazines, newspapers, or books, or studying for other classes/doing other homework during a conversation with you.

### DANGEROUS BEHAVIORS IN PERSON

- Racist or otherwise exaggerated (not just expressed once to press a button) thoughts such as, "Women should be barefoot and pregnant," "Gays are an abomination to God and should be punished," "Muslims are all terrorists and should be wiped off the earth."

- Bullying behavior focused on students in the waiting room or outside the office or in the residence halls.
- Direct communicated threat to staff or another student such as, "I am going to kick your ass" or "If you say that again, I will end you."
- Prolonged non-verbal, passive-aggressive behavior such as sitting with arms crossed, glaring or staring at staff, and refusal to speak or respond to questions or directives.
- Self-injurious behavior such as cutting or burning self during a meeting or exposing previously unexposed self-injuries.
- Physical assault such as pushing, shoving, or punching.
- Throwing objects or slamming doors.
- Storming out of the office or room when upset.
- Conversations that are designed to upset other students or staff such as descriptions of weapons, killing, or death.
- Psychotic, delusional, or rambling speech.
- Arrogant or rude talk to staff or other students.
- Objectifying language that depersonalizes the staff or other students.

While the list is a helpful starting place, it is important to understand this as the floor, not the ceiling, the beginning, not the end of our discussion. There are certainly other behaviors that could be included on this list. There are arguments to move some listed disruptive behaviors into the dangerous category with additional context.

Beyond being able to identify these behaviors, we want the reader to understand a rather straight-forward concept. *Manage and de-escalate the crisis; pass the information to the BIT/conduct office.* This is the key to handling most crisis events that occur inside and outside the classroom. There is a need to deal with the immediate threat of violence or lower level disruptive behaviors and then there is a need to share this information forward with the campus conduct office or BIT.

To highlight this concept, let us share a story from our travels. The Registrar of a large urban community college shared a story to highlight the usefulness of some of our training on separating the student from the larger crowd, building supportive alliances, and listening to the student's frustration:

This student, who was like 17 or 18, and her mother, a woman in her 40s, came into our office. The student was very upset about not being able to register for a class she needed because there was a financial hold on her account. I had the student and her mother come into a side office we use for privacy and explained the situation. The student became increasingly irate and stood up and threw her chair against the wall. I asked her to leave and take a walk while I talked with her mother. The student walked and calmed down some and her mother and I worked out a plan that could have the hold released from her account. I gave the student a chance to talk about why she had gotten so upset and she shared how she felt trapped, panicked, afraid, and stuck. The three of us talked and the student apologized for getting upset and the situation resolved nicely for all involved.

Perhaps, you've a similar reaction to this story. It's nice that you resolved the crisis. In fact, that is quite wonderful. But what about the chair? Have we sent some message to the student that this kind of behavior is tolerable in our office?

What if, in this case, this is the student's go-to way of asking for help? Going all World Wrestling Federation (WWF) on anyone who disagrees with her and tossing a chair at the wall? While the registrar did a nice job of applying our crisis de-escalation concepts, she left out the second part of sharing up the information with the team or the student conduct office. For us, we would suggest a slightly different resolution to this story.

I talked to the student about how happy I was that things had worked out for her and the situation was resolved with her getting into the class she needed. I also shared how I was concerned that she was so angry that she had thrown a chair in our office. While we had resolved the one issue with the class, it is the university policy that I must send an incident report to the conduct office/BIT on what happened and she would have to meet with someone to explain her actions. I shared that I would put a good word in for her in the report, that she explained why she got upset and that she was remorseful. I also shared with her that while I'm glad this worked out for her today, this could have also resulted in campus police being called and her being arrested. The behavior was that concerning.

While we have discussed the behaviors that are disruptive and dangerous for staff in a face-to-face setting, many of our colleges and universities have staff that work with students through email or phone. The following are lists of disruptive and dangerous behavior that occur via email or phone.

## DISRUPTIVE BEHAVIORS VIA EMAIL OR PHONE

- Student posts non-relevant spam or unrelated personal advertising material in email or on website or social media page for the department.
- Frequent interruption of the staff questions with non-relevant comments or off-topic personal details on phone.
- Inappropriate or overly revealing pictures shared with members of the online community through the profile or staff email/website.

- Choosing a screenname or profile name that is offensive to others such as smokingthedope420@university.edu or assman69@university.edu.
- Emailing or making comments while drunk or intoxicated. Conducting phone calls while under the influence of alcohol or other drugs.
- Arrogant, entitled, rude, or disrespectful emails or messages to staff or other students.
- Arguing points of contention or asking for special treatment after the staff requests the student to stop.
- Inciting other students to argue with the staff over policy or other related expectations.

## DANGEROUS BEHAVIORS VIA EMAIL OR PHONE

- Racist or otherwise exaggerated thoughts such as, "Gays should be stoned like back in bible times," "Men should go back to playing football and stop thinking so hard. Leave the mental heavy lifting to the ladies in the class," "Muslims and Mormons are cults and should be wiped off the planet," emailed or discussed on the phone.
- Bullying and teasing behavior through messages, emails, or online hazing.
- Direct communicated threat to staff or another student, such as, "I am going to kick your ass" or "If you say that again, I will end you."
- Prolonged passive-aggressive behavior such as constant disagreement with everyone and everything related to departmental policy, challenging the staff's credentials, refusal to respond to questions or directives.
- Mentioning of self-injurious behavior, such as cutting or burning self or suicidal thoughts or intentions in emails or on social media.
- Threats of physical assault such as pushing, shoving, or punching.
- Threats of online assaults like hacking a website, sharing personal information, or posting pictures online without permission.
- Conversations that are designed to upset other students, such as descriptions of weapons, killing, or death.
- Psychotic, delusional, or rambling speech in an email.
- Arrogant, entitled, rude, or disrespectful messages to staff or other students.
- Objectifying language that depersonalizes the staff or other students.

## A MODEL FOR MANAGEMENT

There are three distinct phases for staff to be aware of when addressing student behavior of concern. These are 1) calming the initial crisis, 2) motivating and inspiring change, and 3) managing the ongoing behavior. We describe the approaches in detail in Chapters 3, 4, and 5.

## The First Phase, Outlined in Chapter 3, is Calming the Initial Crisis

This entails adopting a calm, cool, and collected stance in the face of upsetting or frustrating behavior, activating back-up as needed and applying crisis de-escalations skills to address the concerns. This approach is both an art and a science that requires study and experience to accomplish well.

Recall Jose, overwhelmed by financial stress who yells at the tutoring staff about not having time to read his paper. Before addressing larger issues of helping Jose plan better and be more respectful in his interactions, a key crisis de-escalation concept is to move from solution to listening. Jose is overwhelmed and the way to start an intervention with him is with hearing more clearly why he is overwhelmed before adding to his stress.

With Lina, struggling with homesickness and the potential for suicide, the Resident Advisor should be focused on making sure Lina has an immediate assessment for suicide with the appropriate clinical staff. Other issues such as her homesickness and missing class are important, but the central concept is ensuring a solid referral to a safety assessment.

Carlos, our war veteran experiencing odd anxiety related to his paperwork, starts with the staff adopting a calming approach that does not worsen the anxiety or contribute to his stress. There is less of a crisis with Carlos, yet his case reminds staff that starting from a position of being calm, cool, and collected in the face of odd behavior is essential.

## The Second Phase, Discussed in Chapter 4, is Motivating and Inspiring Change

Once the initial crisis has been addressed, the staff can adapt a bit more of a cheerleading/supportive role with the student, helping them with problem solving and overcoming obstacles. This should be done with an appreciation for the values and boundaries that are set forth as part of the job description. In other words, how does the staff member encourage the student to begin to develop their own critical thinking skills to better problem solve the difficulties they encounter?

For Jose, once the initial crisis of the paper is handled, he is someone in desperate need for guidance and support to learn how to better navigate the system. He likely is moving from crisis to crisis and barely staying afloat while at school. There may be frustrations he is struggling with related to family finances, being a non-traditional-age student or perhaps a hint at societal frustrations given his "bad hombre" comment as it relates to the 2016 presidential election.

Lina is another student in need of helping guidance and supportive mentoring. This may be found within the counseling center following her suicide assessment or perhaps afterwards with a caring staff member who helps her put her struggles in a different perspective. Lina is feeling trapped and in need of someone to help her understand her choices, relieve some of the pressure, or help see the pressure around her in the larger context of it not being this bad forever.

Carlos, like Lina, may need a more serious referral to on or off-campus counseling support to develop some better coping strategies with his anxiety and worry related to his study. He does well academically, but may be having trouble adjusting coming back from his service. A careful referral doesn't make assumptions about Carlos' behavior, but rather finds the best match for him to better get a handle on his worry in a productive way, addressing the larger pattern of behavior.

## The Final Phase, Explored in More Detail in Chapter 5, is Related to Managing the Ongoing Behavior

In many ways, this is one of the more difficult challenges for staff. The initial crisis is resolved and staff have done all they can to form a relationship and help the student develop critical thinking and problem solving skills. But. They. Keep. Coming. Back. The behaviors don't change and staff begin to become stressed to the point of burnout attempting to deal with the behaviors in front of them. In this stage, we encourage the use of additional resources, exploring supportive philosophies such as positive psychology, goal setting, and building self-care capacity for staff and departments.

For Jose, staff may be all too aware of the challenges facing non-traditional students who are trying to balance work, family, and academics. It is not the single student who presents with these problems that overwhelms, it's the seeming pandemic of students struggling in a similar manner. It is not the single drop of water that gets us wet, but rather the torrential downpour. While helping Jose individually is a good starting place, this phase encourages the development of networks of support for non-traditional students who may not utilize traditionally "houred" services as well.

For Lina, with her homesickness and depression, we look for ways to identify problems early to match interventions before the situation becomes worse. This may involve the counseling center or student affairs staff investing in a suicide-gatekeeper program to connect struggling students to existing care networks. It may involve training residential life staff in para-counseling support techniques.

Offering more focused veteran services for students returning from combat and adjusting to college is one way to help students adjust to the new requirements facing them. Carlos may be one of many students struggling with this transition and they may be able to support one another in a group setting or offer advice based on shared experiences.

In scenarios where there is the potential for violence or the need for further follow-up, we encourage staff to share this information with the student conduct office and/or the campus BIT. Staff are, and should be, concerned that some behaviors can escalate to targeted violence on campus. These types of threats are handled well by Behavioral Intervention and Threat Assessment Teams (BIT/ TATs), groups of concerned faculty and staff who meet on campus to discuss at-risk behavior, rate the behavior on a risk rubric, and develop intervention strategies. Threat assessment and BIT concepts are discussed in more detail in Chapter 6.

## PRACTICAL EXERCISES

It was important to us to not write a dry book that simply reviews theory. We wanted to write a book that helped the reader understand theory, but also immediately find ways to apply these concepts to various challenging cases they face every day within very different departments.

We address these departmental specific advice and guidance in the remaining chapters with a focus on case scenarios that apply directly to residential life staff (Chapter 7), academic advisors (Chapter 8), front office staff (Chapter 9), case managers (Chapter 10) and student activities staff (Chapter 11). We review some of the unique challenges found in addressing student behavior within the department focused on in each of these chapters. Each chapter contains five–six scenarios giving the reader practical advice through the three phases discussed in Chapters 3, 4, and 5: 1) calming the initial crisis, 2) motivating and inspiring change, and 3) managing the ongoing behavior. Chapter 12 offers the reader a bit of a "kitchen sink" approach to several additional departments such as admissions, marketing, public relations, custodians, food service, parking, and grounds staff. Each chapter also contains discussion questions designed to keep the reader thinking and engaged in the material during training opportunities.

## MOVING FORWARD

This isn't easy work. It's our hope that this book offers some practical and tangible advice and guidance to make it easier to assist those students who come to you in need.

We understand the difficulty: those feelings of anger at admissions for letting in students who clearly aren't ready to be at college; that chilling moment when you realize you may be the only one at the college able to help change the trajectory of a student who is quickly, and with certain emphasis, circling the proverbial drain.

We wanted to write a book that offers solid advice from the decades of experience we have accumulated helping students be successful at college. We wanted to write a book that will allow you to laugh and breathe a little, as many of the tools and approaches we suggest are important tools for your own self-care and well-being.

Since most of our content will be focused on the dangerous and the disruptive, we included a few light-hearted moments and stories along the way.

We also have a little secret for you. Your authors are children of the '80s. Big hair, Bon Jovi music, John Hughes movies, the original Super Mario Brothers, Up-Up-Down-Down-Left-Right-Left-Right-A-B-START, easy bake ovens—you get the idea. In that spirit, we gained inspiration from all things '80s for our quotes and examples. Surprisingly, some of our favorite characters in '80s classic movies offer us examples of student behavior that stretches us to our limits.

We think these examples offer a memorable way to teach many of the central concepts of this book. Even if you're not a child of the '80s, we hope our unique approach will keep you engaged throughout the book, looking for those hidden '80s references and, most importantly, help you remember important techniques and skills in your most difficult situations.

# Chapter 2

# Understanding Student Backgrounds and Experiences

> Gordie: Do you think I'm weird?
> Chris: Definitely.
> Gordie: No man, seriously. Am I weird?
> Chris: Yeah, but so what? Everybody's weird.
>
> *Stand by Me*

When we say "students," we need to start with the essential idea that each student brings with them a set of unique experiences. Whether these are rooted in generational diversity, cultural differences, sexual orientation, geographic distance, past experiences in the military, mental health conditions, or physical disabilities, it is helpful to understand these differences as they provide insight and assistance to managing potential disruptive or dangerous behavior that we encounter.

In addressing disruptive or dangerous behaviors, one of the first and most important aspects of successfully managing a crisis or creating lasting change is being able to view the situation from the other person's perspective. While this is never 100 percent achievable, we would encourage staff to make every attempt to look through the eyes and experiences of the students they are trying to help. Not because you have to, but rather, because this provides you a better insight into addressing the scenario in a manner that increases the success of your interventions.

Imagine a student from a different culture coming to college. They struggle with how to navigate the various policies and procedures of a department. Imagine this stress as cumulative: piled high on top of homesickness, trying to adjust to a new diet or climate or different predominate religion. These differences are both challenges and opportunities when reaching out to students to help.

This chapter provides a whirlwind tour of the differences we have found to be most prevalent for higher education staff to have a better understanding of to manage the challenges they encounter. This is not a definitive chapter on the background and experiences students bring to the campus environment, but instead a starting place to better understand some of the perspectives and potential motivations we encounter.

## GENERATIONAL DIVERSITY

> Lelaina Pierce: I was really going to be somebody by the time I was 23.
> Troy Dyer: Honey, all you have to be by the time you're 23 is yourself.
> Lelaina Pierce: I don't know who that is anymore.
> Troy Dyer: I do. And we all love her. I love her. She breaks my heart again and again, but I love her.
>
> *Reality Bites[1]*

For the first time in contemporary history, four generations of employees work side by side, bringing to the workplace their own unique set of talents, needs, and expectations (Toossi, 2012). A natural extension of this phenomenon is the changing workplace itself, as each generation brings its own set of values, priorities, and work styles. Keeping pace with these changes, while attempting to understand the differences in the generations is the focus of this section.

Whether you are the staff working with a younger student population, or perhaps a younger staff working with older, non-traditional students, the challenge is to better understand how each generation might approach conflict, change, challenges, and authority. While we don't want to foster stereotypes or assumptions, beginning from a place that seeks to better understand how a different generation approaches stress or difficulty will help increase the success of our interventions.

A generation can be defined as the aggregate of all people born over a span of roughly twenty years. Pioneers in our modern understanding of generations, Strauss and Howe's work in *The Fourth Turning* (1997) moves us beyond this static definition, to weave in intersections of place, time, and age (or development) as a more accurate way to describe the generational phenomenon. They describe a generation as being comprised of the twenty-year span, plus the commonalities of developmental stage (childhood or early adulthood) and *location in history* (historical events and social trends). This shared developmental/historical experience tends to produce a similarity of *common beliefs and behaviors* (in the workplace, this may be seen as work styles, attitudes, and priorities). Owing to an awareness of these common beliefs and behaviors, members of a given generation are said to have a *common perceived membership* in that generation.

A most effective way to demonstrate this phenomenon is to ask members of a specific generation about a historical event that occurred during their childhood or early adulthood. For example, ask a Boomer for their account of the day that John F. Kennedy was assassinated or of Martin Luther King Jr.'s march on

Washington, or ask a Gen Xer for their account of the events of 9/11 or the slow speed pursuit of O. J. Simpson. Demonstrated in this exercise, one sees that it is the combination of *developmental place in time* layered atop *historical context* that produces the rich and varied tapestry of the generation.

As we begin this discussion, let us address the elephant in the room. You may be reading this chapter to better understand the Millennials that come to your front office or live in your residence halls. In undertaking a discussion of generational diversity, we wish to address directly the topic of Millennials, the special snowflakes you have come to love, and the "helicopter parents" who have emerged, not coincidentally, during our work with Millennials as students. Colloquially, the term describes those parents who are overprotective and potentially stunting to the growth and development of their children. The relationship between Millennial child and parent is, in fact, a defining characteristic of this generation.

It is our opinion that the famously infamous stories we tell over water coolers are representative of a perfect storm of outlier parents. These folks, acting in downright ridiculous ways—calling their kids ten times a day, doing their laundry for them in the basement of the dorm, reading and editing assignments and papers, or yelling at housing staff to provide better accommodations for their child—coalesce against our collective frustration. We observe parents coddling their children, most notably evidenced in the now famous "participation ribbons" that hang ubiquitously in every Millennial's childhood bedroom. *And then, after all of that, we are meant to employ the children of these parents!*

At worst, Millennials are described as lazy, unmotivated, and lacking initiative to complete assignments and work tasks. As with helicopter parents, the argument we make here is that this perception—exemplified by the extreme, not the mean—coincides with our collective frustration around this newest entrant to the workplace generation. We argue that we are the proverbial grandparent throwing up hands and exclaiming, "In my day, we walked to school five miles in the snow, uphill both ways!" (Stay with us!) We challenge our reader to consider the perceived lack of work ethic and the resulting clichés which act in unproductive ways and serve only to foster damaging stereotypes of Millenials, as well as previous and future generations.

## Matures (Also, the Silent Generation)

Matures, now only 2 percent of the total workforce, are the most seasoned generation. They are conservative rule-followers who have lived through wars and seen waves of social change unfold through activism, civil unrest, and the turning tides of time. Matures are the least diverse generation as eight in ten are white (Fry, 2015). Matures understand that everything old is new again and bring with them a sage wisdom informed by age and experience. To younger generations, they may be seen as being out of touch with a fast moving, technology-enabled workplace. Leaders and managers may risk not capitalizing on the talents of Matures as their numbers dwindle and they move toward retirement.

America's seniors are coming back to college to explore unfulfilled desires, expand their horizons and learn to better navigate a more technological savvy world. They bring with them a wealth of experiences and expectations and may struggle at times to adapt to new ways of approaching challenging material. Successful interventions typically involve an acknowledgement of these accomplishments and the adventuring nature found in those willing to come to school despite how new and different things may be. Pairing with Matures and adopting a "we are in this together" approach may provide a useful strategy to affecting change or calming a crisis.

## Boomers (Also, Baby Boomers)

Boomers, now 29 percent of the total workforce, are the largest seasoned generation. Boomers may have delayed retirement, remaining in the workforce in direct response to shrinking retirement accounts resulting from the Great Recession, combined with the uncomfortable sandwich between caring for children at home and caring for their aging, longer living parents. Boomers were counter-cultural civil activists whose blood, sweat, and tears manifest the Civil Rights Act, bore the women's liberation movement and protested the Vietnam War. Owing to their counter-culture youth, Boomers may be the oldest relatable generation to employees, often being well liked and inspirational in their leadership abilities.

Staff may find themselves struggling to honor the historical position of Boomers in the workplace, given they have long enjoyed a position of power and attention there—that may wane as Generation X and Millennials come forward with new ideas, energy, and technological savvy. Approaching Boomers with an appreciation for their ideas and struggles, while partnering with them in finding a dual solution to challenges that present will be a more successful way of addressing a crisis.

## Generation X (Also, Gen X)

Generation X, only recently unseated by Millennials as the largest overall proportion of the contemporary workforce, make up 34 percent of workers and are seen as having big dreams and big hearts. These savvy, cynical problem solvers are liberals who lean left. In youth, they coined the phrase "mean people suck." Gen Xers are the rising tide of young leaders and are effective in this role, often working well at inspiring others to tasks.

Leaders and managers may risk not capitalizing on Gen Xers if they do not secure their buy-in prior to asking for their support, as Gen Xers typically have an aversion to the status quo, rejecting simply doing things because they are told to do so. Latch key kids of high divorce rates raised on *Mr. Rogers* and *Sesame Street*, those in Generation X often find themselves in need of praise and feedback. A swan song for the generation, Kurt Kobain's 1991 "Smells Like Teen Spirit" lyrics, "Here we are now, entertain us," characterized Gen X, as did the film *Reality Bites*.

At the risk of sounding repetitive, the key to successfully navigating a crisis or inspiring change with a Gen Xer will likely lie in staff's ability to acknowledge their approach to a conflict and look for a collaborative and novel approach towards solution. They will often repay kindness with kindness and starting from a position of respect and partnership will often net a more positive gain.

## Millennials (also, Gen Y)

Millennials range in age from mid-teens to early thirties, and make up 35 percent, the largest overall proportion, of the workforce. In youth, Millennials have evidenced lower rates of teen suicide, pregnancy, and abortion, and violent crime and drug use. These digital natives are the most diverse generation; about half are non-white. They are slow to get jobs, buy homes, and marry; having begun their economic lives during the Great Recession, they experienced a lack of economic foundation. Nevertheless, Millennials are optimists.

The Millennials' focus on teamwork positions them well to be future leaders, once professional experience and gravitas can be added to their résumés. Leaders and managers may risk not capitalizing on Millennial staff by presuming short attention spans and even shorter tenure within organizations. Strauss and Howe (2003) suggest that no other adult group possess their team player, high achieving reputation. And, it is against this description that the clichéd "Millennial as lazy and unmotivated" is most concerning. What is true of the Millennial is their determination to work *and* play in ways that previous generations could never have imagined.

When addressing Millennials in a crisis event or forming a more lasting connection with them to guide and mentor their behavior into a more positive outcome, the best advice we can share is to avoid the trap of treating them like Millennials. Millennial itself has become a bit of a trigger word. For many in older generations, there are frequent implications that they are lazy, stupid, unmotivated, or incapable of problem solving. Playing into their sense of optimism and giving them choices is one way to better motivate and inspire a Millennial to change their behavior in a crisis.

## Generation Z

Born in 1995 to 2010, this newest generation on the college campus is composed of true digital natives and the most racially diverse generation in history. According to Seemiller and Grace (2016) in their national study of this generation, Generation Z will have a work ethic similar to that of Baby Boomers, the resilience of Generation X, and be more technology savvy than even the Millennials. Generation Z students do not think of technology in separate items: phone, computer, gaming system. They instead see these items integrated into one tool that connects them to the world.

Generations are products of the society and families in which they were raised. With Generation X parents, this newest generation is used to parent and family influence and involvement in their life and continue to actively look to them as role models, but Generation X parents have learned that they must also help their kids to develop an independence different from the Millennials. When addressing Generation Z as it relates to potential issues of distress or during a time of crisis, messaging and communication with parents remains important as well as offering students the opportunity to involve their parents as mentors in their decision making. This can mean giving the student information that they can share with their parent and an opportunity to talk with them for advice and feedback.

Because of vast access to information and the systems in which they have been raised, Generation Z is an open-minded and accepting generation with a thoughtful willingness to engage with others who are different. They enter our schools with an invigorated sense of empathy, responsibility, and willingness to consider other perspectives that is different from Millennials. With their life experiences in a tough economic climate, they are not necessarily motivated by money, but instead by making a difference and opportunities for advancement (Seemiller & Grace, 2016). During conversations with Generation Z about behaviors of concern, it can be helpful to talk about how behaviors impact others and the campus community as well as the student's opportunity to proceed toward their goals.

Generation Z understands issues of violence, bullying, and discrimination. These are issues they grew up with in their early school environments and they likely participated in related educational sessions and programs in prevention. These students may respond favorably to the idea that the school is working to prevent and get ahead of these types of concerns. Staff should embrace transparency about college processes and information about how these actions enhance overall safety and opportunity for students in order to better engage Generation Z (Seemiller & Grace, 2016).

## Getting in Front of the Conflict

It isn't enough to learn about our generational differences, we must better understand the potential for those differences to turn into harmful generational stereotypes. This occurs when differences in values emerge as conflict within the workplace (also, in any house where a teenager and their parents cohabit).

**19**

Recognizing that our values are the bedrock of who we are, we can see the potential for conflict that can emerge when values differ. We add heat to these generational-based conflicts when one generation supervises, and therefore has power over, the other. Understanding the generational differences that exist across the workforce and the potential for conflicts that arise out of these differences is a leadership skill critical to anticipating and addressing them.

Moving forward, staff should learn and question more about their generational expectations and how these interact with others at the point of crisis. This is best accomplished prior to the crisis or disruptive/dangerous behavior occurs, during those slower times, during training events and orientations. Again, understanding another's perspective gives an opportunity to respond to the crisis or management event more wisely with a higher chance of success. We are not suggesting a person's generational viewpoint gives them cart blanche to behave badly, but rather insight for those attuned staff to better manage the crisis.

## NON-TRADITIONAL STUDENTS AND ADULT LEARNERS

I'm getting too old for this shit.

Roger Murtaugh, *LethalWeapon*

When offering training on non-traditional students, a woman in the back of the room joked, "You mean old, right?" And yes, older students are one of the many categories of non-traditional students who find their way into the classroom. But there are others who take "the path less traveled" into college, and this, more than solely age, is a better way to think of "non-traditional."

These other students include those who:

- don't enter college directly from high school;
- attend college part-time;
- work full-time while enrolled at college;
- are financially independent;
- have dependents other than a spouse (usually children, but sometimes others);
- are single parents;
- do not have a high school diploma; or
- may be coming back from military service or involved in The Reserve Officers' Training Corps (ROTC).

There are a myriad of reasons a student may take a non-traditional route through college. Some of these reasons are within the student's control, such as the benefits of asynchronous education and the flexibility of distance learning. Other reasons are related to external factors, such as current economic conditions or changes in the workforce that require different skills. Because of economic constriction and a desire to offer education to a wide range of individuals, schools have broadened their admission standards during the past few years (including community colleges and, of course, open-enrollment institutions). This has resulted in increased enrollment.

What are some of the differences and challenges non-traditional students pose for college and universities? Non-traditional students may require more personal connection and understanding of their life circumstances to move forward and achieve academic success (Dill & Henley, 1998; Gearon, 2008). While many non-traditional students come into college highly motivated with the technical skills needed for success, others struggle with basic technology such as sending an email with an attachment or using the cut-and-paste option in Microsoft Word. These differences require individual assistance and care from the professor to ensure the student doesn't fall behind. They may become easily discouraged and begin to think, "I can't do this. This is more than I signed on for. I'm not cut out for this" (Keith, 2007).

Disruptive behaviors may manifest with the non-traditional student related to a variety of reasons. A student might become frustrated by the speed at which material is being presented and frustrated with the staff for not providing them a way to obtain the material they need. They may be frustrated with the lack of deadlines or structure when they need structure to plan for the future or manage their time. They may struggle with balancing the roles of family and student life (Chao & Good, 2004; Greenhaus & Beutell, 1985).

## NON-TRADITIONAL STUDENT EXAMPLE

Imagine Claire, a non-traditional student coming back to school after years in the workforce. Claire feels overwhelmed by the technology around campus and lacks the basic skills to email, edit text in a word processing software program, or post on the online classroom discussion threads. Claire has trouble finding and completing online forms and is frustrated when staff redirect her to a website rather than talking with her.

Her anger grows and she begins to give off passive-aggressive, non-verbal behaviors to the staff such as frowning, grumbling under her breath, and loud sighs each time the staff makes a reference about an online resource or form. These disruptive behaviors have the potential of frustrating other students, interfering with her ability to learn the information, or escalating into more direct expressions of dissatisfaction.

The staff notices this behavior and engages in a conversation with Claire to see what she is upset about. The staff offers to help Claire during office hours to clarify the material and help her with some of the technology issues she is having. Claire flies into another rage. This time she raises her

> voice and yells, "That's just it! You don't understand. I have to work when I'm not here. I can't stop by your office because I'm either at work or watching my kids. That is why I'm so frustrated when I'm trying to get help and you move through the material so quickly!"

The stress of balancing work schedules and family life can contribute to non-traditional students feeling hopeless when trying to access support services (Kohler-Giancola, Grawitch & Borchert, 2009). Many campus offices post office hours strictly during the 9–5, M–F block of time. Tutoring and academic support, financial aid, and counseling services are often limited to traditional hours during the week. This can make it difficult for non-traditional working students to come to campus for meetings or support. These students often receive little empathy about the challenges of balancing school, work, family, and commuting (Gearon, 2008).

Hans Selye first defined stress in 1936 as "the non-specific response of the body to any demand for change." Stress is a broad term, impacting the physical, social, cognitive, and psychological parts of who we are. He introduced the term "eustress" in 1975. Eustress is a positive form of stress, usually related to a desirable event in a person's life. This may include planning a wedding, studying well for a hard final, or feeling good about a difficult workout. While stressful, the result reduces the overall stress level for an individual.

These "stress reactions" experienced by non-traditional students are the signs and symptoms that should be received as a "heads up" from their body in times of turmoil. Instructors should look for the various signs of stress that may affect non-traditional students in their classroom. These can include both cognitive symptoms (exhaustion, negative ruminating thoughts, inability to focus on a task, reduction in joy, mental fatigue, feelings of futility, and devaluing of others) as well as physical symptoms (headaches, teeth-grinding, insomnia, irritability, muscle tension, gastric disturbance, high blood pressure, rapid heartbeat).

During trainings, we often remind staff that being fair doesn't always mean equal. Policy and procedure are important, but non-traditional students thrive from a personal connection with staff. They do understand that you have a life too, so even a well-crafted email can suffice, as can a phone call. Identifying early signs of stress and expressing care and concern can go a long way in preventing disruptive and dangerous behavior in an office, residence hall, or campus department.

## VETERANS AND ACTIVE DUTY MILITARY PERSONNEL

> I wanted to see exotic Vietnam... the jewel of Southeast Asia. I, uh, I wanted to meet interesting and stimulating people of an ancient culture... and kill them. I wanted to be the first kid on my block to get a confirmed kill!
>
> Joker, *Full Metal Jacket*

Veterans are and will be returning from active duty to the classroom in record numbers (Wallis, 2012). Staff will be seeing more veteran students in their departments and offices, and in some of these cases, they will be struggling to find the best way to help returning soldiers.

Many vets make the transition into the college environment very well. One distinct advantage to a veteran is that they, unlike many students, understand bureaucracy at a very high level. They've lived it like no other student. Thus, they transition easily into the structured requirements of assignments, class attendance, and discussions (as well as financial aid, advising, etc.).

Others struggle greatly with post-traumatic stress disorder (PTSD) or with the adjustment following the traumatic experiences of fighting for their lives to worrying about completing a math assignment. According to the Department of Defense and *Time* magazine (Haiken, 2013), when compared to their peer groups, veterans (especially combat veterans) struggle at a higher level with depression, substance use, suicidal ideation, etc. This is not to say that all veterans are suffering from mental health issues, but that we should be attuned to their needs.

We should also remember that while these men and women have had experiences that their fellow students and we have not, they will share them as they see fit. Do not call on them and ask them to speak to their experiences. Do not ask them to speak for "all vets." Pay attention to anniversaries and events that may bring certain emotions (Veteran's Day, 9/11, Deployment anniversary—which you will likely not know the date of, etc.). Table 2.1 offers some practical suggestions for staff when working with Veterans.

## TABLE 2.1 Dos and Don'ts When Helping Veterans

| Dos | Don'ts |
| --- | --- |
| Do...ask about their service and ways you could be helpful to them in their adjustment to college. | Don't...pry into the details of their service and ask more questions when they seem uncomfortable. |
| Do...take into account their potential past experiences and be aware of how you address them in a crisis. | Don't...assume all veterans or active duty military have PTSD and treat them with "kid gloves." |
| Do...look for opportunities to refer or connect veterans and active duty military with others who may have served. | Don't...avoid helping, talking or automatically referring them to veteran staff because you haven't served. |
| Do...listen to what they say will be helpful for them and respond accordingly. | Don't...tell them how they should feel, assume their political affiliation or attitudes about past military conflicts. |
| Do...set limits about acceptable behaviors in the office related to threats, physical violence or yelling. | Don't...give veterans or active duty military a "free pass" for bad behavior and avoid using panic alarms and police involvement if the behaviors warrant. |

## DIVERSITY AND CULTURAL DIFFERENCES

> Well, someone's got to break the ice, and it might as well be me. I mean, I'm used to being a hostess, it's part of my husband's work. And it's always difficult when a group of new friends meet together for the first time, to get acquainted. So I'm perfectly prepared to start the ball rolling. I mean, I-I have absolutely no idea what we're doing here. Or what I'm doing here, or what this place is about, but I am determined to enjoy myself. And I'm very intrigued, and, oh my, this soup's delicious, isn't it?
>
> Mrs. Peacock, *Clue*

### Race

When addressing disruptive behavior in an office or in the residence halls, it is essential to be aware of our personal biases and history with interacting with those who may be different from who we are. While it is understandable to be cautious around something unfamiliar or someone new, there is a difference between simple discomfort and reading potential threat into a gathering of students. There's a difference between being cautious in a new city and a Caucasian person locking their car door as an African American person walks by.

Gossett, Cuyjet, and Cockriel (1998) found that African American students perceived significantly more discrimination from the administration, their peers, and staff when compared to white students. While not always intentional, prejudice and discrimination may come from students who've had limited contact with those different from themselves or those who make snap judgments about risk when witnessing African Americans hanging out in a group or dressing differently from what they are accustomed to. Ancis, Sedlacek, and Mohr (2000) found that African American students perceived significantly more racial tensions and separation than did white and Asian American students.

While staff are not expected to have a detailed understanding of all the cultural and racial differences that exist, a starting place is a term called cultural humility. This means taking a moment and putting your own race, your own culture, and your own background on hold and instead having a focus on what the other person may be experiencing given their unique background and experience.

Wherever you may stand politically on the issue of Black Lives Matter, one could argue chanting that in response "Blue Lives Matter" or "All Lives Matter" is problematic. Not because these other statements are not true, but because they lack a sense of cultural humility. When someone makes a stand that Black Lives Matter, they are expressing a sentiment about their history and experiences of cultural marginalization. When the response to such a statement is a claim that someone else is important too, it naturally has the effect that the original statement didn't matter to the listener.

Take the example:

Person 1: I really like cookies. They are so good.

Person 2: I like brownies. I think they are good.

Person 1: OK, but I was talking about cookies.

Person 2: Oh, I know, but brownies are more important to me, so I changed the subject.

Person 1: Well, OK then. Bye.

While this seems kind of ridiculous, this example sheds light on why defensive or aggressive responses to someone who is upset about a racial slight or microaggression make things much worse. Staff who are responding to a student who is upset about a racial slight or expressing frustration should not immediately redirect the conversation to their own experiences or try to normalize the student's experience. Instead, they should listen more to the student's point of view to form a stronger sense of rapport.

## International Students

Over 600,000 international students come to the United States each year to study (Hyun, Quinn, Madon & Lustig, 2007). More than half of the international students come from Asia, with the largest representation from China and India (Rothstein & Rajapaksa, 2004). International students have trouble adjusting to their new surroundings primarily because of culture shock (Poyrazli & Lopez, 2007).

When working with students who are in the minority population at your college or university, it will pay to educate yourself about the services (International Student Programs Office, or ISP, etc.) offered by your college. While you do not need to be versed in "all things visa," you should know what topics they have had covered in orientation (and whether they were able to attend); the ISP should be able to help you with this. Also, remember not to isolate them and/or ask them to "speak for all [insert race/culture/ethnicity/religion here]. "Too often, after 9/11 and during the wars, we heard from Middle Eastern and/or Muslim students who were asked to "educate the class" about their culture or religion. Can you imagine asking a Southern Baptist student to speak for all Protestants? Asking a white student to speak for all Caucasians or Americans of European descent? We would never do that to them; why do this to an international student?

We need to recognize that the cultural norms and mores of their home country are different from ours. Attitudes towards women, dating, clothing, and individuals of other cultures and religions are just a sampling of the issues. Even attitudes toward interacting with authority figures or policy discussions are different in different regions in the world. Thus, it is imperative that staff provide clarity about the expectations in these areas. But it must be made clear in a fashion

**25**

that indicates that the staff is just clarifying behavioral and academic expectations for all students, not just for the international students.

International students face a range of adjustment problems in addition to culture shock including homesickness and understanding the requirements of a new academic environment. The effects of homesickness are often negative and can include loneliness, sadness, and adjustment issues (Poyrazli & Lopez, 2007). Tseng and Newton (2002) outline four major areas of adjustment for students. These include 1) general living adjustments such as food, housing, financial transactions, and transportation, 2) academic adjustment to the university system and developing the skills they need to be successful, 3) adjusting to the cultural norms and behaviors, and 4) personal psychological adjustments such as dealing with feelings of homesickness, loneliness, and feelings of isolation (Hyun et al., 2007).

These problems can easily drift into campus departments and create challenges for managing behaviors that may be disruptive to the residence halls or offices. One of the biggest challenges for staff may be overcoming the language barrier to communicate with students about department policies and norms. International students may have differing expectations for what is considered normal within the campus community and language differences may make it difficult to communicate these expectations.

When international students struggle with mental health problems such as homesickness, depression, and anxiety, they may be less likely to seek assistance. Hyun et al. (2007) suggest a host of factors for this resistance for accessing services. These factors include a lack of awareness of their needs for mental health services, the retention of health-related beliefs and practices from their home country, and the cultural stigma associated with emotional expression.

Staff who help international students with their transition will be more successful if they work with international support service departments, friends, and advisors. Hyun et al. (2007) find international students rely more heavily on their peers, rather than professionals, for both social support and information about resources. Staff can assist international students connect with their advisor. International students who have better relationships with their advisors are less likely to report having stress-related or emotional problems and are more likely to utilize counseling services (Heggins & Jackson, 2003; Rai, 2002).

When approaching internationals students in crisis, staff should first attend to any language barriers that may exist. This may require enlisting a supportive staff or peer who can assist with translation. This kind of communication can be even more difficult when trying to communicate subtle social norms around behavior in an office or the residence halls. Staff will be more successful in their interactions if they have a working knowledge of the international student resources on campus. There is typically a staff person or department tasked with helping international students through problems that may occur on campus.

## Gay, Lesbian, Bisexual, Transgender, and Queer

Conservatively speaking, there are over 8.8 million gay males, lesbians, or bisexuals in the United States (Chonody, Rutledge & Siebert, 2009). When working with students who are in this minority population at your college or university, there can be challenges that occur around campus or in the residence halls that can make managing disruptive or dangerous behavior difficult. Students who are gay, lesbian, bisexual, transgender, queer, or questioning (GLBTQ) often come to a meeting or living environment with a history of being bullied, teased, and treated poorly by others. This is certainly not the case for everyone, but these students may report lower levels of perceived social acceptance, lower levels of psychological well-being and lower levels of physical well-being (Woodford, Howell, Silverschanz & Yu, 2012).

Staff should be aware of the impact of certain stigmatizing language and how this language impacts GLBTQ students. While the staff would certainly be expected to avoid using phrases such as "That's so gay," they should be aware that the use of this phrase and the negative impact is common on college campuses (Woodford et al., 2012). The word "gay" is frequently used to describe something as stupid, weird, or undesirable. Students who hear or are exposed to this language experience negative effects. Even the term "homosexual" has moved into a questionable realm of propriety and has been replaced by "gay or lesbian" (Chonody et al., 2009).

There may even be the potential for some students to defend the phrase "that's so gay" by downplaying their intent and offering that this phrase isn't meant to be hateful for the GLBTQ population. Certainly, some argue, it is not as hateful as terms such as "fag" or "dyke." It may be that the research supports a continuum of negative experiences following these different phrases; however, none has a place in the college or university setting. Staff are encouraged to develop some language to respond to these arguments before they occur, perhaps including a statement in the department regulations about expectations around community, supporting each other, and being aware of how language may affect different people in different ways. As with sexual harassment language, the issue here is not so much the intent of the statement, but the impact.

Staff should be aware of potential conflicts among groups of different students in their offices and the residence halls. Research supports several groups that more frequently correlated with high levels of anti-gay biases. These include: religiosity, persons who are from the Midwest or South, those from more rural childhood settings, and those who have little contact with gay and lesbian individuals (Chonody et al., 2009). We would suggest these as starting places for awareness and education, rather than blindly assuming anyone from the rural south who is religious hates gay students. That would be an unsupported extrapolation.

When offering education and support to students around GLBTQ issues, Ben-Ari (1998) suggests a threefold education process. This includes "exploring

**27**

one's own history, learning the facts and getting to know lesbians or gay men" (p. 62). This could involve reflective group discussions in the residence halls around understanding early beliefs and messages from family or panel discussions with GLBTQ students to address any myths or incorrect information (e.g., all people who are gay have AIDS and were molested as children).

One approach to addressing the experiences of GLBTQ students prior to conflict in the residence halls could be inviting a campus speaker to discuss these issues. This could involve a program such as Safe Zones. Safe Zones is described at one college as the process where: "A number of faculty and administrators set out to create a network of faculty, support staff, and students who, after receiving training, would display a pink triangle outside their doors as a representation that a member of the LGBTQ community could find therein a resource for information, support, and, if needed, safety" (Alvarez & Schneider, 2008, p. 71).

## First Generation College Students

The definition of first generation college student varies from campus to campus and study to study. It can mean a student who has one or both parents or guardians who did not earn a college degree or did not attend college. Regardless of how they are defined, first generation college students have lower college attainment rates than students with a parent or guardian with college experience (Smith, 2015). First generation college students are often considered an underserved population alongside racial and ethnic minorities as well as low-income students. They may struggle financially, psychologically, academically, and professionally (Banks-Santilli, 2015). As with any population of students, it's important not to generalize and instead consider the individual student's background, experiences, and needs.

While some first generation college students may have very supportive parents or family members as part of their college experience, others will struggle to navigate the college environment from the campus jargon to understanding the resources and opportunities available to them. In many ways, staff should just assume that all students are first generation and need clear explanations of processes and resources important to student success. If a parent or family member is involved in a student's situation, staff should remember that they are likely equally unfamiliar with college protocols. Explaining the difference between what they experienced in the high school environment as compared to the college environment can give them a point of reference for what to expect in terms of involvement with their student.

You can imagine if a student is coming from a community or background with little college experience then the student may not feel supported in their academic goals. At the same time, the student is struggling to feel a sense of belonging in the new college environment. The combined effect of both experiences can create conflict and stress for the student and have a psychological impact (Banks-Santilli, 2015). Skills of empathy and active listening are important to understand why a student is struggling and why they may be behaving in certain ways. Assisting first generation college students in making connections to other students as well as faculty and staff mentors can be a helpful way to assist with their success. These same connections can assist during times of distress and disruption as well.

## MENTAL HEALTH

> Lloyd: How are things going, Mr. Torrance?
> Jack Torrance: Things could be better, Lloyd. Things could be a whole lot better.
>
> *The Shining*

There are a wide range of mental health disorders that keep college students from performing at their optimal potential. Understanding the common mental health disorders experienced by college students may allow staff to better understand and intervene during crisis events.

This section is dedicated to sharing some basic information with staff to better understand some common mental health behavioral difficulties they may encounter while working at a front office, in the residence halls or department. Examples include suicidal behavior, off-topic or poor attention related to a personality or Autism disorder, manic behavior, delusions and hallucinations, eating disorders, and substance abuse. The section focuses on practical advice on how to approach student behavior.

The section is not meant to provide a comprehensive summary of all mental health concerns, just the most common issues experienced by staff. Likewise, the section does not set out to offer a complete review of these six mental health concerns. Other texts offer this kind of substantive review of mental health symptomology, pathology, and treatment. The goal is to provide staff an abbreviated field guide to addressing common mental health difficulties that may arise on campus.

### Depression and Suicide

Students who experience suicidal thoughts often experience depressive symptoms. These symptoms can include difficulty sleeping or eating (either more or less than normal), a lack of interest in activities that they used to enjoy (going to the movies, hanging out with friends) and general feelings of unhappiness and hopelessness for a better future. While students can be depressed without feelings of suicide (often described as a more lethargic unhappiness or dysthymia), it is rare for a student to experience suicidal thoughts without depression.

The degree to which a student experiences suicide is important to understand for staff. For those with *low suicide experiences*, students experience fleeting thoughts of wanting their pain and the frustrations of everyday life to end. These feelings and thoughts may not contain any plan for the student to kill themselves or, if there is a plan, the plan is vague ("Someday I may just start walking at night and never come back"), non-lethal ("I'm going to take five or six aspirin and go to sleep") or far in the future ("Sometimes I think about just ending my life when I finish college"). Students who experience low suicide experiences need to talk with a professional counselor before these thoughts increase. Staff are often able to refer these students for help at the on-campus counseling center or other community resources.

Other students may have *moderate suicidal experiences*. These students spend time thinking, dreaming, and planning about how they will kill themselves. There is a more serious content and tone to their suicidal talk. There are often feelings of hopelessness and sadness about their current life and the direction it is heading. While there is not a current date and method expressed for when they will take their life, they are putting together plans to narrow down this information. A student may say, "I am sad all the time and I don't see things changing. I've been thinking more about stepping in front of a train when I am out walking at night. I don't know what to do." Staff should report this kind of talk or ideation immediately, ideally with the student available for a follow-up meeting with a counselor or other mental health professional.

Students with *severe suicidal experiences* have a plan, date, and time for when they are going to kill themselves. They are not safe to leave alone and have often become so hopeless and full of pain they believe the only relief from their predicament is through suicide. They have struggled with their pain for quite some time and now have a sense of inevitability about their decision to kill themselves. Many times, they write goodbye notes to their friends, give away their personal belongings, and reduce any obstacles that might get in the way of their choice to die (hoarding pills, obtaining a firearm, collecting a rope, and finding a place to hang themselves). Instructors may be able to witness these exchanges. A student may say, "I'm done. I won't be here tomorrow. I just wanted to let you know."

Staff are required to take immediate action with these students to refer them to help. This may involve calling the police or emergency services. The only way to know the level of depression or suicide with a student is to engage them in conversation about what they are feeling. Staff need to ask questions to learn how students view their current situation. This requires staff to engage students in a conversation about their thoughts of depression, suicide, and self-harm.

Depression is more than just a having a bad day. We all can relate to having a bad day, even a series of bad days. Depression is more serious than this. It's as if a weight bears down on the student and leads them to become lethargic, apathetic, and they struggle to see any hope that things will improve. Depression is beyond a bad day or series of bad days. It is an overwhelming burden and all-encompassing sense of dread and hopelessness that surrounds the student. Depression can have both an environmental component and a biological component. Treatment often involves talk-therapy as well as having a medication evaluation. Any student who struggles with depression is at a higher risk for suicide. Staff need to ask direct questions about suicide to any depressed student.

Staff should be in the position to offer help regardless of their department or position. Helping suicidal students is not a function limited to psychologists, counselors, and social workers. Depression can feel like a difficult topic to discuss, so staff avoid talking to students about it because they don't feel qualified or don't have any easy answers for the depressed student. If you notice a student who is depressed, reach out to them and try to help. Work with your counseling center, department head, or campus BIT to keep them informed, and seek out ways you can be most helpful to the student.

Students who are depressed often experience sleep and appetite disturbances. Others experience lethargy or an upset stomach. Sometimes the only outward signs of depression we see are those physical disturbances. Many times, students in college have sleep and appetite problems as well as homesickness, stomach problems adjusting to the food, and feelings of tiredness. The only sure way to know what is depression and what are normal adjustment issues is to talk to the student in question.

Getting someone's help for depression can be a daunting task. Students with depression often lack the energy needed to follow through with the healthy steps laid out in front of them (e.g., getting to therapy, attending class, seeking support from friends, exercising, and staying on medication). One way staff can help is to offer extra support during the early stages of treatment. Once a student begins to recover, it is likely he or she will need less and less support. Staff should also seek support from their supervisor, counseling center, or campus BIT in order to remain positive and effective with the student they are trying to assist.

Remember, some students are very clear about their suicidal statements: "I am going to kill myself" and "I can't live any more. I am going to do something to end my life." More frequently, students make vague statements that provide only a hint of their true intentions, "I don't want to be here anymore" or "I can't live this way; I'm too exhausted to go on." Staff need to have keen detective ears when it comes to listening to students who are depressed and potentially sharing suicidal thoughts.

Sometimes, students express suicidal thoughts frequently. Staff may be tempted to see the situation like the boy who cried wolf. It can be frustrating when a student continually voices a desire to die. However, each suicidal statement must be taken seriously. No staff wants to be in a position of ignoring the one serious suicidal statement in a sea of false statements. Take every conversation about suicide with a student seriously. Ask yourself, "If the student kills himself tonight, have I done all I need to do in order help?"

## Asperger's

Autism Spectrum Disorder (ASD, formally known as Asperger's Disorder) is a developmental spectrum disorder that impacts an individual's ability to read subtle social cues (such as flirting, sarcasm, or teasing) and function in social situations. They may also experience distractions in the academic or residential life setting. This may include sensitivity to stimuli such as florescent lights or loud noises, hyper-sensitivity to living close to other students or being overreactive to small slights or frustrations. Students with an ASD may have very intense, very idiosyncratic interests such as collecting items or obsessive interests in particular subject areas. They may also display odd movements, ways of interacting, or unusual speech tones as they talk.

Students with an ASD and those with social behavior problems are increasingly finding success in colleges and universities. Students are having better success with the additional support they are receiving in college through the Americans with Disabilities Act (ADA) and counseling support. *It's important to understand that all students with ASD are not the same.* ASD is a spectrum disorder, which means that some have very few disruptions and others have extreme difficulty functioning. While a general understanding of the traits and characteristics of ASD can be helpful to better work with the student, these should not be used to "box in" the student and limit their potential.

Staff are not expected to be mental health professionals who determine the exact nature and type of problems a student experiences. Some students may meet the diagnosis of ASD, while others may have social problems, attention problems, or a personality disorder. The purpose of this section is to help staff work more effectively with students who may exhibit behavior that disrupts an office, department, or residential life environment.

Students with these social difficulties, whatever their diagnosis, often experience difficulty and teasing from other students. They may find themselves manipulated in social relationships or being teased because of their interests, questions, or social difficulties. Again, as a spectrum disorder, some ASD students may do very well in college either because their level of symptoms is not particularly severe or they have invested in therapy and social skills training to overcome these differences.

Staff interacting with a student who has ASD should make their communications calm, clear, concise, and consistent. The student with ASD struggles with subtle communications or inconsistent rules or instructions. They may be sad or depressed about how others are treating them and need some added explanation or support to avoid teasing. They may also not notice others teasing them and have difficulty weighing the social costs of their odd or unusual questions or interests.

## WHAT TO EXPECT FROM AUTISM SPECTRUM DISORDER/ASPERGER'S STUDENTS

- Mental health problems have some commonalities, but also have a degree of uniqueness to each individual. Be careful about applying broad strokes. Each student, regardless of whether they have ASD or not, needs individual attention and adaptation.
- Students with ASD may ask odd or repetitive questions that derail the meeting and distract others. They do not do this to annoy. It is their natural way of communicating.
- They are often teased or laughed at by other students who pick on them or talk quietly behind their back.
- They may have poor hygiene or manners. This is related to their inability to empathize and connect to the feelings and perceptions of others (again, be careful not to generalize; other ASD students may take obsessive care of their hygiene).
- They may engage in odd dress or write on their clothes or arms. This may include black or medieval looking clothes. They may speak with strange inflections or use languages based on their reading or computer gaming.
- They may have odd interests (e.g., car motors, Victorian door hinges, or vintage toys) that interfere with them connecting with their peers and engaging in more socially acceptable activities.
- They have difficulty reading social cues (standing to leave, subtle messages to stop talking, non-verbal signals). This becomes even more difficult when dealing with issues that are built upon subtle social cues such as flirting or on social networking sites such as Facebook.
- Their attempts to connect with peers will often seem flat or slightly off. Caring students help these types of students connect and overcome these "quirks." Students who are frustrated or stressed will often ignore or tease the student with ASD.

## Anxiety

What is anxiety? Well, for starters, anxiety is a very useful part of who we are as people. Without anxiety, college students wouldn't study for their tests, talk to their parents, drink in moderation, or even be able to safely cross the street. Anxiety, at its core, helps us set limits on our behavior. Without this limit-setting anxiety, people would say and do whatever they want. That would lead to chaos.

Anxiety provides some important safety limits to our behavior. It keeps us wearing coats in the winter to prevent freezing to death, washing our hands to protect from germs, not yelling at the mixed-martial arts fighter who cut in front of our line. Anxiety is a safety mechanism hard-wired into our brains.

Anxiety becomes problematic when it expands beyond the normal range. Students who experience anxiety disorders may become anxious about filling out a Free Application for Federal Student Aid (FAFSA) form or residential life checklist the same way others normally would become anxious if a tiger ran across campus. Imagine the panic, sweating, tunnel vision, difficulty breathing, and feeling of impending dread. Fight, Flight, or Freeze!

This level of reaction over a form is out of step with the perceived threat. It is exactly appropriate given a tiger on campus. The problem then becomes one of understanding why some students become so anxious and experience panic attacks at the thought of filling out a form, presenting in front of other students, at the prospect of asking someone out or worrying about getting a perfect 4.0 Grade Point Average (GPA) when a 3.3 GPA would suffice.

Anxiety can occur because of early trauma or early expectations about behavior. The anxious reaction (panic attack, continuous worry, paranoia) becomes linked to an idea or event that doesn't need that kind of reaction. Perhaps there was a physical beating that came with talking out of turn when a student was growing up as a young child. This then becomes a connection they bring to college with them.

Another school of thought regarding anxiety is some people are just wired differently. Anxiety is also understood as having a hereditary basis. Regardless of how someone was raised, some people are just more prone to worry about things around them, out of step with everyone else. In extreme circumstances, this hard-wired neurological problem can form a mental illness such as schizophrenia or bipolar disorder. Here the anxiety shows up as paranoia that keeps the student worried and overwhelmed, frightened at every possibility of life-threatening attack.

There is some good news regarding anxiety, whether it is related to a mental illness, learned environmental behavior, or a subtler worry about tests, performance anxiety, or talking to people. Anxiety and panic attacks are very treatable with talk-therapy and/or medications.

Getting help for an anxiety diagnosis often requires a visit to a psychologist or counselor. As you can imagine, this is difficult since the student who needs therapy is already very anxious. The added stress of coming into a therapy office, filling out paperwork, and telling their story to a stranger often prevents students from seeking help for their problems. This is sad, since many who come into therapy for anxiety feel better almost immediately after their first session.

The process of connecting a student to a therapist can be a challenging one. It can be helpful to:

- Make the intake/start process easier by helping research where the office is located, what the cost is, and other obstacles.

- Help the student understand that therapy and counseling are not just for weak students who can't "make it on their own," but a place to receive help and training. Counseling is like going to the gym, but in therapy you work to strengthen your mind instead of your body.

## Bipolar

Bipolar disorder can be a devastating illness for a young person to struggle with while in college. Bipolar disorder involves periods of manic moods that lead to poorly planned activities, a lack of impulse control, and increased risk-taking behaviors. These manic moods may include overspending on credit cards, starting various business ventures, collecting multiple speeding tickets, and a lack of overall stability.

These manic episodes are often alternated with severe depression that can include a lack of energy, hopelessness for a better future, isolation from friends and family, and suicidal thoughts. These manic and depressive periods can occur over relatively short periods of time (days) or can extend over long periods of time (months or years).

Bipolar disorder symptoms increase with stress; often the stress of academic programs combined with the freedom of exploring and learning at a new college or university may be the "tipping point" for a student to have their first crisis. Other times, students with bipolar disorder have been successfully treated for years in high school and hope that a fresh start at college will help them break free from their past behaviors.

Medication often helps those who struggle with bipolar disorder. Medications include mood stabilizers to reduce the rapid cycling between the manic and depressive states as well as anti-depressants to prevent the student from becoming so depressed they commit suicide. Bipolar disorder typically manifests in late-teenage years through the early twenties. Stress often exacerbates the disorder and the stress of adjusting to college life could make the disorder worse.

Many who experience bipolar symptoms are misdiagnosed as only having major depression since the main concern with their behavior centers on their depression and potential suicide. In contrast, some students use the energy during their manic phase to work ahead on their assignments and may seem to be very productive in their academics. Accurate diagnosis and treatment of bipolar disorder depends on clear and objective information from the student.

Family and friends who offer support to those students with bipolar disorder are a crucial element in their treatment. While professional therapists, psychologists, and psychiatrists are important in diagnosis and providing treatment, it is the friends, peers, and family that help ensure the bipolar student remains well and in treatment. One central role for staff is to serve to connect the student to these supports and to help the student avoid isolation from those who care about them.

## Thought disorders

Schizophrenia is one of the most upsetting and difficult mental health problems to address with a student. The media portrays those with schizophrenia as knife-wielding, crazy people looking to stab mothers walking their young children in baby carriages. Schizophrenics are seen as talking to themselves, responding to voices from another place, and presenting a danger to the community as a whole.

Individuals with schizophrenia are very rare (less than 1 percent of the population) and are often so lost in their own internal logic and paranoia that they struggle to relate to those around them. They are often scared of the world and overcome with worry that they will be hurt. Students may be concerned and worried about the odd behavior they notice in other students who have schizophrenia and will need help to understand what the student is experiencing. They may worry about what the student may do and that they might act unpredictably or put others at risk.

Those with schizophrenia (which means "split mind") often have difficulty regulating their cognitions (thinking) and emotions. They may become upset by strange or unseen threats and need an instructor or other students to reassure them and to assist them when they are becoming overwhelmed. For schizophrenic students to be successful, it is essential they have a strong group of supports that have access to their treatment team in the case of difficulty. This often involves case managers and flexible communication among team members. Students with schizophrenia need connection to mental health services such as therapy and psychiatry. This connection to services can help them monitor their illness and obtain medication to help with the symptoms they experience. Helping a schizophrenic student to access care for their disorder can be difficult.

Staff might also have to take on the role of educator and support for the student as they interact with other students. It may be that other students have not experienced an individual with schizophrenia before and are at a loss on how to communicate. Staff can provide a much-needed buffer and assistance during crisis times when a schizophrenic student may struggle more with their communication, thoughts, or emotions. Individuals with schizophrenia may have difficulty in the classroom with dulled emotions or problems concentrating on the assignments and discussion at hand.

Individual's with schizophrenia may wander off in their thinking or respond to odd or strange tangential issues. Students with schizophrenia who are following their medication regimen will be more likely to stay focused and will avoid drawing attention to themselves. Those students experiencing schizophrenic symptoms will often derail the discussion and engage in off-topic lines of thought.

## Alcohol and Addiction

Addiction is a compulsion that perpetuates itself. It can pertain to a substance or an activity. Some of the substances and/or activities that lead to addiction are alcohol, drugs, shopping, gambling, sex, overeating, and smoking. A common addiction students struggle with is alcohol addiction.

How do you know if a student you are working with has an addiction? Addicts are trapped in their behaviors and cannot always simply quit on their own. People often assume that because addiction begins with a voluntary behavior and is expressed in the form of excess behavior, an addict should just be able to quit by force of will alone. However, it is essential to understand that when dealing with addicts, we are dealing with individuals whose brains have been altered by alcohol, drugs, or behavioral abuse.

While there is no absolute scientific formula for identifying when an individual's use or behavior has developed into a full-blown addiction problem, most drug and alcohol or rehabilitation counselors agree that for drug use, alcohol use, or behavioral misuse, there are four distinct stages that may lead to addiction. The four stages are generally acknowledged as:

- Overuse or experimentation of a drug, alcohol, or behavior.
- The misuse of a substance or behavior.
- The abuse of drugs, alcohol, or behavior.
- A drug, alcohol, or behavior dependency or addiction.

While individuals in the first or second stages of use and misuse may not necessarily progress into addicts, individuals in the third stage of abuse are likely to develop full-blown addiction problems.

There are many places that a person can find help with their addictions, starting with helping them understand the impact of their use regarding their life, work, friends, and family. Those who are developing drinking problems may defend themselves by saying "I don't have a problem, look how good this aspect of my life is..." Another way to help is to point them toward the resources that might be useful for when they are ready to change their behavior.

When in college, students can become overwhelmed with the choices they have in terms of alcohol. Other times, there can be rather severe restrictions on alcohol. Developing educational programs and discussions about alcohol use and typical experiences may help get ahead of the problems students may encounter.

It can be hard working with students who don't want help. This can be a central challenge to working with students who are struggling with their drinking, but are not ready to change. The approach of motivational interviewing (Miller and Rollnick, 2002) offers some suggestions to help students who don't want help. These include expressing empathy for their situation and frustrations, rolling with their resistance, and, instead of challenging them directly, finding other ways to talk to them about change, and supporting them when they make good decisions about their drinking. This process is discussed in more detail in Chapter 4.

## CAMPUS SETTINGS

> I never sleep, I don't know why. I had a roommate and I drove her nuts, I
> mean really nuts, they had to take her away in an ambulance and everything.
> But she's okay now, but she had to transfer to an easier school, but I don't
> know if that had anything to do with being my fault. But listen, if you ever
> need to talk or you need help studying just let me know, 'cause I'm just a
> couple doors down from you guys and I never sleep, okay?
>
> Jordon, *Real Genius*

### Community Colleges

Students who attend community colleges are generally either going back to school
to train in a career or preparing to enter a four-year institution. These campuses
typically have less services available for students, opting instead to keep costs low,
and encourage students to seek services off campus. This presents a challenge in
that many community and technical college students face a unique set of trials
related to balancing the stress of family obligations, academic requirements, and
financial challenges.

Staff attempting to help community college students who are experiencing
frustrations and anger should acknowledge the myriad of stresses they are attempting
to balance. While it may seem like a simple issue of not turning paperwork in on
time or having difficulty accessing information on the website, understanding the
depth of stress students are facing can help in guiding our response.

### Online/Distance Colleges

Many students find success at college by taking courses online or through blended
distance programs. Students who are typically successful in these programs are
ones that have excellent abilities at balancing work requirements, multi-tasking and
working towards a goal. They may be working toward a certification program or
hoping to enter a brick and mortar community or traditional college down the line.

Students in online or distance courses may be testing the waters some when
it comes to college and may not have the same commitment as those who are
enrolled. Distance and online colleges often offer less in the way of services and,
like community colleges, focus on offering lower cost courses. The online nature of
the communication can make things difficult when attempting to mitigate a crisis.

Email communication, specifically, is fraught with opportunities to get a
staff member into hot water. You can make a quick response to students who
are demanding and entitled in their email. You can get into lengthy debate on a
listserv or with other staff around campus. Given the potential for problems, here
are some suggestions to avoid the minefield that can be email communication
gaffs and mistakes.

### Don't Email Angry; They Won't Like You When You Are Angry

One of the most common email regrets is an email that is sent when upset or frustrated with a situation. You may receive a message and assume the other person had a tone or attitude attached to what they wrote (and they may very well have) that leads to a quick, knee-jerk response. Instead of emailing angry, make a rule that you will take at least an hour to respond to an email. And after the hour, read your draft response…aloud…to a colleague. It may sound worse than you think. Ask yourself: can this wait until tomorrow?

### Don't Ever Email Negatives: Don't. No. Bad

A good rule of thumb is to avoid sending emails that involve negative, critical, or other general "no" answers. You may need to tell the person no; however, people generally take this kind of information better either on the phone or in person. This approach also minimizes the potential for misunderstanding and gives them a chance to respond.

### Avoid the Same Patterns of Mistakes

We are always a little surprised to find the same people getting into the same problems over and over again with their email communication. Sometimes they come off as too abrupt and annoy people. Sometimes they come off as angry and uncaring. Sometimes they don't fully understand the question or situation and respond to the wrong thing, making everything worse. Ask yourself whether you are caught in one of these loops and try something different.

### Take the Time to Re-Read Your Message Before Hitting Send

Despite the desire to have the technology to "recall" any email, this is just wishful thinking (like good tasting low calorie mayonnaise). Once you hit send, the email is out there. Forever. Fight the desire to clear your inbox and deal quickly with an email response without taking the time to edit. A simple re-read of an email may make all the difference between "I think all of us could benefit from looking at the situations once again" and "I think all of us could benefit from liking at the sittings once again."

### Don't Respond or Send Sensitive Information via Email

Email is a very useful tool to confirm dates, find out about a conference, check up on a project, or ask a simple question of a team member. It's a very bad tool to discuss a student's mental health history, describe a threatening situation, or respond sarcastically to someone who annoys you.

If it's more than a few sentences, stop, step away from the computer, and call the person. Don't write lengthy missives via email, no matter how good a writer you may believe yourself to be. If you have that much to say to another person, take the time to talk with them face to face or over the phone. Like a car with tires out of alignment, the longer you write, the more likely the email will start to swerve to the side of the road. Keep it clear, concise, and to the point.

## MOVING FORWARD

While lengthy, this chapter should serve to provide a substantive overview of how individuals who come from different backgrounds and experiences undergird the reasons they become upset or frustrated with staff. These reasons do not serve to excuse the behavior, but rather give staff an opportunity to better intervene with more success.

In the following chapters, we will take a closer look at responding to the initial crisis (Chapter 3), addressing longer term change and inspiring hope (Chapter 4) and how staff can best manage chronic challenges without becoming overwhelmed or burned out.

## NOTE

1  We know this movie is from 1994, but as Gen X authors, we reserve the right to break our own quote rules.

## Chapter 3

# Calming the
# Initial Crisis

You must chill! You must chill! I have hidden your keys! Chill!!!

Lloyd Dobler, *Say Anything*

Crisis is contextual.

Perhaps you have heard this before, but it bears repeating.

One of the greatest challenges in responding to a crisis is first acknowledging that you are experiencing something outside of your everyday experience. It's difficult to train staff to respond to disruptive and dangerous behavior without first addressing the idea that each staff member, whether male or female, young or old, new or experienced, has a different tolerance for the variety of disruptive and dangerous behaviors encountered in the department or office setting.

Think about what kind of activity you enjoy in your free time. For some, taking a mountain trek to Nepal or going scuba diving at the Great Barrier Reef in Australia is their idea of a perfect vacation. Others consider this a level of Hell in *Dante's Inferno*. Our leisure is defined by our individual tastes and experiences. Our response to a crisis is no different. We each have a unique view of what frustrates us during our day in meeting with students in our office, around the residence hall, or at the front desk of our department. Developing an appreciation of "what upsets you might not upset me" and the corollary—"what works for you in handling frustrating behavior may not work for me"—is a helpful place to start when understanding disruptive and dangerous behavior.

Why is this important? It's important because we can't just give you a checklist of disruptive and dangerous behaviors and a corresponding "if a, then b" approach to handling these problems without considering the context of your worldview. This applies to both what's considered disruptive and what interventions you bring to bear in each situation. One staff member becomes enraged at a student who fails to fill out their FAFSA correctly and on time. Another might pride himself on helping students who struggle with deciphering the government's rules and policies on the FAFSA. One staff encourages questions during difficult conversations and enjoys the challenge of helping students think critically and engage around why we have rules and policy while another staff flies into a rage at the hubris of today's students who question their policies. One uses humor to calm a disruptive student who acts disrespectfully at the front desk while another may threaten to call the campus police for the same behavior.

So where does this leave us? Our goal in writing this book is to create a useful collection of research-based theories and intervention techniques explained through stories and vignettes to identify and manage disruptive and dangerous behavior as you encounter it around campus. We have spent a little time so far clarifying and defining those behaviors that fall into the clear categories of disruption (yelling, rude attitude, or racist or misogynist language) as well as those behaviors that clearly cross the line into the realm of dangerousness (direct threats to harm other students, throwing objects, or slamming doors). We will also set the stage for an open and candid discussion of those "grey area" behaviors that may frustrate some staff, but not others (overly casual attitude, asking questions out of turn, use of personal technology during a meeting, projecting a sense of being owed something, or entitlement).

We will review how to work with these students effectively, now that we have laid a base foundation in Chapter 2 regarding how to understand the individual motivations that may cause the behaviors and how to refer these students for help within the larger campus community. These approaches to address disruptive and dangerous behavior are best understood as a loose collection of tools, applied in each situation with attention toward the utility and efficacy of the given technique. These are the techniques used by staff to confront behavior and achieve compliance in a manner that keeps the peace and redirects the student's inappropriate behaviors back into the norm of the campus community. In more dangerous or potentially violent interactions, the goal becomes keeping the staff member, other students, and the student causing the disruption—in that order— safe from harm.

## THE RIGHT STUFF

The techniques we discuss will require aptitude and appropriateness in their application. Consider this: You can take a wrench and try to use it to cut a board in half, but that's not the right tool for the job. You would be more successful in reaching your goal by using a saw.

Choosing the right approach for the given situation is critical. Yelling back at an escalating, rude, or entitled student isn't the right tool (no matter how cathartic it might feel). Embarrassing a student who is misusing technology when it's their turn in line to be helped isn't the best way to address that behavior. It's using a screwdriver to hammer a nail into a board. You might be able to get the job done, but there are easier, more effective, ways. We will discuss and explore the variety of techniques and tools available while keeping an eye on how to use them in a practical way.

Another point we'd like to make is the importance of appreciating the unique abilities, knowledge, and experience of staff as they apply a given technique. Some excel at using humor to engage a student without offending them. Others' attempts at humor end up feeling forced and often make a crisis worse. Some display genuine concern and caring through personal questions. Some treat their students with a degree of humanity and empathy that immediately garners respect. Others attempt this same stance and end up coming off as pushy or prying to the student. *The right technique, applied to the right situation with experience and skill is the ideal.* A single technique or comment made at the wrong time can lead to an intervention that fails to persuade the student to comply.

There are some essential, foundational qualities to bring about successful management of a crisis. These are "tried and true" stalwarts that prove efficacious in almost every situation. An example is approaching a student with respect and patience. This can be particularly difficult when the student is not treating the staff member with the same respect and patience. Another is a staff who seeks to understand the student's perspective before rushing to offer a response. Setting clear expectations about behavior at the start of a meeting or at the beginning of the year in the residence hall would be a third. These are non-negotiable, effective approaches to taking the fuel away from the fire, taking the wind out of their sails. Like the game of chess, managing a crisis is easy to learn but takes a lifetime to master.

Some more "advanced" techniques require a bit more training and strategic application for success. In wise and experienced hands, these tools of crisis management are extremely effective in provoking thoughtful consideration and growth within the student. These may include the use of humor or probing and personal questions. They may include one-on-one conversations that closely echo those in a counseling relationship. They may involve giving direct advice, setting inflexible limits and boundaries, or the involvement of the peer group to challenge and motivate the student towards change.

To explain further, let us offer the following example. Think about martial arts training. Learning one technique well, say a front punch, might be just the thing for some martial artists. They find it serves their needs. In a fight, they respond with this effective and well-practiced attack. The crisis intervention corollary is the staff member who listens to students first before attempting to correct their misconceptions (or rude or entitled behavior).

This is a tried and true "front punch" that will always yield an effective result. Patiently conveying a concern for a student's mental health or showing empathy in response to their environmental stress is always a better way to begin a confrontation. Practice this technique well over time and you could put down this book right now and have about 80 percent of what it means to handle behavioral disruptions and dangerous behavior.

**43**

Other martial artists may wish to invest more time and energy to develop, say, "a spinning back fist of certain doom." This certainly sounds very effective (and painful), though learning how to do it well requires much more practice and experience, and necessitates a more tactical application. The crisis intervention corollary here may be a staff member who uses humor (or even sarcasm) to de-escalate a potentially dangerous student who is escalating during a meeting, at the front desk, or in the residence halls. It can be very, very effective in the right situation if applied strategically. It also could result in a total disaster if the technique isn't applied correctly.

Carrying the martial arts analogy to its conclusion, any practitioner of martial arts knows the mantra "use common sense before self-defense." Another common misconception is we forget the power of prevention, and the ability to avoid a situation by engaging in good preventive practices. While we will spend a fair amount of time on how to manage disruptive situations, we will also spend time on prevention, as it is critical.

We want to clear up a common problem when new staff ask for advice on how to handle disruptive behavior. Many have sought council from peers and "wise elders" and they have struggled to successfully use the advice in their own situations as effectively. A memorable department director shared how she could get a student back on track when their questions became too passionate or moved away from the focus of the policy. She told us, "Well, I just tell them to shut up." And strangely enough, that worked very well for her. Students respected this motherly figure and her use of sarcasm with some students was very effective.

You can imagine if we tried her approach with our crisis scenarios, many students would take offense and would have called us rude or report us to a supervisor for unprofessional behavior. And this brings us back full circle to the concept of crisis de-escalation being contextual and subjective. What works for some, given their background and the setting in which they apply their approach, may not work so well for others.

Another common problem is that, when we utilize "old" methods to work with new problems, we often fail. Many staff have shared with us their frustration about their "tried and true" techniques no longer working over these last few years. It's because the student has changed. We talked some about these changes with the student population in Chapter 2.

## CHECK YOURSELF

Allow us to make one more point before moving forward. We have noticed an interesting psychological phenomenon over the years. It reminds us of the story about the emperor who had no clothes. Remember that one? He ends up parading down the street wearing not a stitch because no one tells him that his magnificent outfit is just his birthday suit.

Staff are like this sometimes (not you of course—and certainly not us— but some of them out there are like this). Staff get to talk for hours each week to students about rules and policy, often with very little feedback or a need to listen to other viewpoints. The rules are the rules. They have total control of their policy with very little oversight from their supervisors. They are praised for controlling the front desk, keeping meetings short and focused, and being able to do so without assistance. They enforce policy and do so with a degree of authority and assurance that is often un-checked. They receive very little direction in how to manage students who disagree with policy or rules and can develop their own departmental standards, rules, and social mores. It can be a little like *Lord of the Flies* when left unchecked.

This freedom can create some truly great departments around campus. It allows them to lead and create based on their ideas and thoughts. It lets them alter direction and change the focus to accommodate a new situations and concerns. It allows for creative and critical thinking. This freedom has the potential to create unique and flexible learning environments for students.

However, all this freedom can also create some arrogant, entitled, and rude staff that are well defended against criticism, suggestions for improvements, or challenges to their fiefdom (again, not you or us, of course).

Staff may develop serious blind spots in their interactions with students and, by extension, their ability to manage disruption and crisis. These blind spots can be institutionalized when staff are encouraged to control their spaces and handle conflict on their own. There is a not-so-subtle message: "Good staff control their students." End of story.

This is one of the reasons we wrote this book. We want to call some of you out on your behavior because, really, there just aren't that many opportunities for a staff to hear, "Hey, there is a better way to do that." We know that has been our path over a combined forty years of working in student affairs. It has been with the skills we learned in our professions as a college counseling center director and a Dean of Students that we have been successful managing students in crisis. For us, it has been a combination of on the job learning as well as taking advantage of professional development opportunities—everything from learning about threat assessment and trauma-informed interviewing techniques to paying close attention to the changing student population.

Perhaps this message will bounce off your well-defended view of yourself as an excellent staff member. We hope not. We'd ask you to lower your guard just a little bit. Just to see how it feels.

Perhaps we are preaching to the choir and you aren't in need of redirection in your handling of a crisis. You already have these skills and the experience and knowledge to calm students down and redirect negative behavior. If this is so, then we are glad we see eye to eye. Hopefully you can still find something new and useful in this book.

Maybe you are so set in your ways that you aren't looking for new ways of doing things, especially from us or a required reading of a book on behavior management your department head put into your lap.

And maybe—just maybe—this book is for you. Maybe you want to be better at handling the conversation with a student who says she is thinking of killing herself. Maybe you wonder if there is another way to deal with a student who continues to flaunt the rules and acts in an entitled manner at your front desk. Maybe you want to know what kind of behaviors you should handle yourself and what you need to share with your campus BIT (this goes by many names) or Student Conduct Office.

Maybe you want some help to be more effective at your job.

Good. Us too. Let's begin.

## A CASE OF DISRUPTION

Ginny is a first-year college student from an affluent family. She was involved in many extra-curricular activities in high school such as debate club, student government, and varsity swimming. She came to college with a double major and has come close to completing a difficult first semester with twenty-four credit hours. She is told by an academic advisor that she cannot register for a course that she feels she needs to take to be on track during her upcoming spring semester. Ginny becomes hysterical at this idea and begins to berate the advisor and insult them for not knowing anything about her major. The advisor again explains the course she wants to take is not offered and Ginny says, "I could do your job better. This is not what was promised by admissions when I picked your school to attend!"

## SIGN OF IMMINENT DANGER

Could you describe the ruckus, sir?

Brian, *The Breakfast Club*

Why is it important to focus on this switch from everyday life to the extraordinary situation in front of you? Identifying this point of transition allows the staff member to more quickly establish the proper mindset to respond quickly and properly to address the behavior presenting in front of them. Staff who are not able to transition from everyday meeting and conversational skills into the skills required to intervene with disruptive or dangerous behavior will not be as effective in achieving the desired outcome.

When training staff across the country, we stress the importance of not "being right, but also punched in the head." These are the times when a staff member says

"Well, Dylan…I am sorry you are upset, but it clearly says right here in the policy manual—that you have had since the beginning of the semester—that you cannot apply for financial aid funds after this cutoff date…" While the staff member is certainly correct making these statements to the student, they may be missing the subtle changes in the student's behavior such as clenched fists, shifting back and forth, and glaring eyes that signal an impending attack.

Likewise, a key to preventing disruptive behavior from escalating requires staff to bring their attention and focus to bear on the existing behavioral problem. Too often, behavior management becomes a nuisance and frustration for the staff and key questions are not considered in deference to getting back to the content of the rules or policy enforcement ASAP.

When working with Ginny, a natural reaction for the staff would be to return in kind her insulting behavior or to set a firm limit about her behavior. A successful intervention with Ginny begins with seeing her as overwhelmed and not interacting at her best. When staff recognize this, they can conceptualize the problem in a manner that doesn't lend itself to internalizing her expressed frustrations or taking offense. Then staff are better able to respond based on the tools in their kit, rather than in a reactive manner.

When confronting disruptive behavior, some questions to ponder include:

- "Why is this student acting out right now? What might be some causes of their inappropriate behavior (interrupting, misuse of technology, rude or entitled response)?"
- "What are my goals for an intervention from this student? What is the desired outcome of my intervention?"
- "What kind of intervention with this student will bring about the desired effect?"
- "Is this a behavior I should address now or something I should address after the student finishes?"

## BEHAVIORS THAT REQUIRE IMMEDIATE ATTENTION

- A student threatens the staff or another student.
- A student brandishes a weapon or threatens to get a weapon.
- A student raises their voice or yells at another student.
- Disrespectful or rude behavior such as misuse of technology (texting, making or taking a cell phone call in the middle of a conversation).
- A student is clearly intoxicated or appears under the influence of drugs in the meeting or at the front desk of the department.
- Writing and displaying to others obscene or inappropriate artwork.
- A student falls asleep during the meeting.

- A student engages in self-injurious behavior such as cutting or punching themselves.
- A student pushes, hits, or shoves the staff or another student.
- A student exposes himself or herself in the meeting or the front office.
- A student engages in an odd, strange, delusional, or psychotic rant or action (e.g., standing up and writing on the white board everything the staff member says, talking to people who aren't there, etc.).
- A medical emergency such as fainting, a seizure, or vomiting.

## A CASE OF DANGER

Stephano is a non-traditional college student who attends an urban technical college with hopes of working in the hospitality industry as a chef. He comes into the parking and transportation office waving a ticket and interrupts the front desk cashier who is helping another student by yelling, "I'm not leaving this place until this ticket is taken care of. I pay my tuition on time and was told I could park in this spot before my class!" The cashier tells him that she will be right with him and Stephano is having none of it. He yells again at her and says, "I don't have all day like you to hang around and deal with this. I have places to be and need to get to my internship! You fix this!" He crumbles up the paper and throws it back at the cashier. He storms out of the building and swiping several parking brochures off a nearby table on the way out. He shouts, "I'll be back this afternoon to make sure that is taken care of by your office. It if isn't, I will make your life a living hell!"

## SIGNS OF ESCALATING AGGRESSION: WHAT TO LOOK FOR?

Inigo: [during a swordfight] You are amazing.
Man in Black: Thank you. I've worked hard to become so.
Inigo: I must admit that you are better than I am.
Man in Black: Then why are you smiling?
Inigo: Because I know something you don't know.
Man in Black: And what is that?
Inigo: I am not left handed [switches sword to right hand].

*The Princess Bride*

Now that we are ready to shift from everyday mode to emergency mode, let's talk about the process when a student moves from being calm, cool, and collected to throwing things and punching people. While these behaviors are certainly rare in the office or around the residence hall, they do occur. Developing a more detailed understanding of how a student may escalate will provide staff with a broader foundation to understand crisis events and potential dangerousness.

As a student becomes increasingly upset and escalates, they display a pattern of consistent behaviors and observable characteristics that staff should develop a familiarity with to better identify a potentially violent episode on campus. John Byrnes (2002) coined the term Primal Aggression. This is an adrenaline-driven process and occurs as part of a biological reaction to aggression: the production of adrenaline, the increase in the heart rate and the resulting body language, and behavior and communication indicators that we can identify and measure. This is like the concept of affective (reactive/impulsive) violence outlined by Meloy (2000, 2006).

Meloy, Hart, and Hoffmann (2014) further explain this concept here:

> Affective violence, sometimes referred to as reactive, impulsive, or emotional violence, is preceded by autonomic arousal, caused by a reaction to a perceived threat, and accompanied by intense feelings of anger and/or fear. It is a defensive violence, and its evolutionary basis is self-protection to live another day... Predatory violence, sometimes referred to as instrumental or premeditated violence, is characterized by the absence of autonomic arousal and emotion, the absence of an imminent threat, and planning and preparation beforehand. It is offensive violence, and its evolutionary basis is hunting for food to live another day.
>
> (p. 5)

Dr. Howard (1999) in *The Owner's Manual for The Brain: Everyday Applications from Mind-Brain Research* writes:

> A potential aggressor channels his appraisal into some form of coping. The strength of the reaction is a direct function of the validation of the threat and the degree of certainty that the threat will thwart an objective or a goal. It is the emotion of being threatened and the inability to cope with that threat that initiates aggression. The common thread throughout this process is the release of adrenaline.
>
> (pp. 353–354)

Based upon their research, Drs. LeDoux and Amaral believe that,

> learning and responding to stimuli that warn of danger involves neural pathways that send information about the outside world to the amygdala, an almond-shaped gray area in the roof of the brain's lateral ventricle. This area, in turn, determines the significance of the stimulus and triggers emotional

**49**

responses like running, fighting, or freezing, as well as changes in the inner workings of the body's organs and glands such as increased heart rate.

(Laur, 2002, p. 6)

Threat and fear drive affective violence—it is the "fight" in "fight or flight." Grossman and Siddle (1999) have conducted landmark studies, including peer review, on how aggression induces adrenaline's (or Epinephrine's) influence on the heart rate and its resulting body language, behavior, and communication indicators.

Let's see how this works. Remember our example of Stephano. He has already shouted an ultimatum at the staff member, threatening to not leave the building until she solved his problem. He then becomes increasingly upset when a limit is set with him that his problem cannot be immediately resolved. He yells a second time and then escalates his behavior by throwing a crumpled-up ticket at the staff member. He sweeps several brochures off the counter on his way out of the office. He ends his tirade with a final threat to come back and continue his violent behavior.

The adrenaline rushing through Stephano's system has been well studied by Hart (1995) who has conducted significant work relating stress and anxiety to adrenaline. He illustrates that when an individual cannot cope with their anxiety, their mind perceives this anxiety as a threat. Coinciding with Dr. Howard's (1999) statement above, Dr. Hart concludes that, at this point, an individual starts to produce adrenaline, which triggers this escalation in violence.

Affective violence, in its extreme state, is a complete loss of control along with an accompanying rage or panic. This violence is fueled by the perception of frustration, threat, anxiety, and fear. It is adrenaline driven, predictable, and typically represents a progressive loss of control. Imagine a different student, Patti, who is in conflict with her roommate about how to keep the room organized or what time they should wake up in the morning. She yells at her roommate or she smashes her roommate's alarm clock against the floor. The resulting violence is reactive, immediate, and often not well planned out. She did not plan to yell or smash the clock. This is the result of a progressive, biologically driven path towards physical violence. This is affective violence. There is a path here that happens quickly, but it is still a path that can be tracked.

Luck, Jackson, and Usher (2007) presented some interesting research in this area related to emergency department behavior and patients who subsequently became violent. They created a model, called S.T.A.M.P. that describes some of the same behaviors that accompany the primal aggressor prior to an attack. These include "Staring and eye contact, Tone and volume of voice, Anxiety, Mumbling and Pacing" (p. 14). They found these elements of observable behavior indicated the potential for physical violence. Stephano demonstrates almost all of these.

Affective violence is based upon the primal instinct of fight or flight, fueled by adrenaline, and characterized by someone losing control and ultimately attacking a victim. Caution should be practiced when responding to such an aggressor, since it is likely our own adrenaline will spike when faced with this threat. Staff should control their own escalation as their aggression rises in response to a threat. Staff who simply respond with in-kind aggression will make the situation worse and find it quickly escalating.

## IT'S ALL ABOUT ME!

I'm not even supposed to be here today!

Dante Hicks, *Clerks*

You might expect a chapter on crisis de-escalation to begin with a conversation about what to do and how to intervene when someone comes into an office, residence hall, or meeting upset or threatening. That we would begin with a list of techniques to apply or a checklist to implement.

But no, instead it starts with you. It's all about you.

The most important thing we can share about crisis de-escalation is the importance of adopting the proper stance when working with students who are presenting with disruptive or dangerous behavior. Again and again, the most common error we see with staff and faculty alike when they mismanage a crisis situation is responding to the incident in a reactive and emotional manner. They rush to react because the student's behavior is so incredibly rude, entitled, frustrating, or threatening they drop into an automatic response rather than choosing the appropriate response for a given situation.

This begs the larger question of how to remain calm, cool, and collected in the face of chaos. How does one remain "chill," so to speak, when a student is out of control and escalating? How can this be done when everything seems to happen so very fast?

Well, it starts with Goldilocks.

You remember that girl right? The girl with the yellow hair who had a penchant for eating other people's porridge? That little girl offers some useful advice to those looking to find the best kind of stance when it comes to working with disruptive or dangerous student behavior. Finding a middle ground. Aristotle offers a bit of a fancier take on this simple concept: "Virtue is the disposition to choose the mean, in both actions and passions."

That's what we are getting at in this chapter—finding the wise stance as staff working with disruptive or dangerous students. One of our favorite words is equanimity: the ability to have a sense of calm and patience in the face of adversity and chaos. We encourage staff to obtain greater equanimity when approaching difficult situations with students.

Our argument is one for the mean. Find a stance based in calmness, confidence, and a flexible curiosity when attempting to manage at-risk behavior. Like Goldilocks and the porridge, too hot or too cold misses the mark. A staff who approaches

**51**

a student with their buttons pushed and ready for a fight is going to be just as ineffective managing the crisis as a staff member who approaches the situation with a lack of caring and attention. The "just right" porridge is where the staff member approaches the student with a balanced calm, adjusting as the situation demands.

Think back to Ginny. She comes into the office insulting the academic advisor and demanding something that is beyond the staff member's ability to give. He can aggressively insult her in return and send her packing from his office. He can ignore the problem and tell her, "I'm sorry, there is nothing that can be done" and encourage her to file a complaint with the department chair. These are the "too hot" and "too cold" approaches. The middle ground is a caring confrontation with the student explaining the reasoning for the rule, exploring alternative options such as an appeal or another class that could fulfill the requirement, and a follow-up conversation to ensure that they understand their options and that you are here to help solve the problem, not as a barrier to contribute to their problems.

So, you may say, this all sounds well and good. But how does one put this into practice when a student like Stephano just bounced a crumpled parking ticked off your head and is now threatening to come back later in the afternoon to finish things off?

First, let's acknowledge that this isn't easy. As Professor Snape describes his potion class in *Harry Potter and the Philosopher's Stone*, "It is an exact art and a subtle science." As such, it takes both study and experience to accomplish. Breathing exercises and calming messages to focus your thoughts will work better if they are practiced prior to dealing with a potentially dangerous situation. These kinds of cognitive rehearsals are practiced by sports players before the big game, by professional speakers before an important presentation and by musicians and singers before a performance. These methods are more likely to be successful if they are practiced and incorporated into ritual or tradition. Faculty can practice cognitive rehearsal prior to an emotional interaction with a student by practicing cycle breathing and the introduction of calming thoughts and normalizations.

## Apply Cycle Breathing

The process of cycle breathing is used to control the biological changes that occur when a situation begins to escalate us. This involves breathing in slowly to the count of four, holding your breath for the count of two, breathing out slowly to the count of four, and holding your breath for the count of two. The process can then be repeated (or cycled) several times to lower blood pressure and heart rate and to allow the staff member the ability to remain calm, cool, and collected to better manage the situation at hand. It can even be done very subtly, so it doesn't look like you are trying not to come unglued.

With a student like Ginny, you then remind yourself that the best way to address this student's outburst is from a position of calmness. You take a minute to let them talk and quietly slow your breathing as you prepare to redirect the student with a relaxed, "I'm sorry to interrupt, but I have some questions I'd like to ask to better understand the situation and some ideas that might help find a solution."

## Find Calming Thoughts

This process can involve the interjection of calming or peaceful images into your mind that are unrelated to the topic at hand. These can be images from your latest vacation or something that you are looking forward to in the future. This can also involve the interjection of calming mantra or habitual phrases that help center your thoughts and allow you to remain calm in the face of adversity ("I should not take this personally..."). Focusing on the term equanimity and what it means can be helpful in achieving some peace. Let the student vent, this often allows us to hear what the frustration is, and lasts only about ten to twenty seconds (though it might feel longer). While we are listening, we practice cycle breathing, assess the behavior and situation, and tell ourselves what we need to do next. To be honest, we also are assessing escape routes, other "allies" in the room, etc.

Another useful concept to finding equanimity is found in an approach known as "Staying Centered." When managing any situation, it is critical to find your center: geographically, physically, and emotionally. A quick explanation:

- Geographically: Staying centered geographically means finding the "center" point—or becoming it. If you have ever been to a college keg party (it's OK to admit it, you're reading this alone), you know where the "center" of the party is—the keg. Not the dance floor, not the TV (unless the party was to watch a game), not the kitchen. If it isn't, you can make it the center. Simply grab the tap and hold it, don't give out any more beer. It will take five minutes to be the center of attention. In an academic advising office, the geographic center is naturally designed to be the meeting space and the advisor who is offering guidance and support. When a confrontation occurs, it—or the disrupter—becomes the "center." You must put it back on you. This is not done by shouting or through a show of physical dominance, but instead through remaining calm and in control. The other two aspects of "staying centered" will assist in this.
- Physically: This is easier than you may think. Keeping a neutral body posture is critical. Do not "bow up"—puffing out your chest, pulling your shoulders back, lifting your chin, staring hard, etc. "Bowing up" is simply an attempt, in a very mammalian sort of way, to make yourself appear bigger, an attempt to impose physical domination. Unfortunately, it's also an aggressive gesture, and can move the situation away—often quickly—from the desired "middle ground." But you can't go the other direction either, pulling your shoulders in, averting eye contact, dropping your chin, etc. This is called "getting smaller" and will only serve to empower the disrupter, and keep them in the "geographic

center." So, keep your body even. Shoulders in a neutral posture, chin even, eye contact steady, but not glaring, hands in open positions (not clenched, pointing aggressively, or in pockets, etc.). Your voice is equally important here. You want to bring the tone back to the "center." Often dropping your volume to a lower level than normal does this, even when shouted at. This is designed to bring the volume of the conversation back down. No one wants to shout alone. (You may have to repeat this twice or even three times—but never do it more than three. If that hasn't worked, assume the person is no longer rational.)

- Emotionally: This is the hardest one of all. You need to "tend your own garden." This is difficult because it means acknowledging your own personal biases and emotions. For example: Stephano presents very aggressively and demands resolution demonstrating very little patience. He interrupts, demands satisfaction, and storms off all in a matter of minutes. It wouldn't be unusual for you to be a little less patient with a student like this. Add to that an argument with your spouse that morning, and you are starting the confrontation even more "off center." In this situation, the breathing exercises become even more critical. Taking a moment in this situation—or even "tending your garden" before you go into the office—is a great practice to "stay centered."

## SEVEN TIPS TO CALM THE STORM

Buttercup: We'll never succeed. We may as well die here.

Westley: No, no. We have already succeeded. I mean, what are the three terrors of the Fire Swamp? One, the flame spurt – no problem. There's a popping sound preceding each; we can avoid that. Two, the lightning sand, which you were clever enough to discover what that looks like, so in the future we can avoid that too.

Buttercup: Westley, what about the R.O.U.S.'s?

Westley: Rodents Of Unusual Size? I don't think they exist.

[Immediately, an R.O.U.S. attacks him.]

*The Princess Bride*

Based on our experience in psychology, student affairs administration, and our collective experience managing disruptive and dangerous student behaviors, we have condensed some of these ideas into the following seven tips that are useful in de-escalating the crisis.

### Know the Signs of Danger

Prior to a student escalating to a physical attack, there are often several signs, or tells, they share with the target. Knowing these signs gives a staff member some important added knowledge in assessing the likelihood of them escalating into a physical attack. These include a clenched fist, a student moving in and out of your personal space, verbal declarations of an intention to act violently, and the target glancing around the office for something to throw or use as a weapon. People don't simply explode in violence, they escalate over time as their adrenaline floods their system and they become trapped, afraid, angry, or rageful. Attending some of these escalation behaviors can give staff the chance to better respond.

## Keep yourself Safe

There is this myth that we are expected to do everything for our students with little regard for our needs. While this may be true in some customer service scenarios, the exception to this rule is when we feel unsafe with the student. This could be a feeling in our gut or a more direct response to behaviors or direct threats issued by the student. In these situations, it is recommended to consider a safe escape path or removing yourself from the interaction. While we want to keep others safe around us and have a responsibility to intervene when we come across disruptive or dangerous behaviors, our own personal safety is paramount.

## Know your Backup

Have an awareness of what resources are around you in terms of calling for help. A staff member alone in an after-hours office should approach a potentially violent student scenario differently from a staff surrounded by assistance and across the street from the campus police department. Some schools are lucky and have invested well in technology and panic alarms that are fixed in certain locations (think under a bank teller's desk) in the event of a crisis. These are common in financial aid, conduct, counseling, and the registrar's office, anywhere that would be considered a "hot spot" on a given campus. In the event your school hasn't invested in this, other options could involve using a wireless doorbell situated at the front desk connected to someone in the back office who could manually call campus safety. Other creative options involve web-based panic alarms that can trigger a police response from a computer terminal or smartphone. Another option is coming up with a code shared with another worker such as "get me a coffee with extra cream" that is a covert signal to call for help. In terms of practicality, make sure your code word isn't overly transparent like "Bring me the red folder" or "Can you get Dr. Strong on the phone?" An upset student may see through this and become more enraged at the subterfuge.

## Be Prepared

Don't wait until a crisis occurs to think about what you would do. Planning on how to respond to a crisis during the crisis is a bad idea. Think about working in tabletop exercises or example scenarios during staff meetings and orientation events at the start of the year. Think about possible exits around the office or department. Know how to contact campus police and the difference between calling them on a direct line versus calling 911 (sometimes 911 routes to an off-campus response that can take longer).

## Understand Their Perspective

Another approach to keep calm when facing a disruptive or dangerous student is normalizing their behavior. Imagine the student's behavior within the context of their background or experience. While it is reasonable to expect graduate students to have figured out the basics of balancing family, career, parking, and an off-campus internship, first year community college students may have a bit of a learning curve when it comes to acclimating to the college environment. Perhaps the student in question has just received some upsetting news and their behavior would be more reasonable if you fully understood the context of it occurring. This technique does not excuse the student from responsibility for their poor behavior. It is designed to help the staff understand how to help defuse an emotional reaction in the student. For example, when addressing Stephano, understanding some of the reasons for his inappropriate and threatening behavior is the key to thinking through the best approach to address and neutralize the behavior. It is also helpful to understand some of the larger societal, cultural, generational, and environmental stressors that may be at play here that are discussed in more detail in Chapter 2.

## The Biology of Aggression

Earlier in the chapter, we talked about the biology of affective violence and aggression. A central premise of crisis response is this: the earlier we intervene, the better chance we have at success. If a student is escalating and become increasingly upset, there are biological changes that are occurring related to their heart rate, blood pressure, and adrenaline production that limit the student's ability to think rationally and be reasoned with by staff. Identifying and intervening at early stages of frustration and building aggression is easier than waiting until the student is more escalated in their aggression.

## Persuasion and Body Language

When trying to persuade someone to comply with a request, understand that people are more likely to listen and follow the advice of people who they are similar to and have something in common with than to someone they don't know. A first step in crisis escalation is helping the student to see the person they are angry at as a person and not a job title or bureaucratic cog in the larger university organizational structure. Additionally, staff should consider their tone of voice and body language when communicating with someone who is upset and frustrated. Lowering tone of voice, using inclusive hand gestures, nodding, and making appropriate eye contact are all ways to encourage conversation.

## THEORY

Snakes. Why'd it have to be snakes?

Indiana Jones, *Raiders of the Lost Ark*

We all remember poor Indiana Jones falling into that famous snake pit in *The Raiders of the Lost Ark*. His arch nemeses were those slimy snakes crawling all about that pit. Maybe some of you feel the same way here about theory. Our goal in this part of the chapter is to give you a brief introduction to how the theory can apply to one of the case examples we introduced in the start of the chapter. We hope to make this a painless lesson for those who are theory adverse.

### Kohlberg's Theory of Moral Development

Kohlberg's theory of moral development is dependent on the thinking of both psychologists and philosophers that human beings develop philosophically and psychologically in a progressive fashion. The theory holds that moral reasoning, the basis for ethical behavior, has six identifiable developmental stages, each more adequate at responding to moral dilemmas than its predecessor (Kohlberg, 1973). Kohlberg determined that the process of moral development was principally concerned with justice.

Kohlberg's theory specifies six stages of moral development, arranged in three levels.

### LEVEL I: PRECONVENTIONAL MORALITY

*Stage 1*: Punishment Orientation: Rules are obeyed so the individual may avoid punishment.
*Stage 2*: Instrumental Orientation or Personal Gain: Rules are obeyed because obeying rules creates the potential for personal gain.

### LEVEL II: CONVENTIONAL MORALITY

*Stage 3*: "Good Boy" or "Good Girl" Orientation: Rules are obeyed to receive the approval of others.

**57**

*Stage 4*: Maintenance of the Social Order: Rules are obeyed to maintain the social order of things.

## LEVEL III: POSTCONVENTIONAL MORALITY

*Stage 5*: Morality of Contract and Individual Rights: Rules are obeyed if they are impartial. Democratic rules are challenged if they infringe on the rights of others.

*Stage 6*: Morality of Conscience: The individual establishes his or her own rules in accordance with a personal set of ethical principles.

These stages are not the product of socialization—that is, socializing agents (e.g., parents and teachers) do not directly teach new forms of thinking (Crain, 1985). Indeed, it is difficult to imagine them systematically teaching each new stage structure in its place in the sequence. The stages emerge, instead, from our own thinking about moral problems.

Social experiences do promote development, but they do so by stimulating our mental processes. As we get into discussions and debates with others, we find our views questioned and challenged and are therefore motivated to come up with new, more comprehensive positions. New stages reflect these broader viewpoints.

A student like Ginny will be better understood when considering her potential stage of morality. It may be that a central concern with her behavior is related to the good boy/good girl orientation or to the maintenance of social order, where her compliance behavior is driven by expectations about what it means to achieve and that rules are followed to maintain an order and establish predictability. Her frustration at the school's failure to follow through on the promise to deliver a class she needs can be seen in this context, in order to obtain a deeper understanding of why she is upset. Engaging a student like Ginny around her expectations for the class and appealing to her sense of social order and predictability and process may be a useful tool in de-escalating her behavior.

## Chickering's Theory of Identity Development

Chickering's theory of identity development remains arguably the most well-known, widely used, and comprehensive model available for understanding and describing the psychosocial development of college students. Chickering combined this research with some of his previous development studies to generate the seven vectors.

These vectors symbolize the direction and magnitude of college student development. Vectors were chosen as determinants of development, as opposed to stages, because college student development is too diverse and unique to be characterized by specific maps or pigeonholes. Rather, movement along any vector can occur at different rates and can interact with movement along the others (Chickering and Reisser, 1993).

The seven vectors are as follows (Robinson, 2013):

- *Developing competence*: An individual develops within intellectual, physical, and manual skills, and interpersonal competencies.
- *Managing emotions*: An individual becomes competent in their ability to recognize and manage emotions.
- *Moving through autonomy toward interdependence*: An individual develops the ability to have an independent outlook on life but understands successful relationships are based upon interdependence.
- *Developing mature interpersonal relationships*: An individual develops intercultural relations, appreciation for others, and tolerance for those around them.
- *Establishing identity*: An individual processes through their identity to emerge with a healthy self-concept in all facets of identity.
- *Developing purpose*: An individual has a strong outlook on professional life, makes meaning within their own interests, and establishes positive relationships with others.
- *Developing integrity*: An individual can articulate and emulate their own values affirmed as an individual through three stages: humanizing values, personalizing values, and developing congruence.

In addition, one or many of the following institutional controls can influence an individual's vectors (Robinson, 2013):

- *Institutional objectives*: Consistency in policies, programs, and objects can lead individuals to challenge or acceptance.
- *Institutional size*: This influences the degree to which a student has the ability to participate in the larger community.
- *Student–faculty/staff relationships*: Positive relationships facilitate a deeper intellectual and relational identity for individuals.
- *Curriculum*: Individuals who can better relate to their curriculum have an increased ability to encounter situations and critically reason through situations.
- *Teaching*: Involvement of active learning helps students develop better interpersonal relationships and positive intercultural identity.
- *Friendships and student communities*: Individuals learn best from one another and other individuals' situations.
- *Student development programs and services*: The collaborative environment is necessary to provide programs to challenge and support students.

Other essentials in the learning environment can produce an increase in positive development for any student within the campus community. When considering prevention curriculum development, educators must be actively aware of differences, and be willing to create environments where students learn from each other. They should provide opportunities to challenge and stretch individuals' thought processes, while gaining a deeper understanding of themselves and others.

Understanding Ginny's behavioral outburst from the perspective of identity development can be useful to give staff a larger perspective on why she escalated so quickly and became so upset. As someone accustomed to frequent success, Ginny may not have had as many opportunities to manage her emotions related to failure or delayed gratification. As a new student in college, she is on a path toward establishing her identity and sense of purpose. Over-reliance on having things happen exactly as she expects or without challenge are hallmarks of students who are beginning a process of identity development.

As Robinson (2013) points out, the university can also assist students in moving more quickly through their stages of identity development by creating structures and systems that encourage such movement. Creating chances for students to develop staff/faculty–student relationships on a small and personal scale, being consistent and clear with communication and policy, engaging in active learning opportunities, and encouraging peer support are all helpful to the identity development of the student.

## MOVING FORWARD

We hope this chapter offers some practical and theory-based advice for staff who are placed in a position of responding to an immediate crisis. We have offered a summary of the different types of behavioral crisis that may be encountered by staff as well as a more detailed exploration of the biology related to affective violence and seven practical tips to handle the immediate crisis.

Moving forward in Chapter 4, we will offer an exploration of how to motivate and inspire more lasting change with students who challenge us in our departments, front office environments, and residence halls.

## Chapter 4

# Motivating and Inspiring Change

They're not that different from you, are they? Same haircuts. Full of hormones, just like you. Invincible, just like you feel. The world is their oyster. They believe they're destined for great things, just like many of you. Their eyes are full of hope, just like you. Did they wait until it was too late to make from their lives even one iota of what they were capable? Because you see, gentlemen, these boys are now fertilizing daffodils. But if you listen real close, you can hear them whisper their legacy to you. Go on, lean in. Listen. You hear it?... Carpe... Hear it?... Carpe. Carpe diem. Seize the day, boys. Make your lives extraordinary.

John Keating, *Dead Poets Society*

It isn't enough.

It isn't enough to simply develop crisis management skills and learn how to kung fu and Jedi mind trick your way out of disruptive and dangerous problems that come into your office, pound at the front desk, or pinball around the residence halls. While learning the skills to more effectively and diplomatically deal with crisis events is important, even more important is the work of prevention. How do we accomplish this upstream work of advising, mentoring, challenging, cheerleading, and inspiring the students we work with? How do we move beyond addressing the immediate problem and help them grow and learn?

Stringer (1999) offers a brief story about the importance of this upstream work,

The story goes that a man rescued a number of people from drowning in a river. Eventually, he tired of dragging one after the other from the river and walked upstream, where he observed a bully pushing people into the water. He struggled with the bully, who was eventually arrested and taken away. The problem of the drowning people was solved by his "upstream" work.

(p. 140)

The work we do with students goes beyond simply calming them down when they are upset. Staff have an opportunity here to make a true difference in the student's life and have an impact on their behavior, choices, and future. These kinds of conversations with students should not be limited to the counseling staff or the Dean of Students. All staff who work at the institution are educators. They are here to help students think more critically about their actions and leave an impact on young lives.

## BUILDING RAPPORT

Hans Gruber: [on the radio] Mr. Mystery Guest? Are you still there?

John McClane: Yeah, I'm still here. Unless you wanna open the front door for me.

Hans Gruber: Uh, no, I'm afraid not. But, you have me at a loss. You know my name but who are you? Just another American who saw too many movies as a child? Another orphan of a bankrupt culture who thinks he's John Wayne? Rambo? Marshal Dillon?

John McClane: Was always kinda partial to Roy Rogers actually. I really like those sequined shirts.

Hans Gruber: Do you really think you have a chance against us, Mr. Cowboy?

John McClane: Yippee-ki-yay, motherfucker.

*Die Hard*

Imagine a bridge between you and another person. Sometimes these bridges can feel like they are something out of an Indiana Jones movie. Every other plank is missing and there are sharks circling below a 300-foot drop. Other bridges can be strong and made of steel and span great distances. The Golden Gate, the Brooklyn Bridge. Sometimes the bridge of connection is a strong one built well and made to last.

Our sense of rapport with others is like this. There is a metaphorical bridge between each person we are trying to motivate or connect with, particularly when we are attempting to work with a student in crisis. These bridges can be strong and well developed, allowing us more flexibility and room to take chances and challenge the student we are working with to change. These bridges can be almost non-existent and be testing the very breaking point.

There are certain characteristics and attributes that make our bridges stronger. Some of these can be created and strengthened, some just exist in our environment. Imagine you come from the same town or geographic region as the student. If you are of the same race, culture, or ethnicity. If you are the same religion or share a similar political ideology. You may come from a similar socio-economic place or generation. These similarities build connections and make bridges between those we are trying to motivate to change and us. The stronger the bridge, the more our intervention has a chance to take hold successfully.

There are questions we can ask and conversations we can have with the student to establish rapport and build a bridge of connection. Some of these are outlined in Table 4.1. We can also set up our offices and meeting spaces in a way that encourages discussion: with artwork, making a tea/coffee service available or offering small snacks or candies. These convey to students a willingness to connect and provide for them as a person, pointing the way to being open to help in other ways.

Jack Schafer, former FBI Special Agent and author of *The Like Switch* (2015), shares some insights into the establishment of rapport in a wide variety of settings.

## TABLE 4.1 Building a Bridge

| Areas to Explore | Examples |
| --- | --- |
| Similar interests | Do you share a love for a town or place (Venice, New Orleans, Northern/Southern California)? Is there a similar taste in music, love of an author or theater show? |
| Background | Did you grow up in a similar geographic region, town or area of the country? Is there a shared culture, music, attitude or food from that region? For example, joking about people from New Jersey knowing each other by their exit number on the parkway. |
| Sports | Are there similar sports teams you both like? Are there differences that could also be avenues for connection (say debating the merits of the Yankees vs. the Red Sox)? |
| Create a space | Be open to listening to their perspective and creating a nurturing and supportive place for them to share. While there may not be much in common, simply listening to another's perspective creates these opportunities. |
| Be vulnerable | Sharing aspects of your life, family, background and interests can be one way to communicate with students that you are open to discuss things and curious about their experiences as well. This does not have to be something overly personal, but rather something that shows you as a person to the student. Even a collection of little pink flamingos, pez candy dispensers or a picture of a family pet in your office can help build connection. |
| Stories of success/failure | Most of us have attended college and have stories of success and failure related to our personal experiences getting through college. Are there opportunities to share some of these stories, times where you might have thought you'd never graduate or struggled with a challenge at school? |

While most staff will not find themselves trying to flip a double agent or engaging in espionage, the concepts outlined in the book offer some practical observations about how we go about assessing what is happening around us. Schafer (2015) writes, "Our brains are continually scanning the environment for friend or foe signals" (p. 25). These friend or foe signals can be learned and are useful for staff attempting to establish rapport with a student prior to giving advice, mentoring behavior, or attempting to bring about change.

These signals should be used cautiously with an awareness of cultural and generational differences in how people interpret certain behaviors such as offering verbal nudges, body proximity, or a genuine smile.

Some examples of friend signals we send to others to communicate a desire for a relationship and that we are interested in what they are saying are listed here.

- Eyebrow flash is a quick up-and-down movement of the eyebrows that lasts about one-sixth of a second (brief and not staring).
- Head tilt to the left or the right is a nonthreatening gesture. This is a strong friend signal.
- The smile should be genuine with upturned corners of the mouth and upward movement of the cheeks accompanied by a wrinkling around the eyes. Insincere smiles tend to be lopsided.
- Isopraxism is mirroring a person's body language.
- Inward lean is when people lean toward people they like and distance themselves from people they don't.
- Head nodding communicates to those speaking that they should keep talking.
- Verbal nudges reinforce head nodding and encourage the speaker to continue talking (e.g., "I see," "Go on…," "Tell me more," etc.).
- Focused listening requires those conducting interviews to not let distractions interrupt their attentive listening.

In addition to these friend signals we can send to better establish rapport, Schafer suggests we do something similar, albeit perhaps more unconsciously, to send foe messages to the person we are having a conversation with in our office.

- Elongated stare or eye contact that lasts more than a second can be read as aggressive.
- Body scan/elevator eyes is a sweeping head-to-toe gaze often seen as intrusive because the person doing the looking hasn't earned the right to invade the other's personal space.
- Eye roll sends the message you think the individual is stupid and not worth listening to.
- Eye squinting, furrowed eyebrows, and facial tension are associated with disapproval, uncertainty, and anger.

Schafer shares a success in getting an asset in the field to share information with him, "He spoke freely and honestly not because he was forced to talk, but because he liked me and considered me his friend" (p. X). He continues with this equally important observation, "if you want people to like you, make them feel good about themselves" (p. 77). We can learn to send friend signals to those we are working with and reduce the number of potential foe signals in order to strengthen the rapport between us.

Finally, from the arena of threat assessment and interviewing, Meloy and Mohandie (2014) identified five steps to build rapport with the subject (see Table 4.2). While most staff will not be conducting a threat assessment or attempting to learn information useful in an ongoing law enforcement operation, these techniques are useful in building a bridge with the subject.

## MAINTAINING ROLES AND BOUNDARIES

> If you can't say anything nice about anybody, come sit by me.
>
> Clairee Belcher, *Steel Magnolias*

One challenge facing staff as they work with students is developing an awareness of the boundaries and roles they have. When helping, there is a tendency to lose

### TABLE 4.2 Techniques to Build Rapport

Smiling: This is a universal gesture of goodwill regardless of culture, nationality or religion. Research indicates that individuals who receive a smile from another feel accepted and not judged.

Listening carefully: Most people do not listen to each other in an open and patient manner. If the interviewer is attentive, is nonjudgmental, and shows interest in other people, a very positive emotional dynamic will be put in place, even if the interviewee is very distrustful and hates what the interviewer represents (e.g., the Federal Bureau of Investigation, Americans, infidels).

Finding something in common: Identify a characteristic that is shared between the interviewer and interviewee and point that out. It could be marriage, a child, a common geographical area visited, a certain amount of education, or interest in a certain sport. Find it and say it.

Mirroring the interviewee: This refers to mimicking the interviewee's body language and words, which takes attention and practice. If it is done too obviously, it will be noticed and rapport will not arise. It may mean sitting the same way, making similar gestures, using some of the same words, even using similar emotional tones of voice.

Avoiding blunders: Allowing the soles of one's shoes to face another person is considered an insult in Arabic cultures. Displaying a cold and unfriendly demeanor is considered an insult. Conveying impatience, such as glancing at one's watch or tapping one's fingers on the table, is considered an insult. Certain gestures may be an insult. Study the culture and know what the blunders are (Nydell, 1996).

one's sense of self and fail to appreciate the limits of what we can do for another person. We attempt to help and can occasionally lose track of what is considered professional and within the scope of our ability to help. Likewise, we can find ourselves setting overly restrictive boundaries that keep students from seeing staff as real people capable of understanding.

There is a bit of a goldilocks principle here. Having overly strict boundaries or limits with students is analogous to the porridge being too cold. Here a staff member shares so little about themselves and their experiences that the relationship suffers. They adopt an all business professional persona and create firm and definite boundaries that convey a sense of distance and foster a lack of connection. Conflicts escalate more quickly and students often feel emboldened to act out against the staff in more aggressive and potentially violent ways as they don't see the staff as a person, but rather as a position.

Having few or little boundaries is the porridge too hot. Here the relationship is fluid and overly casual and close. Limit setting becomes difficult and both staff and student are emotionally involved with each other. While this kind of friendship and close relationship can work well during good times, when limit setting needs to occur or the student doesn't fulfill expectations in a timely manner, the overly close relationship becomes a hindrance to connection and developing a solution.

As you might imagine, the answer here lies in the "just right" approach. Having appropriate professional boundaries with students is essential, yet these boundaries should have some flexibility as well as emphasis on the student connecting to the staff on a personal level. When students see staff as partners in a process and as those advisors and mentors who have walked the difficult path ahead of them, the staff have more success at building a bridge of connection with students. This requires staff to adopt an approach to sharing aspects of their lives and experience, without crossing over into over-sharing or developing dual relationships with the students they are helping.

## A CASE OF DISRUPTION

Logan is a sophomore business major who comes from an affluent alumni family in the community. Logan is entitled and feels as if the college owes him an education based on the donations his family has made to the school. He often gets into insensitive arguments with front office staff, his advisor, and professors about how he is a legacy and has paid their salaries several times over. He does mostly B/C work in his classes and often is marked down for attendance and lack of completing assignments. Logan has had several conduct violations related to underage drinking on campus in the residence halls and excessive pranks involving thousands of dollars of fines and damage. Logan is generous with other students and is quite popular on campus. Logan lacks a clear sense of focus and most see him as a rudderless party boy who will someday take over the family business no matter what he does at college. Logan most recently came into some conduct trouble when he paid an overdue parking fine of $189 with pennies. He brought several students in the office with him to pour the pennies onto the cashier's desk. The sack of pennies, weighing close to 25lbs fell out of Logan's hand and onto her wrist. The cashier was taken to the hospital and had a hairline fracture and sprain from the incident.

## THE TECHNIQUES OF MOTIVATIONAL INTERVIEWING

Wax on, right hand. Wax off, left hand. Wax on, wax off. Breathe in through nose, out the mouth. Wax on, wax off. Don't forget to breathe, very important.

Mr. Miyagi, *The Karate Kid*

Motivational interviewing, or Motivational Enhancement Therapy (MET) was developed by Miller and Rollnick (2002) and used primarily with mandated alcohol treatment to help people change addictive behavior. Their approach is useful when there is a disconnect between the goals of the therapist and client or, in our case, between the staff and the student. It is an adaptable approach to working with those who haven't yet recognized their behavior needs to change. There are five key concepts that make up the foundation of motivational interviewing. These are meant to be used based on need and do not have a hierarchical application. These are the expression of empathy, development of discrepancy, avoiding argumentation, roll with resistance, and supporting self-efficacy.

The *expression of empathy* involves a conversation with the student that attempts to both understand their perspective (empathy) and communicate an understanding of that perspective (expression of empathy). This expression of empathy respects the student's point of view, freedom of choice, and ability to determine their own self-direction. Suggestions for change are subtle from the instructor and the ultimate change is left up to the student.

In the scenario with Logan, expressions of empathy can be used in several different ways. Staff could help Logan explore his college experience and how it might feel to have his choices made for him by his family, how others may see him as a one-dimensional party boy, or his potential feelings of regret or guilt around how his prank went awry with the staff member ending up being hurt. Another way to use empathy is to help Logan see a bit more from others' perspectives how the impact of his behavior affects them regardless of his intent. While he didn't set out to hurt the staff member, his actions ended up doing just that. Helping Logan better understand how his actions unintentionally cause harm to others would be a helpful aspect of his growth.

*Development of discrepancy* is the process by which the staff helps a student understand that their current behavior won't help them achieve their desired goal. The staff explores with the student the consequences of their actions in a neutral manner avoiding sarcasm or a condescending tone. The student should become aware of their choices and begin to explore the advantages of choosing a different way to interact.

It is likely Logan has little insight into how his current behavior of drinking, pranking, and missing classes is impacting how he is seen by others and his academic goals. The focus in helping Logan develop discrepancy involves engaging him in a discussion about his life goals and how these are lining up with his expectations. It may be that Logan lacks much insight into what his life goals are and how his current behaviors are either in synch or out of synch with them. Helping Logan better define what his goals are leads to a conversation about how his current behaviors support or detract from these goals.

The third technique of motivational interviewing is called *avoiding argumentation*. This is probably the easiest technique to understand, but the most difficult to put into practice. When you argue back to the student who is arguing with you, neither of you are listening to the other. Let's say that again: if a student is arguing with you and you argue back, they are not listening to you. They are thinking of a retort to what you are arguing. So, don't do that. It doesn't help. Be clear about your expectations and follow through with consequences of the student's behavior.

Arguing with Logan about his behavior will be counterproductive and will increase his tendency to be defensive and resistant. Staff should catch themselves before falling into this trap when addressing Logan and his choices. Two examples are shown below.

## Bad Interaction

Logan: I don't see why this is such a big problem. It's not like I went out of my way to hurt the woman taking the money for the parking tickets.

Staff: Well, your intent doesn't really matter here, does it? You hurt her and that's the fact of what happened.

Logan: Well, the parking ticket was stupid, so I suppose the school should expect a stupid response to stupid action.

## Good Interaction

Logan: I don't see why this is such a big problem. It's not like I went out of my way to hurt the woman taking the money for the parking tickets.

Staff: Listen, of course you didn't start the day out thinking about hurting the cashier.

Logan: No, I didn't.

Staff: Can I ask what went through your mind when the bag fell out of your hands?

Logan: I mean, I didn't want to hurt anyone. It's not like the cashier was even the one who gave me the ticket. I was trying to make a statement because I felt like the office had taken away all my choices. They threatened to suspend my account if I didn't pay this ticket. But when that bag fell out of my hand, yeah, I worried about that. I didn't set out to hurt anyone. I'm sorry that happened.

The fourth technique is called *roll with resistance*. Staff are encouraged to avoid meeting a student's resistance to change head-on. Instead, they should try to engage the student in new ways of thinking about the situation. Perhaps trying to evoke new solutions to the conflict from the student. Lack of motivation or an unwillingness to change and be positive are understood as normal developmental responses, and interventions are designed to avoid becoming mired down in the students' lack of developmental growth and personal responsibility to change.

Logan has a long history of being argumentative with staff and resistant to critical messages about his behavior. Helping Logan see his behavior differently and get to a place of being willing to change requires avoiding springing the well-placed traps he has a history of placing in conversations. To this end, staff could even visualize Logan holding out a loaded mouse-trap to the staff trying to bait them into taking the cheese. Staff should remain focused on keeping a sense of balance and equanimity in the face of Logan's trickery and stay focused on the goal, which is to lower Logan's defensiveness and resistance and help him see his behavior through a different lens.

The final technique of motivational interviewing is *supporting self-efficacy*. This involves helping the student understand that change is possible and there is the opportunity for a better outcome in their future. Staff and faculty encourage and nurture growth in the student, finding times and opportunities to "catch them doing well" and praising this behavior with hopes of shaping future positive behavior.

Despite Logan's history of party-going, missing classes, and his prankster ways, there are likely positives Logan displays with others around campus. This might be related to his generosity (albeit that includes buying underage students alcohol) or his ability to form positive social relationships and achieve popularity on campus. Building from these strengths may give staff a key to working with Logan and shaping more positive choices.

## A CASE OF DANGER

Eduardo is a fifty-two-year-old construction worker who was injured on the job (leg fracture) and decided to attend a two-year community college to look at new career options. This was six years ago and he is still at it. Eduardo takes one or two classes each semester and tends to either obtain a D or drop the class. He often monopolizes class discussions and becomes angry when people don't listen to his point of view. He prides himself as being "from the streets" and doesn't hold back on his colorful language and hostile trash talk with other, younger students of a similar background. The college has a student lounge and lunch area to be used between classes and Eduardo gets into a confrontation with the cashier about her overcharging him for his lunch. He yells at her and attempts to bring other students into the argument. A younger student tells him to "shut the hell up, old man" and this enrages Eduardo. The two continue to yell at each other and spill over a lunch table, when university police are called to calm the conflict.

## THE APPLICATION OF CHANGE THEORY

Cindy Mancini: The moon looks different now, it's not as mysterious or romantic as before.

Ronald Miller: I'm sorry I ruined it for you.

Cindy Mancini: You didn't ruin it, you just changed it I guess.

*Can't Buy Me Love*

Another approach to working with the often frustrating and difficult process of encouraging a student in crisis to change their current behavior lies in the work of Prochaska, Norcross, and DiClemente (1994). Their book *Changing for Good* is a powerful one that is often used when teaching courses in psychology or adjustment and personal growth. The concepts are universally helpful when looking to answer the question "Why don't I (or this person in front of me) change their behavior?"

Their approach outlines how people move through various stages before becoming ready to make lasting change in their lives. This can help give a sense of perspective and understanding about why a student may be repeating difficult or frustrating behaviors. When we teach these concepts, we ask people to pause before going on and think about a behavior they have tried to change in their life. This can be something they are currently struggling with (perhaps smoking, watching too much TV, not getting enough exercise) or something they have tried to change in the past. Please do this now; it will provide a personal connection as we move through the five progressive stages.

## Pre-contemplation

At this stage, the student is unaware that there is a problem and hasn't thought much about change. Faculty can help the student increase their awareness of their need for change through discussion. They also can help the student understand how their behaviors may be impacting their life.

This stage of change is one of the most challenging for staff to address in their students. The problem, as you may be able to anticipate, is everyone else seems to know that the student has a problem except the student themselves.

Eduardo is a good example of a student who likely has very little insight into his behavior and how it impacts others. A common mistake staff make is telling the student to behave differently and moving too quickly to the fourth stage of change, the Action stage. At the stage of pre-contemplation, Eduardo does not have an investment in changing his behavior, as he doesn't understand or have an awareness of how his behavior is disruptive and impacting those around him. When a student is at the pre-contemplation stage, the challenge becomes helping them think more about what they do and how it impacts others.

## Contemplation

This is the most common stage of change for students to be in. The student has thought about change and is getting ready for movement in the near future. The student realizes their current behavior is not in their best interest, but is not yet ready to begin their plan to change. The student isn't happy about their current state and wants things to be different, but has not yet explored how to do things differently or take action to make changes in their life.

In this stage, staff can motivate the student and encourage the student to think in more detail about how their behavior is having a negative impact in their life. They should explore ways they might plan for change and what resources could be helpful in implementing change.

Eduardo may begin to develop an awareness of how others see him in the classroom. For example, his advice may continue to fall flat on the younger generation and he may begin to understand that others don't respect him in the way he feels he deserves. Eduardo may also begin to appreciate, albeit slowly, that his academic progress of D's and dropped classes over six years is falling short of his personal goals. At the contemplation stage, staff should ask open-ended questions to help Eduardo better understand how his behavior is not getting him to achieve the goals he wants to achieve. While he may not quite be ready to change his behavior, and approach his relationships and classwork differently, he becomes increasingly aware that his current behavior is not in line with his ultimate relationship and career goals.

## Preparation for Action

In this stage, the student is aware of a problem and is ready to actively create goals to address the problem behavior in their life. Plans and goals should be focused, short term, and designed to be updated and altered to ensure the student's success. Plans should be measureable and something the student can monitor and understand if they are moving forward, static, or moving backward. Staff can help the student brainstorm and update their plans to ensure a better chance of success.

Here, Eduardo not only has an awareness that his current behavior is problematic and keeping him from reaching his goal, but he now has a commitment to change. This commitment should be seen like a small spark catching on some dry tinder. It needs nurturing and support for the fire to become fully engaged. Staff at this stage should encourage and support Eduardo's self-reflection and desire to do things differently, and help him identify obstacles and challenges to changing his behavior. The pathway to action requires preparation and discussion to better prepare for the up and down, forward and back nature of change.

## Action

This stage of change is where the student puts their plan into action to change their behavior. The student will attempt to alter their negative behaviors and develop new positive behaviors to replace them. Staff can support the student in trying out these action steps and encourage them to keep trying, despite setbacks and the potential failures they may encounter.

Action is often the stage we want to start with when helping students; however, it is rare a student is already at this stage when we begin to help. Eduardo may find himself looking more closely at action if his behavior is brought into light related to a conduct action by the school or an academic probation related to his class performance. When Eduardo is ready to change, the staff's role is about supporting this change and keeping the momentum going. Change is always fraught with setbacks and unforeseen challenges. Helping Eduardo keep positive and not become overwhelmed with the effort required to bring about change in his life is key to the intervention.

## Maintenance and Relapse Prevention

Here the goal is to continue successful plans and repeat those action steps that work, while adjusting things that don't. Change has occurred for the student, and there has been a reduction in problem behavior. They maintain their successful change and reduce the risk of falling back into bad habits. Staff can help bolster the student's success and develop awareness of potential obstacles that could lead to relapse.

Eduardo is either successful in changing his behavior or he is not. If he is successful, the staff's role becomes helping him maintain his change and avoid falling back to bad habits. If a bad behavior recurs, staff help him see this as a small obstacle or a temporary setback rather than something that undoes all of his past positive work. If Eduardo slips or relapses, staff help him see this in the larger construct of the process of change—slow and steady wins the race, two steps forward and one step back.

## CHALLENGING IRRATIONAL HOPELESS THOUGHTS

Well, what am I supposed to do? You won't answer my calls, you change your number. I mean, I'm not going to be ignored, Dan!

Alex Forrest, *Fatal Attraction*

The psychologist Albert Ellis (2007) is best known for his work in Rational Emotive Behavioral Therapy (REBT), where the cognitive-behavioral concept of irrational and catastrophized thoughts was first developed. This concept suggests that we all have the potential to engage in irrational thoughts that can be catastrophized (raised to extreme and unrealistic levels) that then have a direct impact on our feelings and behaviors.

Activating events can happen in a variety of settings. These could occur through daily hassles that the individual encounters in the environment (daily work stress, financial worries, self-esteem), life changes (graduation worries, family divorce, or conflict, being away from home the first time), environmental stresses (construction noises outside the dorm, heating or cooling problems in the residence hall, frustration from living in close quarters with other college students), chronic pain (from past surgery, illness, or injury), or acculturation stress (moving from another country or geographic region, living in a religiously different area).

A simple example is the woman who spills some coffee on her blouse prior to a presentation. The woman then believes, irrationally, that everyone in the room will notice the coffee stain and therefore assume that she is a "slob, unprepared and generally unorganized person." She catastrophizes the irrational thought and takes it to an absurd conclusion. She then does more damage by acting on this thought and allowing herself to become distracted and disorganized during her presentation.

Likewise, some students become so preoccupied and irrationally fixated on their social connections that they fall into the trap of extrapolating a bad, unfortunate experience into one that is horrible and life-changing. A student is teased or bullied and begins to believe everyone on the entire planet is against them.

## THE POWER OF REFERRAL

> Dr. Leo Marvin: You think he's gone? He's not gone. That's the whole point! He's never gone! [Leo opens the door; there's Bob]
>
> Bob Wiley: Is this some radical new therapy?
>
> Dr. Leo Marvin: YOU SEE?
>
> *What about Bob?*

A central premise of this book is found in the idea that no one is going about correcting disruptive and/or dangerous behavior from students in a vacuum. Any staff or faculty who are working with student' behaviors should see themselves as part of a larger process, not individual actors.

Many of the problems we encounter in higher education are circular in nature. Those who work in higher education appreciate the unique nature of the "college student stories," though we also know many of these stories remain the same. Students push against authority. They test limits. They behave in immature ways. Some are isolated and angry at the world. Some are bullied. Some are teased. Others are clearly not ready yet to get the most out of their college experience. Think of every referral you make to counseling, conduct, the ADA office, or the campus BIT as a start of a circle. Think of the initial referral as an arc drawn on a piece of paper. The other half of that arc is making sure the referral "sticks" and the outcome is satisfactory to you as the referral source. Think of closing the circle.

At the heart of this, we are talking about an exercise in personal responsibility paired with a little healthy paranoia. Don't assume that the problem has been dealt with because you haven't seen the student for a while. Attend to the silences, and never let a student "fall through the cracks." To assume that a student is doing better because no one has heard from him in a while is a fatal flaw in follow-up. Staff need to be thoughtful and concerned with student behavior as they are on the front lines when it comes to violence prevention in higher education. While reporting concerning behavior in their office or department is a first step, following up on the reports to ensure that some kind of action or next step has been taken and/or sending a report on how the student is doing (better, worse, the same) helps to ensure the closing of the circle to prevent any students from falling through those cracks.

### Counseling Referral

Counseling services are varied at different colleges and universities. Some are non-existent; some are no more than academic and career support centers that can also address some minor mental health wellness issues such as stress, time management, or organization skills. Some out-source counseling to an Employee Assistance Program (EAP) or Campus Assistance Program (CAP). Other centers provide top-notch psychological testing, assessment groups, and individual treatment, as well as facilitate in-patient admissions for suicidal students.

Issues referred to counseling run the full gamut: from anxiety disorders to depression to drug abuse to schizophrenia to academic stress to trauma; if it happens in the "real world," it happens on campus. A quality director of counseling should be glad when calls come from staff or departments who share concerning emails, upsetting behaviors, or simple requests for consultation or a presentation to the department. Poor directors see these phone calls as frustrating annoyances; taking them away from their important work. Referrals work better when you have a receptive director of counseling.

One approach is to invite counseling staff into your department to give a lecture or presentation about their services or a topic related to a content area. Referring a student becomes easier when the staff have a good understanding of what counseling can and cannot do for students, who the counselors are in the department, and how counseling should be de-stigmatized for students as a source of help, not a label or judgment.

## Disability Referrals

Students often struggle with academics in the classroom or interacting with staff in offices around campus because of a disability. These disabilities are protected under the ADA and students can obtain an outline for reasonable accommodations through their campus Disability Support Services Office (DSSO), a centralized office charged with responsibility for determining appropriate accommodations for students who have registered and qualified for those accommodations. (Note: It is not the purview of the staff or professor to determine what accommodations are appropriate. Doing so may put the professor and the institution at risk of violating the ADA or other anti-discrimination laws.) These accommodations may include note-takers, extended test time, a change in seating location, access to specialized textbooks, specialized instructions, or additional appeals for common processes or applications.

While it is a student's responsibility to obtain these accommodations through the DSSO, many students don't understand how to go about obtaining an assessment or setting up a meeting with the ADA office (despite the information sent to them and given during orientation; this may shock you, but students don't always read everything we give them to read). Students may also be concerned about being stigmatized as a "student with a disability" and therefore have a desire to be successful in their coursework on their own. This may be a noble gesture on their part; however, as the class becomes more difficult and the work more challenging, students may find themselves quickly treading water far from shore. Caring staff can share their point of view on accommodations early in the semester and departments serving students should invite the ADA coordinator to offering a training to staff explaining the services they provide to the students.

## Conduct Referrals

Staff occasionally refer students directly to the Student Conduct Office (SCO). Most schools handle behavioral concerns such as disruptions and rude or threatening behavior through the Code of Student Conduct. These reports are sent to the conduct officer, a meeting is scheduled and sanctions are given or a formal hearing is scheduled. Alternatively, some colleges and universities choose to handle minor disruptions without involving conduct or the police and expect staff to manage the behavior directly.

Immediate referrals (phone and online incident reports) to the SCO and/or the campus conduct or the police are expected if a student is threatening, violent, or aggressive in a department or office. Campus conduct referrals may also happen quickly for racism, harassment, or excessively odd or strange behavior that disrupts the academic environment. Most schools adopt a developmental, educational, or restorative justice approach to addressing student conduct violations in order to foster a sense of learning, growth, and redress for those impacted by the student's behavior.

## BIT Referrals

Referring students to the campus BIT depends on the policy and procedures, rules and regulations your campus has set up in terms of reporting expectations. The rule of thumb for staff about reporting behavior to the campus BIT goes something like this: "If you aren't sure, do it."

Most campuses want information shared with their BIT and see a well-functioning BIT as one that analyzes and triages potential reports into low, moderate, and high levels of concern. The BIT (and/or in some cases, Threat Assessment team) then takes the information and sorts through it to develop an action plan. There are times when this action plan results in the team taking no direct action with the student but taking a "wait and see" stance. Other times, a team may seek to gather more information from available resources such as other professors, an advisor, admissions officer, residence life, campus safety, or the counseling office.

Some suggest having staff be more restrictive in terms of what they report to the BIT. While sharing an incident where a student who gave off a rude or entitled vibe while requesting a form from a front office staff is probably a solid example of over-reporting, it becomes quickly evident that most other disruptive and disrespectful behavior may contain some of the early signs or indications of a potentially more serious behavior problem. This isn't always the case. Students can often be eccentric, frustrating, annoying, or difficult, and present no need to be involved with a campus BIT action plan. However, it is our opinion that the campus BIT is in the best position to sort through this data from staff and then decide about next steps based on their process.

So, when at a loss about what kind of behavior you should report to the BIT, in the end it comes down to just this: "Do it." A more detailed discussion of staff working with a campus BIT is included in Chapter 6.

## Title IX

The same type of reporting exists under Title IX. When a staff member learns of any gender-based discrimination (which would include sexual assault, harassment, bullying, relationship/domestic violence, etc.), even if the incident is dated, they should notify the Title IX Coordinator. The good news for staff is this: telling your SCO and/or BIT will likely get the information to the Title IX Coordinator. Some campuses have provided faculty with a brochure to give to students who may be the victim of discrimination—check with your Title IX Coordinator (you have to have one by law) for more information. But, like with the BIT, the rule of thumb here is, "When in doubt, report."

## Academic Advising/Support

One of the biggest challenges facing students is the stigma attached to asking for help with their academics. Students come to college and university with differing levels of preparation and often need support and addition tune-up advice when first arriving on campus or when facing a hurdle during a particularly difficult class. Staff and faculty all around the university should be well versed in how to access these services and how best to ensure students are able to make that first appointment for assistance.

These referrals to academic support services are more successful when the entire campus community has a good understanding of how these services are used and why seeking support is a sign of resilience and success and not of weakness. When staff are aware of the programs being offered, and can talk about a referral knowledgeably and from a position of stigma-reduction, there is a better chance of the student feeling comfortable and able to ask for help.

## MOVING FORWARD

Following the initial crisis, staff look to the bigger picture to take part in bringing about change in the student's life. Whether you like the term mentor, advisor, helper, coach, advocate, or cheerleader, all have the underlying desire to assist the student in a solution-focused and positive manner to overcome the challenges that face them in their progress and the college. Using some of the techniques outlined in this chapter such as rapport building, motivational interviewing, change theory, setting boundaries, and making the appropriate referral, staff can become effective agents for change in the student's life.

The next chapter looks more closely at ways to maintain change over time and build resiliency with those students for whom change comes more slowly. Working with those who are our frequent fliers can be a stressful and frustrating endeavor, so we offer some advice on how to best manage chronic problems.

# Chapter 5

# Managing Ongoing Behaviors

I'll be back.

*Terminator*

In some ways, managing disruptive and dangerous student behavior would be easier if staff only had to de-escalate crises and did not have to interact with students again. This is rarely the case, and ultimately, it is not how we want to approach these situations.

Students who are successfully persisting through the college experience are generally less at risk than students who are being removed from campus and forced to break what connections they have with a more stabilizing environment. This is not to say that schools should continue to allow a student to disrupt or endanger a campus community, but it highlights the idea that the connections and resources available on a college campus generally provide more opportunities to engage with a student, monitor their behaviors, and work to support student growth and development.

Staff in residence life, student life, academic advisors, and case managers have a high likelihood of working with a student throughout the college experience, but even front line staff or staff working in departmental units such as financial aid or the bursar's office may find themselves dealing regularly with the same student. We hope that the experience of working with students and seeing them change and grow is a positive one, but unfortunately, we know that sometimes our ongoing interactions with students can be trying and difficult for staff, if not disconcerting and worrisome.

In many cases, staff may be tasked with interacting with a student regularly during the course of their job responsibilities. The first type of long-term management of student concerns includes working with students who experienced crisis or trauma and are continuing their enrollment or returning from a short break. The second group of students involves those who continue to exhibit repeated behaviors of concern and are actively engaged with BIT or conduct staff through coordinated interventions.

In most cases, students are on an improved trajectory where staff should be watching for setbacks and obstacles to their care plans. In other scenarios, repeated interactions can create a drain on staff energy and resources especially if student behaviors do not seem to improve or even worsen. These "frequent flyers," students who we seem to have the same conversations and interactions with over time with little change, can cause frustration and annoyance in staff.

Staff play an important role in the ongoing follow-up with students after a crisis. Our goal is for staff to be working in coordination with the BIT or conduct office to echo messages encouraging positive change from the student. This chapter shares techniques and strategies to deal with the ongoing management of student behaviors and how to encourage student development and growth while being realistic about staff time, energy, and roles.

## ADOPTING A TEACHER MINDSET

First learn stand, then learn fly. Nature rule Daniel-son, not mine.

Mr. Miyagi, *Karate Kid*

Maybe you remember watching Mr. Miyagi in *Karate Kid* with his innovative and creative approaches to teaching. From scrubbing floors to washing cars, his techniques to help Daniel learn were intentional and tailored for his student. When thinking about how to manage ongoing interactions with students who have previously been distressed or disruptive, it is helpful to embrace the mindset of teachers outside of the classroom, creating environments where students have the opportunity to establish new behavior patterns, learn, and develop. We are not suggesting that a staff member should work beyond the scope of their position or responsibilities, but if staff are in a role that requires ongoing interaction with the same student, it is helpful to keep in mind some foundational concepts of learning and student development.

Mr. Miyagi might have taken some notes from Professor Nevitt Sanford. Sanford's developmental framework outlined the influence of challenge and support on a student's development (Sanford, 1966). We can learn a couple of critical concepts from this work. First, for learning and development to occur there is a need for a student's existing perceptions and understandings to be challenged. A person's existing way of doing things must no longer work in the same way so that they are challenged to identify new ways of being.

In *Karate Kid*, Daniel experiences a major transition to a new school and town as well as bullying, intimidation, and even violence from other students. These are difficult experiences that we would not want for a student, but they are also the catalyst for reaching out to an unexpected source of new knowledge in Mr. Miyagi and a motivation to learn the new skill of karate. Here, we can see that it is not only the challenge that is needed for learning, but also a readiness to achieve something new.

**80**

Why do students react so differently to the same challenges? Why is a challenging incident debilitating to some but the inspiration for change to another? There are obviously a number of reasons for the different responses, but Sanford (1966) highlights the importance of support and stability to balance the new challenge. Support does not mean confronting the challenge for the student or taking on tasks for the student. Instead, Sanford suggests that when we find support through stabilizing factors we are then better able to manage the challenging experience, grow, and develop. The support can come in the form of resources or people that make the challenge more manageable. The role of the staff member can be in helping a student to identify the support structures available to them that can provide stability during a time of new growth and change.

## THE FREQUENT FLYER

Money never sleeps, pal.

Gordon Gekko, *Wall Street*

Let's consider the story of Daylon and his ongoing financial difficulties. Daylon is a first-year student who is attempting to come to college with little to no financial support, other than financial aid. Daylon connects with an academic advisor during orientation activities who helps him to complete the FAFSA and works with him to apply for housing. Daylon's parents are not with him at orientation, and it seems like he has little family assistance or support.

Because his FAFSA is late, he is unable to financially cover the costs of on-campus housing. The academic advisor reaches out to the Housing Department and is able to make arrangements for Daylon to move into the halls while waiting for his financial aid to be awarded. When he is eventually awarded his aid, it comes in the form of a refund check. Instead of first paying his outstanding housing and meal plan bills, Daylon uses the refund check for personal purchases and food, so he remains "in the red" with the institution.

Daylon's story offers us a glimpse at the positive and negative aspects of making exceptions for students related to institutional processes as well as the importance of helping students to learn how to navigate processes instead of allowing them to sidestep them through our support and assistance. Daylon did not become familiar with the FAFSA process or the processes related to paying for his education, and he ends up making a poor decision related to his financial aid refund. The academic advisor had the best intentions asking for an exception for the student to live in the halls while waiting for funding, but it sets in course a pattern of interactions with Daylon where he takes less and less responsibility for his college enrollment.

Throughout Daylon's first year, he approaches numerous staff across campus in different units about his inability to afford food for himself, even though he has a campus meal plan through his aid package. Because the staff are not communicating to one another about their interactions, Daylon receives a number of different special accommodations from departments. One department puts money on his student meal plan card for him. Another purchases food for him from their personal account. In February, Daylon does not complete the FAFSA for his second year as directed and is again late applying for aid.

As summer approaches, Daylon says he has nowhere to live for the summer and requests summer housing. He does not have aid for the summer, and staff again work with him to make last-minute aid requests and to settle him into summer housing. Daylon is also not doing well academically and is on academic probation from his first year at the college. Here we have the staff attempting to help Daylon, but again, reinforcing his pattern of reliance on others.

In the fall, Daylon is selected for verification as part of financial aid processes and struggles to complete the required paperwork to be awarded his aid. During this process, he is also required to provide information from his parents as part of a parent loan he received. This is the first indication that his parents are in part associated with his college enrollment.

Again, he is allowed to move into the halls while processes are resolved. Daylon is starting to become depressed over his academic performance and financial situation. During his second year, he starts to complain to other students and staff about his distress and lack of options even demonstrating indications of suicidal ideation. His behaviors are finally reported to the campus BIT, and the BIT case manager reaches out to Daylon.

## REPORT, REPORT, REFER, REFER

Adam: Well, how is it you see us and nobody else can?

Lydia: Well, I've read through the Handbook for the Recently Deceased. It says "live people ignore the strange and unusual." I myself am strange and unusual.

Barbara: You look like a regular girl to me.

*Beetlejuice*

Sometimes the idea of reporting student concerns and making good referrals can get lost especially when staff are interacting frequently with the same student. Here, we want to reinforce the importance of regularly reporting concerns related to students to your campus BIT or conduct offices without delay, as well as updating on shifts in the student's behaviors or attitude. Also, staff should focus on maintaining a consistency in communications to the student, especially related to the resources and options available to them.

In Daylon's scenario, he is interacting with staff and students across campus related to a variety of concerns, but it is not until his second year at the institution that a report is made to the campus BIT. What were some of the warning signs? He is unable to navigate financial aid processes on his own. Several exceptions are made related to deadlines and requirements to live on campus and to pay for enrollment. He is also making verbal statements about his own hopelessness over his situation to students and staff. By reporting these interactions to a campus BIT, the team can gather more complete information about Daylon's situation.

Even after the initial report, the continued interactions with Daylon would be important to observe for shifts in his attitude and behaviors. What we would suggest is that, in these frequent flyer situations, you develop an ongoing conversation with your campus BIT or conduct staff where you are sharing regular updates on your communications with the student and are able to quickly report any critical shifts in behaviors. For example, staff could report on Daylon's inability to take responsibility for his financial aid paperwork and deadlines combined with his statements about a lack of food.

As staff, we get caught up in our daily routines. In your role, students may often struggle with navigating a certain process or system. You may frequently see students distressed over finances or other issues. Every student can feel, on bad days, like a frequent flyer. In Daylon's case, staff may have been used to seeing him come in and ask for help, so they did not see it as something to report to the campus BIT because it was his typical behavior.

We would also ask here that you give some thought to how you can identify the outliers in your work. Think about how disruptive, distressed, or dangerous behaviors look in the context of our own environment. Talk with your campus BIT about what behaviors to report and create a list more specific to your unit or department. Recall the student situations that escalated after your interactions and what some of the indicators were when the student was working with staff in your department. Most importantly, we do not want you to become oblivious to the indicators of concern in our ongoing interactions with students.

Staff should also be reiterating the same messages to Daylon across the various departments. Frequent flyer students have a knack for honing in on staff inconsistencies in directions, processes, and policies. If the financial aid staff are indicating Daylon must have his paperwork completed by a certain date, those same messages should be given by other staff involved in residence life, academic advising, and case management.

Similar to ongoing reporting is the concept of ongoing referrals. The earlier chapters provide referral sources and resources for the stages of calming the initial crisis and motivating and inspiring change. Don't underestimate the value of repetition in referrals for students. You may feel that a student has already been told about a service available to them, or the student may have previously declined to utilize a certain department suggested to them. We would argue that it's OK to make the referral to the student again. It's possible that the timing is better, and the student is more receptive to the advice. Something about how you describe the service or referral may be different from how another staff member described it, so the student may find it more appealing hearing about it from you. Students are often bombarded and distracted by the numerous options and resources available to them. Repetition and consistency in our messaging to students about what might be helpful for them can increase the likelihood that they will pursue the referral. With that in mind, review the referrals in Chapter 4 to see if one of the suggested items may assist with your "frequent flyer."

## POSITIVE PSYCHOLOGY

> Who do you think they give me? The Dalai Lama, himself. Twelfth son of the Lama. The flowing robes, the grace, bald... striking. So, I'm on the first tee with him. I give him the driver. He hauls off and whacks one – big hitter, the Lama – long, into a ten-thousand foot crevasse, right at the base of this glacier. Do you know what the Lama says? Gunga galunga... gunga, gunga-lagunga. So we finish the eighteenth and he's gonna stiff me. And I say, "Hey, Lama, hey, how about a little something, you know, for the effort, you know." And he says, "Oh, uh, there won't be any money, but when you die, on your deathbed, you will receive total consciousness." So I got that goin' for me, which is nice.
>
> Carl Spackler, *Caddyshack*

Martin Seligman founded the positive psychology approach in 1998. In modern psychology, treatment is normally focused on a client's symptoms and difficulties. In contrast, Seligman's post-modern work studies people who live happy and successful lives and looks to teach their strengths to others. The approach is highlighted by a quotation from the British philosopher Thomas Troward (1847–1916): "The law of floatation was not discovered by contemplating the sinking of things, but by contemplating the floating of things which floated naturally and the intelligent asking of why they did so."

Staff have the potential to focus on where the student is failing to complete forms on time or follow expectations in the residence halls. In fact, traditional approaches to management and leadership that are overly focused on failure will do well to take a cue from this approach. The positive psychology approach suggests that while we respond appropriately to the negative, we should spend an equal amount of time looking at the qualities that enable individuals and communities to thrive. It encourages us to seek ways to support and connect to positive influences and supportive communities.

Staff make a mistake when they become singularly focused on identifying negative behaviors, monitoring students for slip-ups, and trying to control their office like a police officer walking his beat. Although we need to fill out incident reports and hold students accountable for their behavior, we must primarily attend to qualities that make our students healthier and focus on the positive attributes of those who overcome obstacles and manage their stress effectively. It is here that we will find ways to help other struggling students overcome their difficulties. Positive psychology doesn't suggest replacing departmental rules or objectives related to behavior, but instead to supplement them, and encourage staff to attend to a student's potential and see negative behaviors as speed bumps on otherwise positive journeys.

## HAPPINESS AND SUCCESS

Barbara: We're very unhappy.

Juno: What did you expect? You're dead.

*Beetlejuice*

Happiness and success are such basic concepts that we often assume that they imply a common understanding. But what does it really mean to be happy and successful?

We find ourselves in relationships with students who beat themselves up over a single mistake or bad interaction with a staff. We find ourselves talking to other staff who have many friends in the office and are well respected by colleagues. Staff who have it all together when helping others and avoiding conflict. What does it mean to be happy? What does it mean to be a success?

Research tells us that people who express gratitude on a regular basis have better physical health, optimism, progress toward goals, well-being and help others more (Emmons & Crumpler, 2000). Likewise, people who witness others perform good deeds experience an emotion called "elevation," and this motivates them to perform their own good deeds (Haidt, 2000). Staff can use this information to create an office environment that emphasizes these types of activities and interactions.

Staff could try the following exercises with a student. They could ask the student to imagine that everything has gone well in their classes and encourage them to think about what it would feel like to accomplish their life dreams and goals. They could ask the student to write down three good things that happen each day and think about the causes for these good things. These positive-focused activities and exercises could help shift the student to a more optimistic way of seeing their academic work on a day-to-day basis. You can see how using these strategies with our frequent flyer case, Daylon, could be an effective way of trying to revive his academic intentions.

Positive psychology suggests that we help students build on a positive experience to develop healthy traits and to ultimately create or connect with healthy institutions and communities. An example could be a student who struggles in a class, but is committed to being on time to appointments for tutoring. This attention to detail is a positive trait that could be nurtured to improve other aspects in their life.

The difference between people who are successful and those who are not, often depends on how they see failure. We can help students see failure or mistakes as temporary setbacks along the longer journey of academic success. How often do we remind students that they are not alone in making these mistakes? Do we remind them that other students have struggled to master their academic challenges and have gone on to excel and flourish? That other students have also had trouble making friends or have felt so angry with someone they wanted to hit that person, but have gone on to deal with those feelings and do well at college?

When we talk with students about failures being temporary setbacks, we often don't make it the conversation's primary focus. Although many of us would agree that we should encourage hope in those we interact with, how often do we actually focus our energy on it? In his book, *Making Hope Happen,* psychologist Shane Lopez (2013) describes the "Hope Cycle" as one that includes goals, an idea of where we want to go, our individual agency, our ability to shape our lives, and pathways, how we find appropriate routes from where we are to where we want to be. When we apply this concept to the academic environment, we can agree that staff and students, as well as departments and institutions, benefit when staff and students see hope in their future, and experience their work and academic progress through the lens of the Hope Cycle.

## What does it mean to be happy?

Seligman (2006) suggests there are three kinds of happiness all people are able to achieve. The first is found through pleasant engagement, where the individual is encouraged to find as much positive emotion as they can around them. They are then encouraged to try to amplify and be mindful of these good things, savoring them, and stretching them to last longer. Some of us are better than others appreciating the good around us. All of us typically adapt to positive things in our lives, and the experiences habituate and become mundane after so much repetition. Even paradise would become tedious after enough time.

The second form of happiness, which should be seen as an addition to the first, rather than a replacement, is living a life of engagement. This involves finding something we love—work, parenting, love, leisure time, or hobbies. As we engage in these activities, we lose ourselves in what many refer to as "the zone." In the literature, this is described as "flow"—that place where we feel a sense of inner clarity, focus, concentration, and being outside of ordinary reality (Csíkszentmihályi, 1990). We live life as a work of art, rather than as a chaotic response to external events. A life filled with flow experiences is likely to be a fulfilling and happy one.

Examples of flow would be gardening, playing music, learning to dance, reading a book, or playing a video game. The individuals lose themselves in the activity and they are engaged and focused on what is in front of them.

The third form of happiness is the highest form and should be seen as further progression from the first two conditions; not replacing them, but building upon them. This third stage of happiness is understanding the meaning of your life. Knowing what your highest strengths are and using them to belong to and join in the service of something larger than you are. It is finding the perfect job where you can be engaged in the everyday, but also give back to others and the larger community.

While it won't be found in any student handbook, one task staff has is helping the student find their passion in their lives. When they are passionate about their work, it moves faster and doesn't feel like work any longer.

Tennyson describes this sense of purpose and direction as The Gleam:

> Launch your vessel, And crowd your canvas, And, ere it vanishes Over the margin, After it, follow it, Follow The Gleam.
>
> Alfred Lord Tennyson, *Merlin and The Gleam*

## GETTING A HANDLE ON ANGER

> Don't mess with the bull, young man. You'll get the horns.
>
> Richard Vernon, *The Breakfast Club*

Anger is a monster we all must wrestle with from time to time. In the same way a wrestler trains to be more effective in their sport outside of the match, students should be encouraged to set themselves up for success when it comes to managing situations where they may become angry. Nay (2004) offers the following list of five S- "anger intensifiers" that students can gain better control over prior to experiencing anger or frustration.

### Sleep

Students in high school and college are notorious for not getting enough sleep. This lack of sleep makes them irritable and reduces their ability to be flexible and positively focused when approaching negative stress or activating events. Staff should assist students in discussing their underlying difficulties with sleep (lack of exercise, inconsistent sleep schedule, and substance abuse) and how these lead to difficulty in getting enough rest.

### Stress

The body feels stress when reacting to change and frustrating situations. High stress levels lead to higher irritability and difficulty in responding flexibly and positively when dealing with activating events. Stress is cumulative and builds up to dangerous levels, setting the stage for the next activating event; eventually it might lead to an explosion. When college or high school students engage in too many tasks, struggle to balance competing deadlines, and are surprised by life events like problems at home or relationships ending, they are at risk for intensifying their aggressive responses.

## Substances

Alcohol and caffeine can dramatically intensify our emotions. College students are surrounded by these substances offered at parties and advertised through energy drinks and study aids. Substances increase irritability, and they decrease impulse control and frustration tolerance, both of which can affect how stressful events can be perceived. They can be overused to reduce stress and ultimately make the situation worse.

## Sustenance

Students often struggle to eat a healthy diet and maintain proper exercise. When trying to balance class work, relationships, social life, athletics, club memberships, and family, it is easy to see how good nutrition and exercise quickly fall by the wayside. Too much sugar and junk food may also increase mood swings and intensify aggressive behaviors.

## Sickness

When students become ill, their ability to cope with stress is reduced. Pain and discomfort increase their arousal and irritability and decrease their ability to think clearly. Poor nutrition, lack of exercise, and increased stress leads to a weaker immune system and a higher potential for sickness.

Addressing a student's overall wellness, sleep, eating, stress, and substance use has the potential to help reduce their existing problems. In the same way a gardener ensures the right soil, sunlight, water, and nutrients for plants, addressing anger intensifiers can be useful to support other cognitive behavior therapy efforts. If we return to Daylon's regularly occurring concerns related to finances and other university processes, you can imagine that helping him regain balance in the ways outlined here would allow him to refocus on academics and the resources available to him.

## MAKING A PLAN AND STICKING TO IT

I love it when a plan comes together!

Hannibal, *The A-Team*

One approach that works well with students is walking them through a clear and well-thought-out plan to best illuminate their path moving forward. We have found William Glasser's (2001) work in Reality Therapy particularly helpful when working with Millennial students. He offers a system based on Wants, Direction and Doing, Evaluation, Planning (WDEP). A helpful worksheet outlining this approach is included in Appendix B.

## W = Wants and Needs

Here we look for the desires and direction the student wants to head in. It's no good developing a plan to move forward with a student to reduce disruptive behavior in an office, department, or residence hall without first ensuring that they have an interest in changing the behavior. Help the student understand that by changing their behavior, they can improve their success in achieving what they want.

## D = Direction and Doing

Assess what the student is doing and the direction these behaviors are taking them. Students who act out in the residence halls, ignore rules around alcohol or substances, or disrupt other students from studying are not engaging in behaviors that will help their long-term academic success. Help the student understand that their current behavior is going to result in them remaining at school and will ultimately keep them from reaching their goals.

## E = Evaluation

Make an evaluation of the student's total behavior. Is the behavior taking them closer to their wants and needs? Have they implemented change in their behavior? Is that change successful?

## P = Planning and Commitment

Assist the student in formulating realistic plans and make a commitment to carry them out. As with most change in life, this will often be a "two steps forward, one step back" process.

So, what does a plan end up looking like? What are some of the qualities of a successful plan with a student that is designed to change behavior and reduce campus disruption? Again, Glasser (1975; 2001) shares some thoughts on the qualities needed for a successful plan with a student. These plans are:

- simple: broken into small, easy pieces;
- attainable: realistic and can be accomplished;

**89**

- measurable: can be assessed and evaluated;
- immediate: involve short-term goals that occur soon;
- controlled by the planner: ensuring adjustments;
- consistently practiced: repeated until habits form; and
- committed to: involve buy-in and investment.

When developing a plan for corrective action with a student, focus on these aspects of the plan to ensure a higher rate of success in the student's follow-through. A student who does not buy into the plan, or who cannot see the immediate progress of their behavior related to the plan's success, will likely fail to achieve the goals.

## DEALING WITH IRRATIONAL THOUGHTS

Another approach to help students who are having ongoing difficulty adjusting to college or stressful events around them can be found in Albert Ellis' (2007) work in REBT. REBT was developed by Ellis and is useful to assist students in identifying irrational thoughts that the student has in reaction to activating events. The REBT approach can be described in terms of A-B-Cs: these are Activating events, Beliefs about these events and the Consequences of these beliefs.

*Activating events* can be anything from a relationship argument, getting cut off in traffic, spilling coffee on your favorite shirt, or having your computer crash. These events cannot be prevented, they just occur throughout our lives. It's our *beliefs* about the activating events that lead to increased anxiety, panic, and negative consequences. We cannot change the activating events in our lives, but we can change our beliefs about the activating events and the resulting *consequences* of our behavior.

Staff can help students to identify beliefs about activating events that end up increasing their panic and paranoia about the future. They can be encouraged to appreciate that there will always be upsetting activating events that we will have little control over and that we should instead focus our energy and effort on finding alternative ways to think about the activating event in order to increase the likelihood of positive consequences.

This is easier when staff can empathize and help all involved to move away from escalating aggressive behavior. For example, we are less likely to be aggressive toward the driver of a car that cuts us off when we understand that the other driver may be rushing his pregnant wife to the hospital. Our aggression is dissipated because we acknowledge that we might act in the same manner if we faced a comparable situation. A student who is frustrated by a professor for receiving a failing grade on an exam is likely to be less aggressive if the reason for the grade is clear and the student can acknowledge that the quality of work merits the grade that was given.

Ellis' A-B-C's are helpful for both staff and students in managing their emotions and finding alternative ways of thinking about upsetting events. This can be done directly by teaching student's the A-B-C's with examples.

A: Activating events
B: Beliefs about these events
C: Consequence of these beliefs

## Negative Example One

A: You wake up late and don't have enough time to get to a tutoring meeting you scheduled.
B: You would have to rush to the meeting and believe you will get yelled at by the tutor because of being late.
C: You skip the meeting altogether and dig yourself into a hole.

## Positive Example One

A: You wake up late and don't have enough time to get to a tutoring meeting you scheduled.
B: You gather yourself and go late, hoping they can still see you. You stay and apologize to the staff for oversleeping and take the blame.
C: You have a mark against you for coming late to an appointment, but the tutor respects you for taking responsibility for your action.

## Negative Example Two

A: You text a friend who doesn't respond back after several attempts.
B: You become more and more angry and begin to fume about them ignoring you.
C: You leave several angry voicemails and refuse to talk to them.

## Positive Example Two

A: You text a friend who doesn't respond back after several attempts.
B: You think of some other reasons they might not be texting back like their phone is off, broken, or they are sleeping.
C: You find something else to occupy your time and your friend texts back later— apologizing for not getting back to you.

## FOUR STRESS CONTROL TECHNIQUES

Another approach to planning comes from the Navy SEALs. During their "hell" week training, SEALs are taught four key stress control techniques that help them cope better with stress and stay focused on their goals (Blair, 2008). While our students are unlikely to be headed out on combat missions, there are some takeaways from the SEALs that are helpful to share with students.

## Goal Setting

This is the process of encouraging clients to have a clear picture of their goals and creating a way to see progress toward them. This can be done through journaling about progress or creating a chart of successful times they coped with activating events or were able to reduce their escalation phase. The client should be encouraged to focus on an immediate, measurable goal.

A SEAL trainee might focus on "I need to make it to the next hill" or "I just need to stay under for another 5 seconds... I can do another 5 seconds." A student may need to focus on getting through a class without arguing with the professor or "making it through a disagreement by finding a way to step out of the situation and not get upset." For students struggling academically, this would mean looking over all of their assignments and setting up a plan to attend to each one in turn for a set period of time. In this way, the student stays focused on the task at hand and avoids worrying about becoming overwhelmed by the next assignment on the horizon.

## Mental Rehearsal

Students should be encouraged to mentally imagine themselves being successful at a particular interaction that in the past caused problems. It is easy to imagine Navy SEAL trainees visualizing successful missions or accomplishing a goal. Sports psychologists teach this technique for basketball players to improve their foul shots. Students can complete the following steps:

1   Clearly visualize a conflict where you could become aggressive or continue to escalate.
2   Visualize responding calmly and avoiding an escalation or allowing frustrations to develop. Focus on the best possible response, such as "Well, that is certainly one way to see it. I don't see it the same way, though."
3   Imagine obstacles to a successful interaction. Possibly imagine another student pushing or yelling back. Visualize the best possible response.
4   Repeat this process several times a week until you begin to see results.

## Positive Self-Talk

This will assist students in developing an internal "cheerleading team" that can help push them during difficult times. The student should identify a supportive person in their life—a cheerleader— and then imagine that person mentally accompanying them during a conflict. While the conflict is going on, the student can imagine the cheerleader saying, "You got this one. No way are they going to push your buttons. Calm and cool. The more they push, the more you relax."

## Arousal Control

By taking slow, deep breaths with controlled exhalations, individuals communicate to their bodies that they are not in a panic situation (fight/flight/freeze) and that they must maintain control. This process is similar to what expectant mothers, Navy SEAL snipers, and meditating monks use to control their biological functions. As with any technique, practice and repetition are key.

## WORKING WITH PARENTS

Phone home.

*E.T.*

For general staff reading this book, it would never be your position to contact parents regarding a student concern. This is a role left to a Dean of Students, conduct officer, or other administrative position. These individuals will consider the influence of the Federal Educational Rights and Privacy Act (FERPA) on parent notification as well as the overall likelihood of improving or harming the student's situation. However, we want to take a moment here to note the possibility, especially with "frequent flyer" students who are regularly on your radar, that parents or family members will be involved in our interactions and planning with their student.

While this is not a book on dealing with parents, we have outlined a few tips for you below to help any staff member interacting with parents or family members of students.

- Don't overreact or underreact to the idea of FERPA-protected information. Refusing to talk to parents or family members because "everything" is FERPA-protected is generally not the best approach to working with parents. In most cases, there are ways you can listen and provide assistance without any FERPA concerns.
- Begin by thinking about what information in your position is FERPA-protected. It might include items such as student grades, academic status, phone numbers, and other personally identifiable information. Review your college or university policies related to directory information and FERPA for a complete understanding of student records and privacy at your institution.

**93**

- Think about what type of information you have that is not FERPA-protected. This might include directory information as outlined by your institution, but moreover, it includes general facts and information related to how school processes work and what resources are available to students.
- When contacted by a parent, start by acknowledging the limitations in terms of what you may or may not be able to share, but offer to listen to their concerns, and identify ways to assist them. More often than not, just the process of taking time to listen and understand the parents' concerns about the student and explaining institutional processes will be a sufficient way to assist the parent and the student.
- Give the parent options for how to talk with the student about the situation. Can you give them specific processes or resources to talk with the student about? Can you point them to campus resources available to assist parents or family members with college life?
- If conversations are moving beyond the scope of your position, be ready with a referral to a more appropriate staff member on campus. Parents and family members may not understand institutional structures. They can become easily frustrated and just contact the President's Office because no other course of action was suggested. Instead, provide a specific name and contact information for either a Dean of Students, campus BIT, or academic or student affairs administrator who is more suited to assist them. You should also immediately notify the person that you suggested the parent contact and share information about the situation and why you referred them over.

## EYES ON THE ROAD AHEAD

> It's 106 miles to Chicago, we got a full tank of gas… it's dark, and we're wearing sunglasses.
>
> Elwood Blues, *The Blues Brothers*

When you are planning how to get from point A to point B on a trip, perhaps you use Google Maps or another app that gives you directions to your destination. When managing the ongoing behavior of students, being thoughtful about how students will get to their ultimate destination in education can also be helpful. Google Maps does this by highlighting on your map areas of potential concern such as accidents, traffic, or construction. When planning for students, we should also think about potential potholes in the road ahead. We should be thoughtful about triggering events or situations that may serve to reactivate the student's previous behaviors of concern or potentially re-traumatize the student. Being proactive about these catalyst moments for student behaviors can help staff get in front of difficult situations and conversations with students.

In Daylon's case, financial aid deadlines and housing deadlines regularly caused problems for him. How can we be aware of these upcoming deadlines, increase his awareness, and still not give him constant reminders, or do the work for him? Some options might be working with Daylon in advance to update the calendar on his phone with important dates and deadlines, ensuring that he is receiving regular communications from these departments and is checking the correct email addresses, or suggesting that Daylon schedule appointments as the deadlines approach with staff who can assist him with questions or concerns.

Here are a few other examples of triggering activities that staff can better anticipate in their travels with students:

- Student is struggling academically: Time periods when the student receives grade information become important.
- Student has conflicts with a faculty or staff member: An awareness of when they will need to interact again can help staff to prepare for the outcome of the meeting.
- Student struggles with meetings deadlines or requirements for university processes: Attention to these approaching deadlines allows staff to track the student's effort in this area.

An awareness of these critical moments for students gives staff an opportunity to clarify their department processes, increase communication around these time periods, and be more prepared for the student's success or failure. Road trips are more successful when we have a planned route and are ready for potential problems along the way. Navigating ongoing interactions with students can benefit from this same type of planning.

## THE RETURNING STUDENT

> Many of the truths that we cling to depend on our point of view.
>
> Obi-Wan, *Return of the Jedi*

Let's return to Daylon's case. Unfortunately, various interventions did not have the desired impact on his outlook and progress at school. Daylon continued to spiral down and eventually was required to sit out for a semester because of his academic status. We mention this here because some of our most important interactions with students can be during these moments of transition in and out of the institution. These moments give us an opportunity, a checkpoint of sorts, to gauge how the student is doing.

Keep in mind one other teaching concept when you hit the restart button with students. Carol Dweck's (2010) research shows clearly that individuals view learning in two distinct ways. They either see themselves as having a "fixed mindset,"

**95**

believing their intelligence is something they are born with and can only grow to a certain extent, or they have a "growth mindset," believing their capacity for learning can change over time. Students with a growth mindset are more likely to respond to obstacles by engaging, trying new ideas, and using resources. Staff can help facilitate a growth mindset in students by giving them a sense of progress and improvement and discussing challenges as opportunities to learn and grow. Staff should also stay focused on what is yet to come and the long-term opportunities for success available to the student. With frequent flyer students, we can easily fall back into thinking that there is no more room for improvement and learning, and the student may feel the same way. Consider opportunities to invoke the idea of growth back into our conversations to help students see their potential to learn and develop.

The other strategies provided for you throughout this chapter are also well designed for these moments of transition. In a department like financial aid, where staff have worked regularly with Daylon before his suspension, you can see how using techniques related to positive psychology allow staff to "restart" with Daylon. An academic advisor or residence life staff member could use the WDEP planning process with Daylon to discuss better academic performance, financial management, and how to meet deadlines related to housing and financial aid. These same techniques can work well with students returning from voluntary or involuntary leaves from school. Sometimes students are not successful during their initial experiences in college, but this does not mean that a period of time away and a fresh start cannot see different results.

Part of helping well is about seeing students not as broken or as failures, but from another frame. The term *Kintsugi* (or *Kintsukuroi*) refers to the Japanese practice of repairing broken pieces of pottery with precious metals such as gold and silver. When a piece of pottery is broken, it is mended together with gold or silver along the cracks to form something more beautiful than the original piece.

This process reminds us of how things that are broken aren't necessarily worse off for the experience. Not all who wander are lost. The non-traditional community college student who must struggle more than the rest to catch up with technology and balance the competing needs of family, work, friends, and academics. The veteran returning from active duty combat who still has the memories of violence and nightmares competing in his mind with course syllabi and paper deadlines. The first generation college student who fails one of their four classes and continues to learn how to navigate the challenges of university life.

College success is more of a marathon than a sprint. Those who can balance competing needs have the scars and experience to show what they have overcome and achieved. When you ask those who have been successful at college, they tell stories of missteps, failed attempts at papers, classes, and exams, and the importance of concepts such as resiliency, perseverance, and persistence. People who achieve work hard and overcome obstacles. They do not do things perfectly, but instead can pick themselves up, brush themselves off, and take another step toward their goal.

It's the story of the itsy-bitsy spider. You remember that little guy. Rained on. Knocked back down the water spout. But in the end, he persevered and overcame the obstacles placed in front of him. The sun came out and he tried, and tried again. Success comes to those who don't give up and instead have realistic goals about perfection.

Staff are in a unique role to encourage students with these stories and metaphors. Helping the students understand that failure is nothing more than delayed success. They teach students there will be temporary obstacles in the path, but these obstacles are just that, temporary challenges, not permanent barriers. Staff are encouraged to share their own personal stories of missteps, challenges, and failures in their journey. These stories help build a bridge of connection with students, showing vulnerability and teaching that achievement is about picking yourself up and taking another swing at the ball.

## BEING TRAUMA-INFORMED

Sarah: Help! Stop It! Help!

Helping Hand: What do you mean "help"? We *are* helping.

Different Helping Hand: We're Helping Hands.

Sarah: You're hurting!

*Labyrinth*

Throughout this book, we address responding to student concerns and managing behaviors, but let's not overlook the opportunity to be more proactive in our delivery and design of services. For students returning to campus after a crisis or others who experience trauma while enrolled, staff who are skilled in trauma-informed processes and care are more likely to be able to engage with these students and form the connections helpful to their future success.

Trauma-informed care is the idea of designing our department processes and interactions in a manner that accounts for the impact of trauma on students. When thinking about our ongoing interactions with students who have previously experienced trauma, these are tools that we can use to increase the utilization of our services for students as well as their overall impact. Staff can utilize techniques and processes associated with trauma-informed care to help create environments better designed for students recovering from crisis and trauma.

Trauma-informed processes have been used successfully in several settings, including medical and mental health care, substance abuse treatment and recovery, homeless and refuge populations, and military veteran services. In recent years, trauma-informed processes reemerged as a critical component of effective and equitable responses to incidents of sexual violence. These same ideas can be used in most campus units as part of their customer service efforts for students. Table 5.1 highlights some of the major elements of trauma-informed care for staff.

## SELF-CARE FOR STAFF

> Life moves pretty fast. If you don't stop and look around once in a while, you could miss it.
>
> Ferris, *Ferris Bueller's Day Off*

We wanted to end this chapter with a discussion about the necessity of staff taking care of themselves to maintain good health, be retained in their positions, and continue to serve students with their fullest capabilities. You probably would not be reading this book if working with students was not something that you found rewarding, but let's face it, some situations and some days are tougher and more draining than others. When I think of the times when it was difficult to leave my work at the office at 5 p.m. or the times where I felt stressed by my interactions with students, I often think of situations like those we have discussed throughout this book. I especially think about those frequent flyer situations that seemed to be reoccurring with little improvement following my interactions with the student. Yet, those same situations were some of the most rewarding when I was able to see a student through a challenge in their life and watch them persevere.

So, ask yourself this question: "Who do you take care of better, your students or yourself?"

Ideally, we want to find a balance between the two, but more often than not, if we are being honest, many of us tend to prioritize our commitment to students over our commitment to ourselves. This chapter is not suggesting that you skip work as often as Ferris Bueller skipped school, or that you turn away from critical situations like those described throughout the book, but it is recommending that you take this concept of self-care seriously and proactively consider how it can impact you and your ability to do this important work with students. Bottom line, our job performance, relationships, morale, ability to think clearly, and overall wellness will suffer when we do not take care of ourselves.

### Step 1: Recognize When You Are Stressed

Stress can be good and bad. Sometimes a little stress can push us to finish a large project and meet a deadline. The challenge of new situations can be stressful, but they also help us to learn. However, stress can also lead to constant, reoccurring thoughts about work pressures, emails, and our interactions bleeding into our personal time. When we are juggling too many responsibilities, we can literally "drop the ball" and miss appointments or fail to keep up with tasks. It can make us irritable and feel dread over the thought of more work. The physical and mental toll can run from high blood pressure, insomnia, and headaches to exhaustion, inability to focus, and other negative thoughts. When we are stressed, we overextend in an urgent and constant manner while draining more and more energy from our systems.

## TABLE 5.1 Staff Competencies Related to Trauma-Informed Care

| Staff Competencies Related to Trauma-Informed Care | Examples |
| --- | --- |
| Staff recognize situations and experiences that create trauma. | Trauma can occur with any event or life experience that threatens a person's life or well-being. The threat can be real or perceived. Events could include war, medical incidents, violent or abusive experiences, loss of loved ones, and natural disasters. |
| Staff acknowledge the array of responses and reactions to trauma. | The impact of trauma can challenge the emotional, physical, neurological, psychological and social functions of individuals. This includes impairments to thinking, decision making, sleep and memory. Trauma victims can present with virtually any emotion from being angry or depressed to disinterested and irrational. |
| Staff are familiar with the long-term impacts of trauma. | Trauma can have a long-term influence on how someone manages their physical and emotional responses, how they see themselves and the world, and how they form relationships with others. |
| Staff consider their office environments and the impact on those who have experienced trauma. | Physical spaces have the ability to feel supportive and safe. Trauma-informed spaces consider entrances and exits, lighting, seating options, and the other sensory experiences of those using the space from smell to touch. |
| Staff are aware of the causes and impact of re-traumatization. | Experiences that require someone to recall the traumatic event can trigger trauma responses similar to those that occurred at or near the time of the actual trauma. Individuals need space and time to begin to heal from traumatic events and experience the complex reactions that occur with trauma. Staff should carefully consider processes that require retelling of traumatic events. Avoid unsupportive responses, attempts at labeling what a student has experienced, or questioning what a student experienced. |
| Staff acknowledge the impact of trauma on family and friends of those who experienced the trauma directly. | Those close to victims of trauma may also experience similar impacts of trauma or their own stressors related to the event. Trauma-informed processes consider how to offer support to friends and family of victims. |
| Staff prioritize student choice and decision-making related to traumatic events. | Victims of trauma have already had power and control taken from them through the course of what they experienced. Staff should consider ways to empower students and ensure opportunities to choose the path or processes available to them. |

continued...

Table 5.1 continued...

| Staff Competencies Related to Trauma-Informed Care | Examples |
| --- | --- |
| Staff focus on student safety and building trust. | Basic safety planning and needs assessment is a critical first step before embarking with students in other campus processes. Staff should also be attentive to rapport building, role clarification, and helping students to trust the people and processes available to assist them. |
| Staff understand the influence of cultural competence in relation to trauma. | Staff should maintain a self-awareness and recognition of their own implicit bias related to their perceptions of students and trauma. Cultural norms influence our response and reactions to trauma and those who have experienced it. |

Source: Adapted from the Office of Violence Against Women, 2013

One type of stress particularly important for the work discussed in this book is "compassion stress" or "compassion fatigue." Compassion fatigue is a decreased ability to be empathetic and assist with other's suffering because of continued exposure to helping someone who has suffered from a traumatic event such as suicidal ideation, violence, or mental health concerns (Figley, 1995). When we are first confronted with these situations, we are committed and involved with the student, assisting them with problem solving, and using our full array of helping skills. Over time, we can become emotionally fatigued in the same way we become physically fatigued which can quickly impact our level of engagement and satisfaction at work. Similar to compassion fatigue, if we do not recognize other work stress unrelated to working with students managing trauma and suffering, we can still burnout. It's called burnout for a reason. Our spark goes out for the work we do. We no longer feel engaged and instead feel hopeless or numb to the work world around us. Stress and compassion fatigue can be managed and reduced; burnout often leads to needing to change jobs or careers.

## Step 2: Re-Read Portions of this Chapter

Earlier in the chapter, we introduced concepts of positive psychology, happiness and success, and Glasser's Reality Therapy. Return to these sections and review this content with your own attitudes and behaviors in mind. We cannot control all sources of stress in our professional lives, but we can manage our responses to those stressors. The tools we identified for working with students can help staff in shifting their own responses to situations as well.

## Step 3: Identify and Commit to New Self-Care Strategies

Below we have shared a list of possible strategies that you can use to better prepare yourself for engaging with compassion in difficult situations as well as for taking care of yourself along the way. Explore this list as well as other ideas and begin committing to healthier patterns of work for yourself and your coworkers.

- Use regular debriefing strategies with those in your work team. Ask questions such as what happened, why did it affect you, and how did you take care of yourself following it.
- Identify "hot button" cases for you and consider options for minimizing your interactions with these types of cases. Example: If you are a sexual assault survivor, it is OK to ask for help or support when dealing with other victims of violence. If a student comes in and reminds you a great deal of a previous difficult situation, can you ask another staff member to step in for you or sit in with you?
- Incorporate periodic moments of relaxation and personal time throughout your day.
- Make a clear transition from professional/work to personal/home. Find ways to disconnect from electronic devices and communications related to work. Be careful about doing work in personal spaces in your home such as the bedroom.
- Monitor and improve other aspects of your health and wellness such as diet and exercise.
- Ask for help from your supervisor. Discuss workloads, reward systems, role clarification, and the support available professionally.

## MOVING FORWARD

When you picked up this book, you may have thought it would only address your initial interactions with students exhibiting disruptive behaviors. Instead, we hope you are seeing that both our initial and ongoing interactions with students are important to managing student behaviors and promoting student success. In this chapter, we have provided a variety of strategies to employ with students when trying to manage ongoing behaviors and facilitate long-term change. Starting with adopting a teacher mindset and moving to techniques related to positive psychology and rational emotive behavioral therapy, each concept can be applied to a variety of student situations depending on the role of the staff member and the needs of the student. We also acknowledged some of the challenges associated with more frequent and ongoing interactions with students, specifically the impact on staff well-being and self-care. Taking care of yourself is synonymous with taking care of your students.

In the next chapter, we look at the role of BITs in helping staff get out in front of more dangerous behaviors and threats. Sharing information forward is a critical part of keeping the campus safe and identifying the puzzle pieces that may add up to a larger concern in the future.

# Chapter 6

## The Campus BIT, Threat Assessment, Dangerousness

> Go that way, really, really fast. If something gets in your way, turn.
>
> Charles de Mar, *Better Off Dead*

### A BIT ABOUT BIT

You aren't in this alone.

Most schools around the nation have invested in BIT/TATs whose expressed mission is to identify, assess, and manage threat and dangerousness on campus. Your job here is to ensure the team knows about crisis events, however small, that occur within your departments, offices, or residence halls. In fact, the first stage of any BIT/TAT work is ensuring the community knows about their process and what to report forward to the team.

Following the tragedy at Virginia Tech in 2007, there has been a push to formalize teams of staff and faculty at institutes of higher education to assess potential threats to campus security. It is estimated that over 80 percent of four-year colleges and universities have such teams (Eells and Rockland-Miller, 2011). Depending on the mission and purpose of the team, they may also seek to identify at-risk students to provide services and connection among existing departments.

Teams existed prior to the shooting in 2007, but these teams had their focus on helping at-risk students find support on campus, or on critical incident/emergency response following natural disasters, explosions, and fire. Teams existed in the forms of campus "moms and dads," administrators who were serving as de facto parents independently, and as ad hoc "student of concern" teams who operated without protocol or objective measurement. The evolution from here led to protocol-driven, objective measurement teams. One of the first was formed at the University of South Carolina, designed initially not to prevent shooters, but to identify students who were in the early stages of "moving toward" crisis, work with students exhibiting self-injurious behaviors or ideation, and to prevent self-injury and suicide.

Second and third generation BIT/TATs encourage the community to report at-risk behaviors to be reviewed by a group of professionals trained in various areas of expertise such as conduct, psychological evaluation, residential life, campus safety, medical issues, and the legal perspective.

Colleges and universities need to implement threat assessment teams. These teams are essential to identifying threats, reviewing the nature of the threat, and mitigating the risk. The ASME-ITI (2010) American National Standard encourages the following: "It is recommended that Threat Assessment Teams be put into place on campus to help identify potential persons of concern and gather and analyze information regarding the potential threat posed by an individual(s)" (pp. 9–10).

There is some debate in the field around the name of a given team in relationship to its function. Threat Assessment Teams (TATs) are said to focus primarily on identifying threats to campus safety. Behavioral Intervention Teams (BITs) focus on identifying behaviors of concern and providing intervention strategies and action plans to address the behavior. Other names reflect attempts to improve communication between departments such as care, Campus Partners, Networks, Risk Assessment, Student of Concern, and Care and Concern teams.

A central question for teams to wrestle with is the development of a mission or purpose statement. These statements focus the discussion of the team's cases and corresponding actions. For example, a team's mission that reads, "To identify and intervene with students who pose a threat to the campus community" will be more focused on violence and danger to the community. A team that has a mission "To identify and assist at-risk and struggling students become more connected to services" may have a stronger focus on student assistance and may even be concerned with retaining the student's enrollment at the university rather than dangerousness.

Deisinger, Randazzo, O'Neill and Savage (2008) suggest the following for a mission statement: "Identify a student, faculty member, or staff member who has engaged in threatening behaviors or done something that raised serious concern about their well-being, stability, or potential for violence or suicide" (p. 47).

The background experience of the team's membership also has an impact on the mission. Some TATs become focused on law enforcement and police response, others on mental health risk, and all seem focused and concerned with the legal and policy implications of their decisions. Regardless of the background of the team members, there should be a respect for the interaction between the law, mental health, and law enforcement. This creates opportunities for departments to work together and reduce isolated communications.

These isolated communications occur when each department on campus focuses on their own individual mission, policy, and rules without seeing themselves as part of a larger, more complex system. Communications that focus primarily on a single department to the detriment of seeing threat assessment and behavioral intervention as a campus-wide issue are said to be operating in a "silo."

Much like the tall grain silos that are spotted throughout the Midwest, they are single structures serving their function, separated from the larger overall system.

Meloy, Hoffmann, Guldimann, and James (2011) further define this danger: "there is always the risk of a 'silo effect'—different domains of behavior are never linked together or synthesized to develop a comprehensive picture of the subject of concern, conduct further investigation, identify other warning behaviors, and actively risk-manage the case" (p. 19).

Randazzo and Plummer (2009: 56) write,

> one of the biggest pitfalls to avoid was the usual tendency of higher education institutions to operate in information 'silos,' with different departments and offices taking steps on their own to handle situations without knowing the bigger picture or factoring in steps that other departments may be taking. One of the most important roles that Virginia Tech envisioned for its threat assessment team was to facilitate information sharing across departments and offices and to break down some of those silos.
>
> (p. 56)

Much of the benefit of the creation of a team can be found in the simple act of having the diverse department staff and faculty gather weekly to discuss their concerns. While there are important trainings and more advanced ways to develop these interactions to become more efficient, useful, and focused, the heart of the BIT/TAT will always be bringing together these busy, over-scheduled professionals with the purpose of trying to make the campus a safer place.

We have found staff are more likely to buy into a concept if they understand the greater purpose behind their participation. For example, have you ever gotten those little messages on your computer after something crashes that say, "We would like to send an error report? Continue or cancel." We never send it. We don't understand where it goes or what is done with the information that is sent. We don't have any buy-in to the process. We assume our message doesn't mean anything. We think it is added to some great digital pile of messages from around the world. Like the messages sent in tubes on the island from the TV show *Lost*. They are a big pile of wasted messages with no clear purpose.

Reporting information forward to the team, regardless of how small the incident or even if the problem seems to have been resolved in your office, is essential. In fact, this is one of the most important concepts of this entire book. Keeping information from the BIT/TAT that could prevent potential violence is one of the biggest mistakes staff make. See the information you hold like a puzzle piece that gives the team another small part of the larger picture. Teams that work well nurture the campus community to report and respond in a preventative manner to mitigate the potential risk.

## CASE STUDY: GRACE

Imagine Grace, a student who comes into the registrar's office to sign up for a French history class offered next term. Grace is an odd student who is often the butt of teasing from others. She seems to struggle with social interaction, speaks with an odd inflection, and often interrupts the staff with off-topic questions and lengthy rants about her understanding of French history and why the course is important. Grace is smart and often shares insightful and articulate insights about French history, but the problem is in her timing and delivery. She comes across as arrogant and disconnected when talking to staff who have tried to help her register, but can't seem to get her to stop talking long enough to get her to listen. These conversations don't go well and Grace responds with a sullen and snarky mood when interrupted. Grace becomes frustrated and shouts, "I'd like to have you put your head down on a wooden stump and use a guillotine to cut your head off." Staff ask Grace to leave the office. She leaves, slamming the door in the process, and mutters "bitch" under her breath.

## CASE STUDY: CARLOS

Imagine Carlos comes into academic advising and tutoring help for his Anatomy and Physiology class. This is a required course for nursing students. It is a difficult course and about a third of the students find the course so hard they have to take it a second time in order to achieve the required C grade to be accepted by the nursing program. Carlos has failed the first test and shares his worry about being kicked out of the nursing program due to a poor grade. Staff encourage him to study harder and to perhaps visit the campus tutoring center to assist with his studies on a more regular basis. He tells them how important the nursing program is to him and that he has always dreamed of being a nurse. Carlos says that he has been increasingly anxious in class and struggling in the lab assignments. On a dissection project the next day, he runs from the classroom in a state of panic, worried he was going to make a mistake. He doesn't show up for the next week and misses a study session before the second exam. He opens the following email he sends the tutor on his phone:

> Thank you for trying to help me. I have failed and I am a failure. I don't know what I will do, but I wanted to thank you for your kindness if I don't see you again. Please donate my lab dissection tools to a future needy student. I won't need them. Goodbye.

## ADDRESSING GRACE AND CARLOS

Grace has made a clear threat against a staff member and engaged in some rude and disrespectful behavior in front of a waiting room of students. Her outburst will likely have little positive impact on her social status among her peers. How should her threat be handled? Could there be a mental health component to Grace's social behavior? What happens when Grace comes back later in the day to try to register again?

Although Grace has made a threat against a staff, "death by guillotine" would likely require massive funding and carpentry knowledge. While the nature of the threat may not indicate a high lethality event (compared to Grace threatening to shoot her professor with her father's .38 revolver he gave her so she would be safe at college), her poor reaction to the staff's redirection of her poor social behavior and off-topic discussions is a concern. Grace may have a history of social difficulties or a diagnosis of a mental health disorder such as an ASD/Asperger's. Reporting her threat to the Student Conduct Office or BIT will allow for further investigation and potential referral to support services such as counseling and/ or the Disability Support Office on campus. The threat, while likely not a high concern for the staff, may be a first step to connect Grace with support services. Though not likely dangerous, Grace's disruption requires some intervention.

Carlos presents with a mixture of anxiety and depression. Is Carlos dropping the class or is Carlos thinking of killing himself? Should you report this behavior to someone? Is it appropriate to ask Carlos directly about suicide? Is that your role as staff?

His note suggests two potential suicide concerns (giving objects away and a veiled threat of "I don't know what I will do" and "Goodbye"). While these may be the only hint we get prior to Carlos going home and putting a gun to his head, it may be just as likely that he has decided to drop his Anatomy and Physiology class and is thanking his tutor and saying goodbye since he no longer will be in the class; his behavior could be a simple expression of shame that he is having to change his major. As with threat assessment, suicide assessment requires further questioning of Carlos such as asking him: "When you say 'I don't know what I will do' and 'goodbye', it makes me think you might be thinking of killing yourself. Is that what you mean?" Given the academic difficulties, apparent anxiety, and depression observed, a referral to the counseling center or BIT is essential for Carlos.

## THREAT ASSESSMENT AND VIOLENCE

Kreese: Sweep the leg.

Kreese: Do you have a problem with that?

Johnny Lawrence: No, Sensei.

Kreese: No mercy.

*The Karate Kid*

We want to share a little bit about the concepts of threat assessment and violence. We've already shared what it's not (e.g., predicting future attacks best done by profiling students based on some list of characteristics). So, what is involved in assessing threatening behavior that a faculty reports from their classroom? What happens next after your referral/report? It's important you know because we think faculty having this knowledge helps you better understand the referral process.

*Threat or risk assessments* can be performed by clinical or non-clinical staff who work in the areas of human resources, workplace violence, law enforcement and executive protection. Threat and risk assessment techniques examine the individual to determine their risk to the greater community through asking contextual questions about the nature of the threat and risk, using computer-aided models and assessing risk factors used to determine a level of potential dangerousness. Threat assessments generally take place when a communicated threat has been made.

Determining whether an individual is organized or disorganized in his behavior or communication allows the evaluator to determine the relative level of risk for an impending attack. Turner and Gelles (2003) write:

> In cases where the level of organization of behavior and communication is rated as high, the author has stuck to a single theme that is continuous, linear and logical… disorganized communication with a multitude of messages jumbled together… from a risk point of view… such ideas usually represent a decreased risk for a planned, effective attack.
>
> (p. 96)

There are several concepts threat assessment professionals look for when determining how dangerous a person may be. These are assessing the organization/disorganization of a threat, the degree of fixation or focus on target, and the presence of an action or time imperative.

## Organized or Disorganized

In a college setting, the difference between an *organized* and *disorganized* threat profile may be seen in Nathan, who has frequent arguments about the uselessness of liberal education and how the administration forces students to take classes they don't need and will never use. He targets his arguments only to professors who teach courses he doesn't see value in, such as remedial math. He argues against having to take the class multiple times and expresses frustration at being cornered by the administration to complete this class to graduate. Nathan's thoughts are organized, linear, and follow a logical pattern. Contrast this to another student who believes her professors and administrators are "out to get her" and who might be just as likely to be upset with a professor as she will be with her dentist, the police who pull her over for speeding, or her parents who think she should change majors from education to business. Her outrage and potential threats lack any kind of continuous or linear direction.

## Fixation and Focus

Turner and Gelles (2003) also suggest individuals with a *fixation and focus* to their threats present a higher risk than those who lack these traits. Fixation relates the degree of blame and how it is attributed. Imagine Grace (our guillotine wielding student) begins to blame all social problems on her drunkard, narrow-minded, idiotic peers who don't understand her. If Grace also blames her social problems on her high school friends who just didn't care enough to know her, her rural geographic location, and the limited travel opportunities she had because of her parents' limited finances, there is little evidence of a fixation.

Focus occurs when an individual with a fixation, such as Grace, who blames others for her social problems, begins to zero in on the single staff member who prevented her from registering for her French history class. She might brood about the encounter, making notes and planning ways to get back at the staff. The focus of her fixation would increase as she ruminates about cutting off their head with a guillotine. This staff member becomes responsible for all of her troubles, perhaps beginning to establish the irrational thought process of, "If I can only get rid of her, all my problems will be solved. I'll stand up for myself and show everyone they can't walk on me."

## Action and Time Imperative

The *action and time imperative* relate to the impending nature of a potential attack. The action imperative, according to Turner and Gelles (2003), "refers to the need on the part of the person to take personal action to resolve the situation when the person has determined that all other avenues (administrative, legal, criminal, etc.) are not going to help with the resolution" (p. 97). Carlos knows he isn't doing well in the class, given his anxiety during the dissection lab and failing the first exam. He knows he must do something or he will end up being kicked out of the nursing program. Things can't continue the way they have been. His performance so far in class gives him an imperative to take action. The time imperative gives a sense of urgency to the action imperative. Will something occur today, several days from now, a week, or a month in the future?

Turner and Gelles (2003) write, "Here, the person has not only determined that he or she needs to act to harm the company, but that this action must be taken soon or within a near time frame." Carlos may begin to feel this time pressure as he misses the study session for his second exam. He knows that if he misses the exam itself he will not be able to complete his class and will not fulfill the requirements for the nursing program. He begins to see his dreams and desires fall apart around him. This drives him to a sense of desperation and hopelessness that results in his email and potential suicide threat. The time imperative is Carlos' belief that missing the second exam is a critical juncture. He has both an imperative to take action (do something) and a pressing time event (second exam) that may drive him to a suicide attempt.

## TEN RISK FACTORS FOR TARGETED VIOLENCE

All you have to do is follow three simple rules. One, never underestimate your opponent. Expect the unexpected. Two, take it outside. Never start anything inside the bar unless it's absolutely necessary. And three, be nice.

Dalton, *Roadhouse*

There isn't a list of characteristics that we can cross off a checklist to determine who the next school shooter will be. Those who have engaged in extreme rampage violence at high schools and colleges over the last decades include good students and failing students, socially well-liked and socially isolated, male and female, bullied and popular, Caucasian, Asian, and African American. The Federal Bureau of Investigation (FBI), Department of Education (DOE), Department of Justice (DOJ), Secret Service, and several threat assessment experts (Albrecht, 2010; Meloy et al., 2011; Meloy & O'Toole, 2011; O'Toole, 2000; Turner & Gelles, 2003; United States Postal Service, 2015; Vossekuil et al., 2002) all agree that profiling a certain type of individual won't work when it comes to identifying rampage violence in high school and college settings.

The Secret Service, DOE, and FBI offer this:

The threat assessment process is based on the premise that each situation should be viewed and assessed individually and guided by the facts. Judgments about an individual's risk of violence should be based upon an analysis of his/her behaviors and the context in which they occur. Blanket characterizations, demographic profiles, or stereotypes do not provide a reliable basis for making judgments of the threat posed by a particular individual.

(Drysdale, Modzeleski & Simons, 2010, p. 37)

Another expert in threat assessment, Dr. Mary Ellen O'Toole, wrote a book called *Dangerous Instincts* (O'Toole & Bowman, 2011). She introduces the term CTD to represent Concerning, Threatening, and Dangerous behavior. She presents several concerning behaviors that are based on her work as an FBI profiler and, while not exhaustive, provide an excellent place to start when considering a person's risk. These behaviors are, "impulsivity, inappropriate or out of control anger, narcissism, lack of empathy, injustice collecting, objectification of others, blaming others for failures or problems, paranoia, rule-breaking, use of violence, thoughts and fantasies of violence, drug and alcohol problems, poor coping skills, equal opportunity coping skills and thrill seeking" (pp. 181–182).

One of her concepts that we have found helpful in understanding those who develop plots of revenge and intricate schemes to inflict harm on others is the "injustice collector." O'Toole describes this individual as "a person who feels 'wronged', 'persecuted' and 'destroyed', blowing injustices way out of proportion, never forgiving the person they felt has wronged them" (p. 186). They kept track of their past wrongs and are often upset in a manner way beyond what would typically be expected. They hold onto past slights, many back as far as childhood, and see the world from this "singled-out perspective" and often have poor coping skills to deal with their frustrations.

In 2012, Van Brunt completed a book entitled *Ending Campus Violence*, in which he reviewed over ninety incidents of violence that took place in high schools and at college campuses. Based on that research, we have developed ten general concepts to attend to when it comes to what kind of behaviors or situations most commonly lead to violence. While not an exhaustive list, this is a helpful starting place for staff to better understand the nature of more extreme violence. It also should be shared that these can be classified as warning signs or red flags for further investigation.

Simply raising these red flags does not imply that the student in front of you will be the next Jared Loughner (Tucson/Pima shooting), Steven Kazmierczak (Northern Illinois University shooting) or Seung-Hui Cho (Virginia Tech shooting). However, these are the concepts we suggest to staff when they want a list of ways to prevent violence in their departments and living environments on campus.

- *Attend to potential leakage* related to a planned campus attack. This leakage may be overheard conversations, shared comments on social media such as Facebook, Twitter, and YouTube postings, or a directly communicated threat through a class journal, blog, webpage, or e-portfolio. Staff are in a unique position to "overhear" students who may be planning an attack. The news frequently covers high profile, high body count rampage shootings that occur in educational settings, but often reports little about the thwarted attacks prevented by a student or staff member who took a threat seriously.
- *Attend to work conflicts and terminations* with fellow staff and academic failures and program dismissals with students. Emotions run high in these tense conflicts. These events should be seen as potential contextual tipping points for violence. A fellow staff who doesn't receive a positive performance evaluation or who is publically embarrassed in front of the other office staff can be at a tipping point for violence. A denial of financial aid or separation from an academic program such as nursing or teacher certification could be

the catalyst for a desperate student who sees no other way out but to kill or take revenge on those they deem responsible.

• Investigate and closely monitor *unrequited romantic relationships* that lead to isolated, irrational behavior. Several cases involve violence that either began with or were driven by the frustrated passions of unstable individuals. These situations can trigger explosive bursts of anger or methodical and carefully detailed plots of revenge. Staff are often able to witness some details of these intense arguments and fights in the departments where they work.

• *Look for manifestos* or large societal messages that indicate a deeper, entrenched view of the world or call to action. Many of those who plan violence do so under the rationalization of some greater cause or message they are trying to communicate. Their attacks and killings are in some way designed to release their larger message or call others to action for their cause.

• *Identify those who feel hopeless or are irrational in their logic.* Many of those lost down the path toward violence fall out of connection with others who have the potential to refute their pessimistic logic and offer alternative views of the world outside of violence as an escape from pain. Identify students who are isolated and out of connection with others. Find ways to try to engage them and, if such engagements are unsuccessful, consider a referral to the campus BIT.

• *Watch for all bullying behavior* (perpetrator and victim) and attend specifically to bullying behavior that creates isolation and an environment where a smoldering individual grows more dangerous in his thinking. All those who are bullied (or who bully) are not destined to become the explosive attacker or the sociopath causing harm for pleasure on a grand scale. However, some who are bullied carry these scars and wounds with them and eventually seek revenge. Staff should attend to and report bullying behavior that occurs in their department or residence hall.

• Look for gaps in *students who need mental health services* on campus. While those with mental illness are not more likely to commit violence on campus, a protective factor to prevent this violence can be found by ensuring proper treatment. This involves timely access to the appropriate care in a quantity that can have an ongoing positive impact.

• Though rare, be concerned about the sociopath and those that *take pleasure in harming others and expressing obsession-filled hate and threats of violence* towards individuals or groups. These behaviors may manifest in teasing behaviors in the residence halls and the classroom, practical jokes that are taken too far and a lack of remorse when caught hurting others.

• *Pay attention to small hints and dropped information.* Those who engage in violence rarely just snap; violence is often the end product of months (if not years) of planning. It is important to identify those on the path to violence at the early stages of ideation and planning rather than the later stages of acquisition of weapons and implementation (Deisinger et al., 2008). Extreme violence is rarely an impulsive decision; rather it is the culmination of much thought and planning.

- *Watch for the hopelessness and desperation* to escape pain that occurs in suicidal individuals. This is also present in most who engage in extreme violence. While all suicidal people do not kill others when they attempt to kill themselves, it does appear that most who engage in extreme violence end up taking their own life in the process. The isolation and distorted thinking about escaping pain and, perhaps, a romanticized escape from this world appears to accompany many of the attacks.

## MOVING FORWARD

This chapter offered a brief overview of how a campus BIT/TAT may address threat on campus. Most staff on a college campus will not be in a position to conduct a detailed threat assessment on a student, but having the knowledge of these critical risk factors and an understanding of how the team functions helps create front line staff who can identify concerns early and share these concerns with the team.

In the second half of the book, we explore specific applications of the concepts outlined so far, with case scenarios specific to residence life staff, academic advisors, front office staff, case managers, student activities staff, orientation, marketing, custodians, food service staff, parking, and grounds staff.

# PART II

# PRACTICAL
# APPLICATION

In the second half of the book, we approach an assortment of departments to offer practical guidance and advice through scenario-based examples. To introduce these remaining chapters, we thought it would be helpful to bring in a close friend of ours, Poppy Fitch, Associate Vice President, Student Affairs at Ashford University. Besides having decades of amazing student affairs management and leadership experience, Poppy typifies what it means to be a staff member who excels at addressing disruptive and dangerous behaviors around campus.

The example below offers you some insight into the format we will use for the case studies in the remaining half of the book. After the introduction to the chapter, each scenario will include a case narrative explaining the details of the scenario, and will address the three phases of calming the crisis, motivating and inspiring change, and managing the ongoing behavior. The scenarios end with some discussion questions to allow staff to have a conversation about the case and find some additional takeaways.

## INTRODUCTION

More than twenty years ago I started my career in higher education as a student worker in the disability services office of the local community college I attended. This job helped me in many ways: to feel connected to my campus, to cement my position as a member of the community, to gain a greater understanding of the experiences of people with a variety of disabilities, and to develop my skills as a listener. But, most of all, this position helped to establish a foundation for my professional practice. Even now as an administrator, I see it affecting the ways I approach every student and every staff interaction.

Although this story is about a student who experiences significant mental health concerns, it is applicable across the spectrum of mental health issues, and is particularly important to front line college and university staff as we continue to see a rise in the number of students who experience anxiety. In fact, a survey by the

Association for University and College Counseling Center Directors (AUCCCD, 2016) found that during the 2015–16 academic year, more than half of the college students who visited campus counseling centers reported symptoms of anxiety.

## Narrative

It was a big day; the rest of the office staff was away at a professional development event and I was alone in the office for the first time since beginning my position as a student employee in the front office of the disability services office. I was confident, I was ready, and I was sure nothing could throw me off my game. Enter Debra.

Debra was a well-known member of the campus community. She was a larger than life woman with a bright smile, a booming voice, and a flair for the dramatic. Debra experiences paranoid schizophrenia and has an affinity for the staff in the office. On that day, Debra arrived like a summer storm, sudden and unexpected. More than a dozen plastic shopping bags hung from her arms, seeming to carry all manner of belongings, but with nary a book or notebook in sight.

"What's happening Debra?" I asked.

"What's happening?" she answered in an animated voice that dripped with sarcasm. "What's happening is that they are trying to steal my things!" and to this day I am certain that Debra believed I should have known that *that's what was happening.*

In response, I asked too many questions: "Who is trying to steal your things?", "What are they looking for?", "Why do you think they are trying to steal your things?" and so it was that during my inquisition, I became suspect as well. Debra's focus turned to the empty office. "Where's Michelle? Where's Jennifer? Where's Mimi? Where IS everybody?" Debra demanded. I answered that they were all away at a workshop, but I could see that this was troubling to Debra, as tears welled in her eyes.

"They're trying to steal my things and NO ONE is HERE TO HELP ME! WHAT ARE YOU GOING TO DO ABOUT IT?" she bellowed.

## Calming the Initial Crisis

For Debra, the familiarity of the staff and the environment of the office provided a place of respite. "Debra, would you like to have a seat? You can sit anywhere you like since folks are out of the office for the day," I offered. In this brief exchange, I was able to provide Debra with information that helped to set an expectation for what would come next: none of her trusted folks would be available.

For a time, Debra paced the entire space of our building. She peeked into the windows of each office and around cubicle walls. Debra's breathing was rapid and shallow. She rambled, sometimes straying into the incomprehensible. I was scared and woefully unprepared.

I asked myself what I would want if I were in her shoes. I found a box of Kleenex and offered her a glass of water. She accepted and eventually settled into a seat in a corner of the office. When the moment was right, I discretely sent a message to the Administrator on duty. While I awaited his arrival, I sat in comfortable proximity to Debra. I was careful to take deep, even breaths. Eventually, Debra's breathing caught pace with mine and we sat quietly for some time.

## Motivating and Inspiring Change

Emotional escalations happen to us all. Whether student, faculty, or staff, we all fall victim to our emotions from time to time. In Debra's case, the underlying issue could be traced to her disability. For many students, frustration, fear, or anxiety are the root cause.

Although rarely articulated in a job description, I see the role of front line staff as being in the best position to receive the blunt end of these escalations. For this reason, staff are in a unique and powerful position to demonstrate care for students in their time of need. But, how does this connect to motivating and inspiring a change in behavior moving forward? Paradoxically, I believe the answer to this question is in resisting the temptation to save the day.

Working through difficult and frustrating experiences helps us to build the capacity to navigate them more effectively in the future. Students who are upset or in crisis most definitely need to feel heard and to know that they are not alone. They need strategies to help them self-regulate and a support system to help them navigate toward solutions that are appropriate for them. They need to feel a sense of self-determination and agency. What they do not need is a savior.

## Managing the Ongoing Behavior

Managing and responding to mental health concerns is a complex component of the job of front line staff. The role I played on that day, and for the years since, has had to do with understanding and accepting my part in the overall equation. In the case of Debra, it wasn't perfectly executed, and you can bet both my heart and mind were racing during the time we spent together.

In Debra's case, attending to her feelings of safety and security, as well as her physiological needs, were the order of the day. Whatever was troubling her, the disability services office was there to provide support. Because I understood that, I could see that my job was to be a calming presence in the midst of her storm.

## DISCUSSION QUESTIONS

1   What went wrong? In this scenario, what would you have done differently to come to a more positive outcome?

2   What worked? There were three specific interventions that seemed to support Debra in her moment of crisis. What are some interventions that you use when working with students in crisis?

3   This scenario provides data from the Association for University and College Counseling Center Directors (AUCCCD) Annual Survey. How can staying up to date on larger trends in higher education help support the capacity of front line staff? What are some ways that you do so?

We hope this example is a useful one and sets the stage for the remainder of the book, both in terms of format as well as the underlying message that comes through from Poppy so well—successful interventions often begin with a sense of caring and love for the person you are attempting to assist. This approach, leading with love, is a powerful one that is a thread that ties through many of our examples in the remainder of the book.

# Chapter 7

# Advice for Residential Life Staff

Screws fall out all the time, the world is an imperfect place.

Bender, *The Breakfast Club*

Not all schools are lucky enough to have a residential campus. We say lucky, because residential schools have a significant advantage over non-residential settings in that they can reach out and follow up with students more easily when problems occur, as well as look for larger patterns of behavior given the 24/7 nature of the campus.

Most traditional campuses follow a similar administrative structure including a director of residential services, professional staff called Resident Directors (RDs) that oversee various halls and structures, and student workers who serve as Resident Advisors (RAs) who watch over smaller groups of students on each floor of the hall. Community colleges have recently begun developing some residential capacity for a small percentage of students on their campuses.

Common problems addressed by residential life staff include roommate conflicts, mediations around living conditions, responding to mental health concerns, relationship difficulties, and alcohol and substance abuse violations in the halls. Staff often receive some of the most intensive and detailed training related to mediation, para-professional counseling support, suicide gatekeeping, mental health first aid, conflict de-escalation skills and community building techniques. These trainings are often done in collaboration with existing campus departments such as counseling, health, police, student conduct, Title IX, and disability services.

Many schools experience a wide range of diversity in their halls which brings with it a series of challenges as well as benefits. Students may come from different cultures or geographic regions, practice different religions, have opposing political or social justice ideologies, a wide spectrum of socio-economic differences, distinctive sexual orientations, mental or physical disabilities, and generational diversity. This backdrop can provide unique opportunities to grow and learn from our differences while simultaneously offering potential flash-points for conflict and frustrations.

## PRACTICAL EXERCISES

As RAs are some of the best trained and most experienced staff in terms of addressing both disruptive and dangerous behavior, this chapter is designed to highlight some more challenging case examples and offer advice related to the three phases of 1) calming the initial crisis, 2) motivating and inspiring change, and 3) managing the ongoing behavior, as outlined in Chapters 3, 4, and 5. Discussion questions are also provided for each of the case studies to help facilitate training and discussion.

## THE HONEYMOON IS OVER

### Narrative

First-year students Marcy and Kara were best friends at the start of the year. They bragged to other students on the floor how well they were matched, how their sleep and class schedules lined up together and how they had come from similar small towns. They had few conflicts as the school year begun and they started to adjust to college life.

Sadly, their honeymoon phase was short-lived. Marcy's biology major turned out to be much more demanding than she first anticipated. Kara met a boy she started dating and began arguing more and more with Marcy about time alone in the room with her new boyfriend. Marcy feels sleep deprived and frustrated that Kara doesn't get her need to spend some more time studying in the room. Kara has been missing class recently, going to off-campus parties more and is struggling in her academics.

Their fights and arguments have recently increased with the two of them loudly shouting at night, slamming books and chairs around the room and having other students ask the RA to tell them to be quiet. Kara tells Marcy, "just study in the library. That's why it's here. I don't see why you have to be such a bitch about this." Marcy shouts back, "Maybe if you cared a little more about college and less about sleeping with your boyfriend and getting drunk, you'd understand why it's nice to have a quiet place to study."

### Calming the Initial Crisis

Setting limits with Kara and Marcy about expectations around how they communicate with each other and how they need to behave in the residential community is a central goal for the RA. The fights have already begun to escalate to include some physical altercations and likely will continue to escalate without intervention. A divide and conquer approach may be useful, with the RA meeting alone with each roommate and allowing each of them to talk more about their frustrations. Clear limit setting about noise levels and how they resolve conflicts (no shouting or throwing things) is also important to set expectations about them remaining roommates and being able to continue living on campus.

## Motivating and Inspiring Change

The larger issue with these two is addressing the underlying conflicts that have arisen based on their stress and challenges adjusting to campus. What started out as a roommate conflict is now an opportunity for a caring and aware RA to make important referrals for Marcy to academic support regarding her stress and workload and to assist Kara with finding a balance between academics, social activities, and her boyfriend.

## Managing the Ongoing Behavior

This will likely not be an issue that has a miraculous and immediate resolution. More likely, Marcy and Kara will continue to rub against each other and cause frustration and conflict. With intervention and referral, the RA should be able to keep the conflict within a reasonable spectrum and that situation will improve. If the situation does not improve, it may become necessary to consider conduct action related to their disruptive behavior or discussions about switching roommates or mediation between them in the counseling center, if this is an available resource. Additionally, the RA should see this roommate conflict as a marathon, not a sprint. As such, they should seek regular supervision and support to ensure their responses do not become reactive or stress-produced.

## DISCUSSION QUESTIONS

1   Think back to Kohlberg's (1973) moral and Chickering's identity (Chickering and Reisser, 1993; Robinson, 2013) development mentioned in Chapter 3. How might this apply to understanding some of Marcy and Kara's behavior?

2   It would be reasonable to assume this behavior will likely have an impact on other students who live on the same floor as Kara and Marcy. What are some ways the RA can address these concerns?

3   Based on our conversations in Chapter 4, what Prochaska et al. (1994) stage of change would you place Marcy at? How about Kara? Discuss some of the motivational interviewing techniques that might be helpful in de-escalating the conflict.

# GET OUT OF MY COUNTRY

## Narrative

Ahmed is a second-year chemistry student living with Kyle, a third-year philosophy major. Ahmed was born and raised in Chicago and Kyle is from southern California. They attend a large public university located in the rural southeast. Ahmed and Kyle get along well despite some of their differences. Ahmed is a practicing Muslim and Kyle is an atheist. Both have had an upsetting reaction to recent political events, issues of tolerance for immigrants, and the rise of hate speech around campus.

Ahmed has increasingly become worried about his safety on campus. There have been incidents of swastikas painted in bathrooms on campus, a very public attack on a trans-male student attempting to use a gender-neutral bathroom in the library, and increasing rhetoric about "building a wall" and "sending those people home."

Ahmed comes back from class shaken up at a report that a pig's head was found the night before on the steps of his Mosque. He is aggravated and upset and passionately shares his frustration with Kyle. Ahmed talks to other students about his frustrations. Some are not as supportive as Kyle and others make inappropriate jokes about where the rest of the pig ended up because they love bacon. The next morning, Ahmed finds a cartoon pig logo on a bag outside his door from the local BBQ restaurant, The Lucky Pig. On the bag is written, "Get out of my country, bacon hater."

## Calming the Initial Crisis

The RA has several responsibilities here in the immediate aftermath of this discovery. This incident may very well raise to the level of a hate crime and/or on-campus conduct action so the RA should document what was found and involve campus safety. This immediate action serves two purposes. First, it collects evidence and information that can be used in the future. Second, it shows Ahmed and those on his floor that these incidents are taken seriously and will not be tolerated in an on-campus residence hall. Ahmed has a close friend in Kyle and will likely receive support from Kyle following the incident. However, Ahmed is likely to feel even more worried about his safety on campus and some immediate steps should be taken to help him feel more comfortable in terms of a safety plan.

## Motivating and Inspiring Change

Whether this was an intended intimidatory action or a poorly conceived "prank" by some students who hadn't fully realized the impact of their actions, this incident threatens a core component of most residential life communities—namely the ability to feel safe and tolerate differences among its members. The RA should offer support to both Ahmed and Kyle, as this is an ongoing issue and not one that will be immediately resolved. Additional support may come from on-campus clubs or organizations as well as individuals from Ahmed's Mosque. A key aspect of helping Ahmed is giving him support as well as opportunities to talk safely about his experience, perhaps through a counseling referral. Additionally, Ahmed should be given a way to act related to his frustrations if he wants to express himself or make more lasting change within the college or larger community. This may involve referrals and connection to local political groups or social justice/ action organizations.

## Managing the Ongoing Behavior

These types of attacks on any individual in a community often cause a range of emotional reactions from others. Some feel outrage, others feel these kinds of behaviors are vindicated given terrorist actions abroad. Often, there are strong religious, political, and social justice thoughts and emotions that are stirred by such an event. In addition to supporting floor members, Ahmed and Kyle, the RA, police and student affairs staff need safe places to talk and share their experiences, seek guidance and find solace. On a systems level, increased training on campus related to microaggressions (Sue, 2010), discussions of intent versus impact and opportunities for open dialogue concerning difficult issues are all needed.

## DISCUSSION QUESTIONS

1  Discuss how an issue like this would be handled on your campus. What are some of the cultural, religious, or political issues in your town/gown relationships that might have an impact in how the event is handled?

2  What are some additional ways the RA could support Ahmed through this? How can Kyle be supported? In what ways could other departments (such as counseling, diversity services, study abroad, religious departments) offer support during the aftermath of the incident?

3  If the students who put the picture on Ahmed's door were discovered, how might the student conduct process walk them through Prochaska et al. (1994) stages of change model discussed in Chapter 4?

## A BOTTLE OF PILLS

### Narrative

Kaylee had hoped that things would be different when she went away to college. While she did well in her first two years with her grades, she often felt sad and struggled with having the energy to make friends. Some suggested that she talk to a counselor about her depression, but she was afraid the more she talked about it, the worse it would become.

Kaylee begins to miss some of her classes; she starts spending more time alone and avoids making eye contact with her peers and classmates. She stops showering or making any effort in her appearance and clothes. She says, "I just don't see the point anymore. Nothing matters. Everything hurts and I can't even think about getting up each day. I don't want to feel this way... I wish I could be happy like everyone else. But I can't. I don't want to be here anymore."

The semester goes on and Kaylee misses more of her classes. She is tearful most of the time and is unable to handle any stress. She doesn't leave her room for days. The RA keys into her room to talk to her and finds her with a half empty bottle of iron pills and some anti-nausea pills. Kaylee admits to reading on the internet about how to overdose on iron pills and that she took about thirty pills and some of the anti-nausea pills so she didn't vomit (removing the deadly iron from her system). The RA calls an ambulance and her RD. Kaylee is rushed to the local hospital and has her stomach pumped.

### Calming the Initial Crisis

This is an emergency scenario and the RA works quickly to remain calm, cool, and collected. This gives the RA a better chance of choosing the best approach moving forward rather than reacting rashly to the situation. The RA understands there is an immediate medical risk, avoids a lengthy conversation with the student and gets the ambulance on the way. Becoming hysterical, losing control of the scene, or trying to do everything by herself are things to be avoided. The RA calls for support from the RD as soon as the ambulance is on the way.

### Motivating and Inspiring Change

Kaylee may or may not be back to the residence hall this semester. This depends on several factors: the nature of the suicide assessment, her willingness to seek support and the college's policies on these behaviors. If Kaylee does return, the RA has a key role in watching for future signs of increasing depression or suicide, offering Kaylee support within the RA's scope of practice and realizing that addressing serious issues like suicide and depression are problems that take some time to mitigate effectively. The RA would do well to offer support to Kaylee's roommate as well as other members of the residence hall who have been impacted by Kaylee's behavior.

## Managing the Ongoing Behavior

In this scenario, there is a need for community programming on identifying the signs and symptoms of suicide, how to help someone struggling with depression, and what counseling resources are available to students on campus. This could be accomplished through inviting the counseling center staff to come into the hall or through train-the-trainer programs residential life staff may have had access to in the past. Long-term support of a student like Kaylee should also include making sure she has access to case management services, academic support, and mental health assistance. This may also have been a traumatic event for the RA and RD in responding to Kaylee's attempt, so supportive services for these first responders is essential as well.

## DISCUSSION QUESTIONS

1   Could Kaylee's suicide attempt have been prevented in this case? What steps could have prevented it?
2   Kaylee has not attended therapy or taken medication for her depression. What are some of her reasons for this? How would you work with her to overcome this?
3   What responsibility does the RA or RD have to talk to the other students in the hall about Kaylee's suicide attempt? How can help be offered while respecting Kaylee's privacy? What are some ways the RA and RD in this case could seek support for themselves?

## POWDER KEG

### Narrative

Simon always has been a bit of a hothead. He speaks without thinking and tends to get his way based on the frequency and volume of his arguments, rather than the content. Simon also has a knack for being unpredictable and losing his temper. He gets into arguments with his roommate about not locking the door when he leaves, listening to his music too loudly, and coming back into the room loudly when his roommate is sleeping. Simon doesn't deal well with confrontations about not following the rules. He often becomes explosive and yells when he doesn't get his way. He seems unable to see things from other people's point of view and becomes narrowly focused, only seeing things from his perspective.

**125**

One afternoon, Simon storms out of his room and slams the door closed. His RA pokes his head into the hallway and Simon yells at him, "This whole place is a mess. I'm so tired of this damn school. Someone should get a gun and just shoot all the stupid, annoying people." He leaves the hallway through the stairwell and slams that door as well.

Several other students come out into the hall and look to the RA for guidance on what to do. Some see this as more of Simon's typical behavior. Others see this as an escalation and think the police should be called because Simon just threatened to shoot a bunch of people at the school.

## Calming the Initial Crisis

As with Elvis, Simon has left the building, and there isn't much to be done with him in the immediate aftermath of his tirade. The RA's primary duty here is choosing about reporting the incident up the chain of command or attempting to address and calm down other students on the floor. Calling an RD or someone on the BIT should occur in short order, as this may be the beginning, not the end of Simon's outburst. There is a temptation to make assumptions that this is "typical Simon behavior." Instead the RA should take the incident on its face value of a physical escalation (door slamming), yelling and shouting and a vague threat at a shooting. One could assume that Simon isn't done with his disruptive/dangerous behavior for the day and may need a more immediate intervention to keep others safe. Once a notification goes out to campus safety, the BIT, and/or the RD, the RA can then take some time to talk to other students who are rightly upset about Simon's behavior.

## Motivating and Inspiring Change

Assuming Simon isn't planning a campus shooting and he returns the halls, it will be important to have clear behaviorally defined expectations about his outbursts moving forward. It is unlikely Simon is going to change his approach to dealing with things that frustrate him, so the system has some responsibility to be prepared to address his behavior calmly and consistently when it occurs again. Simon's RA could help him, perhaps in tandem with some mandated anger management, to better handle his frustration tolerance and brainstorm new ways to express himself when frustrated. Again, these skills will unlikely be learned quickly with Simon and will take root better when suggested consistently in multiple voices.

## Managing the Ongoing Behavior

In the long term, Simon's behavior can have a negative draw on the residential community as well as those closest to him with the most pressure to intervene (for instance, his RA or roommate). Support for those addressing Simon's behavior, whether disruptive or dangerous, is important to avoid stress, burnout, and reactive interventions that escalate Simon. Community-wide civility programs may also be helpful to address the behavioral expectations of the community through a more broad-based, public health model. Pairing with additional departments such as mediation, conduct, diversity, and counseling will increase the effectiveness of these efforts.

## DISCUSSION QUESTIONS

1   How would you have handled the initial choice between following Simon, calling the police/conduct/BIT or calming the other students? What are some likely consequences of each course of action in terms of the pros and cons?

2   We mentioned the importance of remaining calm, cool, and collected during a crisis. Assuming Simon didn't immediately storm out of the building, what are some ways the RA could have achieved this state given Simon's outburst? What might be some of the reasons for Simon's way of behaving?

3   Simons age, race, ethnicity, sexual orientation, body size and musculature, or native language were not mentioned in this case. Discuss how some of these issues might impact, for better or for worse, assumptions the RA or floormates might make about whether this was an actual threat to commit a school shooting or simply an inappropriate angry outburst.

## MY BODY IS A TEMPLE

### Narrative

Patience grew up in a conservative Christian home and is the youngest of three daughters. Her parents were rather strict and she often turned to food and reading to occupy her time. She gained weight throughout high school and had little luck with diet or exercise in changing her appearance. Her older sisters often teased Patience and told her to stop eating foods that were bad for her or "the only men that would ever want her would be down at the truck stop." Her mother would use religion to make her feel bad and say, "1 Corinthians 6: 15, 19–20. Your body is a temple, and you are destroying His holy gift to you."

During high school, Patience began to binge—eat large amounts of food—and then vomit, feeling as if she was not only a failure at her weight loss, but a disappointment in the eyes of God. Patience continued this throughout high school and into college. For the first couple years at college, Patience experimented with using laxatives and starving herself by not eating anything but a cracker or two a day for weeks at a time. Her weight would fluctuate throughout the semesters. Patience eventually goes to counseling and with some hard work, gets her eating disorder under better control. She is very excited about the chance to study abroad and works with her therapist to develop plans while studying away at another school.

Patience joins to a religious club on campus and while they do not push her as hard as her mother, this begins a downward trend for her. She begins struggling more with her classes and feels stressed all the time. Her RA becomes concerned at the amount of food she is eating and overhears vomiting noises coming from the community bathroom. The RA brings up her concerns and Patience begins crying, "I just don't know what to do anymore. I thought this was all behind me. I can't do this... I can't do this..."

## Calming the Initial Crisis

This scenario should leave the RA with a level of concern around not only Patience related to her eating disorder, but also some potential suicidal behaviors. Remaining balanced and calm in the face of her disclosure and concern around an uncertain future is a good approach to begin with while talking to Patience. The RA should avoid jumping to offering solutions and instead work towards listening and asking more open-ended questions to better understand what Patience may be going through. In the end, the conversation should involve a consultation with an RD or staff from counseling for an assessment related to suicide risk as well as a referral to help with her eating disorder.

## Motivating and Inspiring Change

Avoiding superficial or glib advice about eating disorders is key when working with Patience as she becomes connected to counseling or additional support. While there may be some temptation for the RA to comment positively on her weight, and give advice about what might have worked for others overcoming disordered eating or depression, the best stance here is to offer support and kindness. The RA can support Patience by helping her feel positive about her choice to seek help and care, and by being a resource that is willing to talk, within the RA's limited scope of para-professional help. Additional training for RA and RD staff may be helpful to assist in helping Patience if she remains in the hall and a potential release of information could even give residential life or BIT staff access to talk with Patience's counselor to offer added support.

## Managing the Ongoing Behavior

Eating disorders are notoriously difficult to treat and often require an integrated team approach to be treated successfully. This may often involve family and mental health and medical professionals working in tandem with the client to provide slow and steady progress. The RA can be most helpful here by ensuring Patience stays connected to care and offering additional support to other members of the residence community who may be lost at what to do to help someone like Patience. In addition, making sure the RA and RD have support as they try to help a student struggling with an eating disorder is key to the long-term success of any plan. Trying to help someone who is stuck in a cycle of good and bad behavior can feel particularly frustrating and hopeless when interventions don't go well or a student relapses.

## DISCUSSION QUESTIONS

1   Talking to someone about very personal behaviors like eating problems can feel intrusive and awkward. Discuss ways to make the conversation more comfortable and how some senior residential life staff have handled these kinds of conversations before.

2   In addressing these problems, the motto "it takes a village" comes to mind. Discuss other departments around campus that may be helpful in terms of training or talking through strategies to manage eating disorders in the residence hall.

3   In Chapter 4, we discussed some of Miller and Rollnick's (2002) Motivational Interviewing techniques. Give some examples of how a few of these approaches would be useful with a student like Patience.

## LIVIN' ON A PRAYER

### Narrative

Tommy had been dating Gina for the better part of six months in an on-again/off-again relationship. They were known on campus for marathon, late night shouting fests in the public lounges that often ended up in late night make-out fests in those lounges. During one of their latest arguments, Gina finally made the decision to break up with Tommy. He did not take this well and the two of them have been having heated arguments about their relationship all over campus.

The situation worsens when Tommy goes over to Gina's residence hall and they get into a two-hour yelling argument. Several students hear them shouting back and forth. They aren't sure what to do and end up calling the RA to let her know that it seems like this fight is worse than the other ones they have overheard.

As the RA is walking down the hallway, she hears a loud crash coming from the room. The RA knocks on the door and there is no response. She uses her key to open it. Inside the RA sees Tommy standing next to a large hole punched in the closet door, holding his first in pain, and cursing at himself. Gina is sitting on her bed crying.

## Calming the Initial Crisis

More than other scenarios that we have seen, this is an example of the importance of keeping calm, cool, and collected prior to intervening. The RA should also be wary of her own safety, given Tommy's punching of the closet door. While there is no blueprint to a successful intervention, the RA could start by asking another nearby student quickly and quietly to get some additional assistance (in terms of police or an RD). Then the RA could take a supportive stance with Tommy and attempt to help him get some assistance for his hurt hand. This does several things immediately, it begins to move Tommy and Gina apart from each other and it shows concern over Tommy, rather than putting him on the defensive related to the punching. If Tommy responds angrily, then helping Gina under the guise of "freshening up" in the bathroom for a moment is another way to separate the two of them.

## Motivating and Inspiring Change

As the case begins, we learn this is an ongoing behavior between Tommy and Gina. In these types of scenarios, it is rare that they resolve quickly with Gina asking Tommy to never to talk to her again and a no-contact order being created between the two. More than likely, they will continue with their off-again/ on-again relationship. Setting boundaries and expectations about how to work through disagreements and/or engaging in conversations with Gina about a potential counseling referral for her to talk more privately about her relationship choices would be a good place to start.

## Managing the Ongoing Behavior

Relationship violence has recently received a good deal of attention under the Violence Against Women Act (VAWA) and Title IX. Colleges and universities are doing more each day to educate students around the signs and symptoms of intimate partner violence (IPV), domestic violence, and dating violence. Residential life would do well to pair with counseling, health educators, police, women's studies and social work to teach students what healthy relationships look like as well as the signs and symptoms of problematic relationships. Additionally, an incident like Tommy's violence has the potential to act as a ripple effect for those with past trauma events. Working with domestic violence is not easy and support services should be offered for all those involved, including the RA.

## DISCUSSION QUESTIONS

1 Given your past training, what are some of the signs of unhealthy relationships? What do you think goes into a healthy relationship? What are some things that have been effective working with someone who was stuck in an unhealthy relationship?

2 Who are the stakeholders in this scenario? Who should the RA be thinking about in terms of providing short- and long-term assistance? What kind of support services are available to students like Tommy and Gina?

3 Discuss some of the barriers that keep students from seeking counseling services when they are having relationship problems. What are some of the ways residential life staff can help to reduce this stigma?

# Chapter 8
## Advice for Academic Advisors

Negative, Ghost Rider, the pattern is full.

Air Boss, *Top Gun*

Academic advisors sit at the intersection of student experiences in and outside of the classroom. It's a busy intersection. Depending on the focus of the advising unit, advisors may see students exploring majors, seeking an override into a course, struggling with financial aid and the costs of college, upset by treatment from a faculty member, questioning academic department policies, filing a degree plan, considering dropping or stopping out, as well as the array of student concerns and questions that travel through any general student service unit.

The best academic advisors embrace helping students as they navigate the twists and turns of college life, even the students speeding through the intersection. Because of the nature of advising roles and responsibilities, these staff are well positioned to observe and report disruptive or dangerous behaviors, and in many circumstances, they can provide or support the interventions for students as well.

Advising structures will vary from institution to institution with some schools utilizing centralized advising where most students see a common group of advisors regularly. Other schools use decentralized models where advisors are located in various academic units and even across the institution in centers for special populations such as veterans, first generation college students, and undeclared students. In some cases, faculty in academic units play advising roles in addition to their teaching duties. Needless to say, an academic advisor's scope of responsibility and interactions with students will vary, but students are still traveling through the advising unit offering opportunities to observe the student's course of travel, progress, and speed.

In many institutions, advisors are already responsible for identifying students at risk and recognizing patterns of student behaviors. The school may use formal, predictive modeling programs to track student progress and pinpoint students who are at risk for failing or dropping out of school. Advisors are also encouraged to note interactions with students and often utilize some centralized record system shared with other advisors. Advisors share a unique perspective with access to information on a student's history and experiences at the institution, and in some cases prior to enrollment. Not only does the nature of an advisor's interaction with students make it likely that they will run into displays of distress and disruption, their access to information about students makes them a critical resource for responding to students of concern.

Also, consider for a moment what activities are mandated for students to participate in at college. In most schools, there are very few requirements for all students. Not all colleges are residential with on-campus housing. Not every student participates in student organizations or student activities. There may not be one class that every student takes, but students do have to register for classes and file degree plans. While meeting with an advisor each semester or year may not be a requirement, it is likely to be one of the reoccurring experiences or interactions shared by most, if not all, students. This positions advisors to engage and connect with students more frequently and consistently than in other areas, an essential component of responding to disruptive and dangerous behavior.

## THIRTY-MINUTE CHANGE

I feel the need, the need for speed!

Maverick, *Top Gun*

For advisors, it can feel as though the day is a blur of thirty-minute segments and students moving in and out of the office. In these brief moments with each student, how is it possible to talk about course selection, major selection, and a degree plan while also answering basic questions about how to register? Not to mention, many advisors are trying to make good campus resource referrals related to areas where the student is struggling such as academic tutoring, counseling services, financial aid, student disability, and student involvement. Then, advisors are also encouraged to discuss career goals, and the benefits and opportunities for career exploration, internships, assistantships, and even graduate school. And, let's not forget, advisors should introduce students to opportunities for study abroad, undergraduate research, and service learning.

As advisors are frantically working down the checklist of topics to cover with each student, how could we ever expect that there would be any time to just talk to the student? An important skill for an advisor is the ability to quickly build rapport with a student and then reestablish that connection in the next meeting. Believe it or not, the time constraint can actually work in the advisor's favor.

A few years ago, *Time* magazine ran an article sharing information about building rapport based on experiences of the former head of the FBI's Counterintelligence Behavior Analysis Program (Barker, 2014). The article summarizes techniques for connecting with people. One tip includes establishing artificial time constraints because people do not want to feel trapped in a conversation that has no end point.

Now, advisors are not trying to recruit intelligence officers, but rapport building is a foundational skill for advisors working with students who have exhibited concerning behaviors, or any student for that matter. The fact that the meeting has structure and scope can actually work in favor of connecting with students.

Instead of worrying about the short amount of time available for students, advisors can focus on the quality of the experience and interaction. Other good rapport building practices (many are covered in Chapter 4) will just enhance the ability to connect with students, such as creating a comfortable office environment and having office decorations and memorabilia that disclose appropriate context about the advisor to the student as well as the critical skills of active listening, open questioning, and validating aspects of the student's story and experience.

In several of the case studies in this chapter, advisors are asked to form connections with students to assist with interventions, and they are tapped to maintain a longer term association with a student who remains enrolled in the institution. Meaning, the advisor needs to be attentive to the shifting demeanor and behaviors of the student as they meet and interact over a period of time. Distinguishing between a student who is maintaining a consistency in attitude and behaviors and a student who is exhibiting elevated behaviors of concern becomes critical for the advisor working closely with an at-risk student. Chapter 5 explores this concept further.

Clearly, advisors can be quite helpful to BITs or conduct officers working with disruptive or dangerous student behaviors. They also hold a great deal of power. It may not feel like it sometimes, but the ability to override a student into a course, maneuver a student's class schedule, or interpret and modify a degree plan are valuable tools when making modifications to help a student. Advisors approached by the BIT or student conduct for assistance in these matters should be open to discussing options to help manage the situation. This does not mean automatically making broad exceptions about student requirements and processes, but it means talking candidly about the pros and cons of different courses of action that may be necessary to assist the student.

## COLLABORATIVE PARTNERSHIPS

You can be my wingman anytime.

Iceman, *Top Gun*

In the case studies below, we highlight the importance of advisors providing good case management and interventions even at the earliest signs of academic and social struggles and how this can prevent the escalation to more serious concerns for students. You will note that the early case studies may not seem disruptive or dangerous and most of the interventions suggested are the types of activities that advisors deploy with students regularly, but we highlight how in these cases, they help to establish further connection with students exhibiting early red flag behaviors; they allow us to gather more information about the student's concern to share with a campus BIT and to identify opportunities to check in with the student at later points to see how they are doing.

Of course, advisors also run into more concerning situations, so as the case studies below advance, you will also see more advanced recommendations such as increased communications, interactions, and referrals to the campus BIT, counseling unit, or conduct office. In all of the scenarios, advisors function as "wingmen" for a campus BIT or conduct officer responding to disruptive and dangerous behaviors. From access to information about the students to establishing rapport and an understanding of the student's academic progress at the institution, the advisor is a valuable team member for responding to concerns.

## PRACTICAL EXERCISES

Academic advisors are on the front lines of student interactions. Despite their position, they do not always have the most detailed training on how to respond to crisis events outside the academic content of their sessions. This chapter is designed to highlight some more challenging case examples and offer advice related to the three phases of 1) calming the initial crisis, 2) motivating and inspiring change, and 3) managing the ongoing behavior as outlined in Chapters 3, 4, and 5. Discussion questions are also provided for each of the case studies to help facilitate training and discussion.

## WHAT'S YOUR MAJOR?

> I don't want to sell anything, buy anything, or process anything as a career. I don't want to sell anything bought or processed, or buy anything sold or processed, or process anything sold, bought or processed, or repair anything sold, bought, or processed. You know, as a career, I don't want to do that.
>
> Lloyd Dobler, *Say Anything*

### Narrative

Lloyd is a second-year student majoring in biology, and he is starting to realize that he does not like his major. He is struggling in his classes and was placed on academic probation. While attending his required advising appointment in November prior to registration for the spring semester, he talks about feeling overwhelmed with the rigor of classes and stuck in his major. Lloyd shares that his mother is a doctor and he feels family pressure to perform better so he can be admitted into medical school. He believes his parents have wanted him to be a doctor since he was little.

Lloyd is uncertain what major he is interested in pursuing, but he admits that he has struggled with most of the science courses required for his major. When the advisor asks Lloyd if his parents know that he is on academic probation and his grade requirements to remain enrolled for the spring, Lloyd indicates that his parents do not know the extent of his academic concerns. He says they will not understand and will stop paying for his classes.

Lloyd becomes very quiet and sad during portions of the conversation where he seems to have trouble seeing any hope related to the situation. At other times, he is more vocal and expresses frustration about his parents' pressure on him. He is uncertain about what to do or what options are available to him.

## Calming the Crisis

Lloyd's story is probably not that unique to academic advisors, but we use it here illustrate the importance of these more common interactions with students about major selection, academic struggles, and parental expectations. Several aspects of Lloyd's interactions with his advisor offer concern. The hopelessness and inability to see a path out of the situation is always an attitude that should raise a red flag. The advisor should use active listening and expressions of empathy in order to gain a full understanding of Lloyd's situation. This may mean putting off some of the other tasks for the meeting related to longer term degree planning or other paperwork.

In this case, calming the crisis means working with the student to identify options and hope with a forward focus. Lloyd and the advisor identify classes he can take for spring that leave him some flexibility without committing further to the path in biology, allowing him to explore some other types of classes to see what may speak to his interests. They also talk through his current course performance and discuss deadlines for dropping one course if he does not do well in an upcoming test. By showing Lloyd how his GPA is calculated, he is able to see that he still has an opportunity to remain academically eligible for the spring.

With the upcoming Thanksgiving holiday, the advisor should also attempt to address Lloyd's concerns about his family's expectations and discuss his plans for the winter break. Connecting with Lloyd through a personal story of the advisor's own temporary setbacks may help to establish additional trust with the student where he is more likely to continue coming to the advisor for assistance and more open to discussions about his family concerns. Asking Lloyd to talk through worst-case scenarios of his parent's reactions to his academic struggles helps him to identify options for talking with his parents about his major. The advisor also suggests that Lloyd schedule to talk to a counselor for ideas about how to talk with his parents, and the advisor schedules a follow-up meeting prior to the winter break.

Following the meeting with Lloyd, the advisor submits a report to the BIT outlining a minor concern about Lloyd's hopelessness over academic concerns and describes the resources and meetings identified for Lloyd. Unless the BIT has other information or previous concerns related to Lloyd, the advisors plan of action is likely to be a sufficient first intervention for Lloyd.

## Motivating and Inspiring Change

In the follow-up meeting after Thanksgiving, the advisor is looking to see how Lloyd's outlook has changed or whether it has remained the same. In this case, Lloyd says that he talked some with his parents about his struggles in biology, and while their reaction was not too bad, they have a lot of questions about his degree plan and where it can lead if not biology. He seems hesitant, but more hopeful than before. Here, the advisor is looking to begin involving Lloyd in identifying options for himself and encouraging self-efficacy. The advisor suggests a meeting with a career advisor and completion of career assessments as a starting point and offers to participate in a phone call with Lloyd and his parents to discuss degree plan questions and options.

## Managing the Ongoing Behavior

After facilitating a transition for Lloyd from biology to a communications degree plan, he seems excited for the upcoming spring semester. A case management issue for the advisor's attention would be if Lloyd finishes the fall term with poor grades that could result in his suspension. Based on Lloyd's previous history and inability to cope with these types of obstacles, it would be important to try to connect with Lloyd prior to winter break to make sure he is doing OK and has a plan for talking with his parents about what occurred.

## DISCUSSION QUESTIONS

1   What are the various signs of hopelessness that advisors may observe in students?
2   How can advisors work with students struggling to identify a major or needing to transition out of a major?
3   Are there aspects of what the advisor did in this scenario that you feel are beyond the scope of what an advisor could or should do? If so, what aspects? How could additional training or support assist an advisor in performing those roles?

# I'M BETTER THAN THIS FACULTY MEMBER

These classes can be real inconvenient!

Thornton Melon, *Back to School*

## Narrative

Travis returned to college at the age of forty to complete a business degree. He worked in his family's business for many years after high school, but he would like to move into a corporate environment and needs the degree to qualify for the most appealing jobs. He has made mostly A's and B's in courses up to this point, but he has struggled adjusting to group projects with younger students and gets frustrated with some course requirements that seem meaningless to his goals. Travis reminds his advisor regularly in communications that he could teach these classes based on his previous experiences, but he is just going to do the minimum to get the degree.

Travis comes to his advisor's office irate and frustrated. He expresses anger that the professor in his finance class is not clear on assignments in class, is not qualified to teach, and says, "The professor is crazy if he thinks I have two hours per night for his course! I'm doing this stuff in the real world with my family business, not just faking it here." Travis needs this course for his major and has already failed the first test that accounts for a third of his grade. He seems overwhelmed and uncertain how to pass the class other than blaming the instructor.

## Calming the Crisis

In this situation, the academic advisor should use active listening and simple reflection and allow Travis to vent and express his frustrations. It is important to avoid confrontation and argumentation with Travis. The advisor may be tempted to remind him that he knew the requirements of the degree before returning to school or to argue with him about the suitability of the instructor, but this will just serve to increase his agitation. Instead, the advisor should try to be proactive and solution focused by helping Travis to narrow down his frustrations and identifying obstacles related to his performance in the course. After a period of venting, the goal should be to try to uncover a win–win situation with the student. The advisor should ascertain if the student plans to continue in the course and how the student plans to engage with the faculty member.

## Motivating and Inspiring Change

In a follow-up appointment with Travis, the advisor would want to monitor his progress in the course and his interactions with the faculty member. A note on the calendar to ask about his performance in the second of the three tests could help to build trust and rapport with the student around the situation as well as serving as an indicator of the student's improvement in the course. In order to head off future frustrations, the advisor could talk with Travis about strategies related to course selection and the amount of time that he has to commit to courses each semester.

## Managing the Ongoing Behavior

The advisor would want to remain attentive to a hardened perspective toward faculty or department policies and processes. If specific interactions with faculty were negative or student behaviors toward faculty escalated, the advisor should report to the campus BIT or conduct office for further assistance. This is a very goal-oriented student focused on degree completion. Win–win solutions should be possible to identify since he is motivated and has shown good academic abilities in courses up to this point.

## DISCUSSION QUESTIONS

1   What frustrations can be common for returning adult students and what strategies have been effective in addressing those frustrations?
2   How can advisors approach student complaints related to faculty?
3   What type of win–win solutions might work for this scenario? What are the hazards and the benefits in trying to create dissonance around the student's current approach in the course?

## LOST AND ALONE

### Narrative

Lucas, a male sophomore student, comes to the office looking for academic help. The advisor was given a heads-up by his supervisor recently about Lucas. The BIT shared with the supervisor that Lucas exhibited some socially odd behavior, particularly related to females around campus. While Lucas did not come into the office for help with his behavior or making friends, this may be a good time to begin a conversation with him about his behavior.

The advisor sat down with Lucas and talked with him about how he was doing on campus. Lucas talked at length about all the women he was asking out around campus and how he was going to get lucky one day. The advisor asked what this meant and Lucas explained that while he was asking out about five or six women a day and while none had said yes yet, he was optimistic that his time would come.

## Calming the Crisis

While Lucas may not see the current behavior as a potential crisis, depending on the size of the campus, he is likely going to have a negative reputation shortly with his odd approach to dating. Although the central reason for his referral is not related to this, the advisor would want to be attentive to what was communicated by the BIT and any specific direction given by the BIT. The focus of the advisor's work should be primarily academic, although there is an opportunity for him to talk a bit more with Lucas about his approach to asking women out. This could involve addressing the directness of his request with women he doesn't know well or the sheer volume of his behavior potentially creating a negative reputation on campus. If the advisor is comfortable starting this conversation with Lucas it is important they share the information back to his supervisor and the BIT.

## Motivating and Inspiring Change

The academic advisor will be more successful in working with Lucas if they are able to establish rapport and connection by being genuine, offering positive regard, and building a bridge by looking for commonalities. After assisting with the academic issue, the advisor could explore his social connections, involvement, and difficulties by using active listening and simple/summary reflection. The advisor has a unique role to help reduce the stigma Lucas may have about accessing counseling services to help him reach his goal of dating a woman. The advisor could support this positive goal for Lucas while helping him learn how to best seek advice moving forward. A referral to counseling to assist with social coaching could also be helpful.

## Managing the Ongoing Behavior

Using the positive psychology approaches discussed in Chapter 5 and helping Lucas focus on behaviors related to his strengths as well as supporting his self-efficacy would be helpful. As mentioned earlier, the advisor would want to remain in contact with the campus BIT and updated on these interactions. With good rapport and connection, future discussions could include a follow-up to see if the student pursued the counseling referral and how social concerns have changed.

## DISCUSSION QUESTIONS

1   How would you handle information that you received about a student from the campus BIT or conduct office? What are the benefits and concerns associated with incorporating that information into your advising plan for a student?

2   What are some questions and statements that you might use to discuss the student's social connections and involvement?

3   What are some strategies that you could use to build ongoing rapport with this student?

## CHECK YOUR SIX

### Narrative

Zach returned to school after serving for the US military in Afghanistan. He is in his final year in a difficult Engineering program. Advisors in the College of Engineering have worked with Zach for several years and have had some difficulties. He often complains about the quality of faculty and the content of the classes, expressing that he learned more in the military, but he has persisted and is close to graduation. The Engineering Department made a number of degree plan changes during the time period when Zach first enrolled leading to confusion among students in Zach's cohort. He has just been notified via email that his degree plan audit indicated he was missing a required course for graduation. In addition, the course is not being offered next semester.

Zach responds to the email about the requirement with an aggressive and concerning email. Excerpts of the email are provided below:

> What a bunch of idiots! How can I have been enrolled here for 4 years and you are just now noticing that my degree plan was incorrect. Let me guess, this is my inept advisor, Patricia Stewart's fault. She better check her six because she does not want to have to see me until this is fixed. I want my entire file reviewed and a meeting with the Dean immediately.

### Calming the Initial Crisis

Advising centers communicate via email with students regularly, and sometimes the news delivered is not good. Typically, it is the responsibility of the student to stay on top of their degree requirements and courses, but advisors know that this can be a challenge for students. It is OK for students to be confused, worried, and even occasionally frustrated as they navigate college life, but it is not appropriate to make threats or intimidating remarks toward a staff member. Upon receipt of this email, the wording should raise concern for the Advising Center. It should be reported to the campus BIT in order to coordinate the best response. Some BITs will offer to contact the student to discuss the email as a first course of action in order to separate it briefly from the Engineering Department since that was part of the catalyst that upset the student. Then the student would be directed back to Engineering with a clear set of directions about who he will be meeting.

If the student were to come to the Advising Center before a clear plan of action was established with the BIT, then front office staff should be aware enough to know how to direct the student. The hope here is to establish good communication with the front office staff, not to put them on edge about a student's presence, but to ensure the initial greetings, requests for meetings, and scheduling of appointments does not further escalate the situation. It's quite likely that the student will be in the office to continue discussing his concerns with staff, and the Advising Center should have direction about who he should meet with and when.

It is not recommended that he meet with his typical advisor, Patricia Stewart, who is mentioned in the email. She should be pulled out of the situation until it is discussed with the student and he is asked about his intentions in the email. Instead, an academic administrator or Advising Center Director could talk with him about his concerns, questions, and options related to the degree plan. The email content could be discussed, but only after establishing rapport and assessing the student's attitude and behaviors in the meeting. Should the student arrive at the office and continue his disruptive, aggressive, or threatening manner, staff should ask for assistance from campus police.

## Motivating and Inspiring Change

After calming the student's initial response and addressing his questions and options related to graduation, the hope is that the Advising Center can begin to recreate a more normal interaction with the student. The Engineering Department should also assess the overall roll-out of the degree plan change and its impact on students. Was it communicated appropriately? Did Zach receive communications about it? The academic administrator can make a determination about making an exception related to the degree plan requirements.

Assigning Zach to a specific advisor who is aware of his history and the action plan moving forward will help to maintain a stability with the student as well as an ability to see if something is off track. His advisor should work to build trust and confidence with the student, but the advisor should also establish boundaries around the student's behaviors. Should Zach become aggressive again, the hope is that the advisor can ask him about the aggression and discuss the impact of that behavior on his overall goals.

## Managing the Ongoing Behavior

This is a student who should remain on the Advising Center and BIT radar until his graduation. Between the various campus departments, there should be some checkpoints for Zach over the next year to see how he is progressing toward graduation and what his plans are after he completes his degree. Being positive and future-oriented will help keep Zach focused on the completion of his goals. Should his behaviors become concerning again, the Advising Center should coordinate options with the campus BIT or conduct office.

## DISCUSSION QUESTIONS

1   What aspects of Zach's email are concerning? What other written communications from a student can you think of that have raised concern?
2   What structures do you have in place with your front office reception area when you need to have a coordinated plan when a student arrives to the office? How do you communicate among other advisors about these plans or issues?
3   When degree plan or program changes have the potential to negatively impact a cohort of students, how do advisors work proactively to head off concerns like Zach's? How are degree plan and graduation concerns communicated to students? Are there better ways to prevent these situations?

## ABOUT A BOY

### Narrative

Ruby has been taking courses at her local community college for about a year. She is dating a boy she met in high school and he has become increasingly possessive, aggressive, and threatening in the past few months and recently became physically violent resulting in Ruby being treated for minor injuries. Ruby missed over a week of classes and has scheduled a meeting with her advisor to discuss her options.

### Calming the Initial Crisis

In Chapter 5, we discuss trauma-informed care. An office environment and staff with these elements in mind are particularly helpful in situations like this. Ruby's advisor should focus on establishing a safe and trusting environment for Ruby to discuss what she wants and to identify options to allow Ruby to return to school. The advisor should recognize that there are potentially Title IX reporting implications and requirements and talk with the college's Title IX Coordinator as well.

### Motivating and Inspiring Change

As Ruby returns to classes, she should be working with the Title IX Coordinator related to her situation. This person will help provide safety planning and other resources. Her advisor may observe Ruby struggling with questions about whether she plans to remain in her relationship with her boyfriend. It can be tempting to try to tell her what to do. The advisor wants to focus instead on identifying resources that can help Ruby process what has occurred, such as referrals for her to talk to a counselor or community agency such as a Women's Protective Services. If the boyfriend is also a student and has classes with Ruby, the advisor will need to work with the Title IX Coordinator on options related to classes and other campus resources.

## Managing the Ongoing Behavior

As advisors establish trust with students, they start to reach out to them with a variety of concerns and requests. In Ruby's situation, it's still important to establish boundaries and expectations related to her student experience. It's likely some exceptions were made to class attendance requirements around the time of the initial incident. Advisors need to be prepared to handle additional incidents that Ruby reports as well as the impact of the relationship violence. What if Ruby reports being anxious and unable to attend class? Advisors will want to consult with a student disabilities staff member about a referral for Ruby to apply for disability accommodations related to the impact of the traumatic situation. At the same time, class absences are not a disability accommodation, so it is important to discuss other ways to support her making it to class. Is she nervous to walk on campus and needs closer parking? Are evenings causing her concern and can she switch to a morning section? Regardless, the advisor should continue to work with the Title IX Coordinator as Ruby's requests and needs shift.

## DISCUSSION QUESTIONS

1   What processes are in place to work with students experiencing medical emergencies, trauma, or other personal crisis related to class attendance?
2   What are your school processes for reporting incidents of sexual violence and other Title IX-related issues? Who would you work with to coordinate a Title IX response? What services would they provide?
3   How do you handle referrals for students who may qualify for disability accommodations? What types of statements and requests from the student are good cues for you to make that referral?

# Chapter 9

# Advice for Front Office Staff

Grace: Hello, Jeannie. Who's bothering you now?

Jeannie: Is Mr. Rooney in?

Grace: No, I'm sorry. He's not. May I help you?

Jeannie: I seriously doubt it. When's he back?

Grace: Well, I don't know. He's left the school grounds on personal business.

Jeannie: What's that supposed to mean?

Grace: Well, I believe that it's personal and it's none of your business, young lady.

Jeannie: [scoffs] Nice attitude.

Grace: Isn't Mrs. Hagel expecting you in Consumer Ed. class?

Jeannie: Probably. [Departs]

Grace: Mmm-mmm-mmm. What a little asshole.

*Ferris Bueller's Day Off*

Front office staff are the unsung heroes of higher education. Whether it is working in financial aid, the registrar's office, parking and transportation, health and counseling services, residential life, library services, student affairs, athletics, or disability services, the staff who serve as the first contact for students coming into a departmental office are often the ones who end up dealing with the lion's share of the difficult and dangerous behaviors we have been discussing in this book.

The most common stories we hear when we travel and offer trainings involve students who are under extreme stress related to academic deadlines, personal challenges, family obligations, emotional strain, or financial worries, who then show up at the office demanding help to fix their problems. Students are commonly described as rude and entitled, lacking patience, and frustration tolerance.

Front office staff can become frustrated with hearing the same story, receiving the same late form, assignment, or payment. They experience more burnout than other staff and often feel a sense of frustration at the school for letting these kinds of students in and are the first to complain about topics like Millennial entitlement.

But they are also some of the best, most caring people we encountered in our travels. In addition, these front office staff have an amazing opportunity to have a positive impact on those students who are struggling in some of the most profound ways. They are the caring surrogate parental figures that offer perspective, kindness, and advice right at the point when students need it the most.

For those who see students at their worst, there is a special opportunity to apply grace in a way that creates a lasting sense of caring, support, and change. While this is not always easy to achieve, when it is done well, students feel cared for and have their problems resolved and front office staff feel as if they have made a significant difference in the life of someone who was struggling. While we can't always change the rules to give the students what they want, we have a responsibility to make sure that students understand their choices and options moving forward. Front office staff have a responsibility to not leave a student in a hopeless, frustrated, and overwhelmed place. There is always an option, a caring referral, or a next step that can be taken. Table 9.1 offers some guidance to staff who are working with students on the phone.

## PRACTICAL EXERCISES

Front office staff are often in some of the most dangerous situations and receive the least amount of training. In this chapter, we seek to highlight some more challenging case examples and offer advice related to the three phases of 1) calming the initial crisis, 2) motivating and inspiring change, and 3) managing the ongoing behavior as outlined in Chapters 3, 4, and 5. Discussion questions are also provided for each of the case studies to help facilitate training and discussion.

## THAT ISN'T OUR PROBLEM

### Narrative

Davis comes into the financial aid office frustrated at an email he received telling him that he isn't eligible to remain enrolled in classes. Davis is a second-year student and depends on financial aid to stay enrolled in school. His family is not particularly supportive of his desire to go to school and have told him that he is "on his own" when it comes to filling out forms. The most recent problem involves Davis' father not giving him his completed tax forms. Davis asked him several times for these forms but his father said, "I told you, I'm not doing this. If you want to go to college, fine. But I'm not filling out a bunch of

**TABLE 9.1 Tips for Handling Tough Phone Calls**

| Scenario | Bad Approach | Good Approach |
|---|---|---|
| Caller yelling and cursing. | Yelling back at the caller or threatening to hang up if they keep speaking to you that way. | Be patient. Allow the caller to finish before responding, and answer their questions in a calm and reasonable manner. Do not respond in kind or threaten them. |
| Caller interrupting you when you are talking. | Interrupting them back or talking over them. Telling them you "can't answer them because they aren't being quiet and listening." | Wait until they finish talking and ask them to clarify issues you may not understand. Do not rush to answer and respond slowly. Imagine the phone call as a microphone on stage. If they want to talk, give them the microphone and wait until they finish. |
| Caller not listening and distracted by other conversations or noises. | Telling the caller that you can't talk to them until they are focused and ready to listen. | Ask clarifying questions and do not respond with answers if you cannot hear the question. Ask them to repeat themselves or explain you cannot hear them. Stop talking if they are not listening. |
| Demand to speak to a supervisor, making demeaning comments. | Telling them you are the only person that they will talk to and that you have already made your decision. | Ask other ways you could try to help them. Transfer them to a supervisor or take their number to have a supervisor call back. |

bullshit paperwork for you. I have my own things I need to take care of here at the house."

Davis comes to the front desk with his phone in his hand. He tells the woman at the desk, "I'm sick and tired of getting these threatening emails from your office. I'm doing everything I can to be able to stay in school. I don't need this from you." Other students gather around and start whispering and talking about Davis' behavior. The financial aid advisor tells him to calm down and stop shouting. She tells him the reason he received the email is because his forms are way past due and he will be unenrolled from his classes. She tells him, "You have already had the maximum amount of outstanding bills for our department. We have sent you literally six emails telling you that this day was coming. You can't go to class if you don't finish the forms that are required for your grants."

Davis becomes enraged at this. "I DID finish all my forms. It's my father who won't give me his tax records. What am I supposed to do? Go to his house and force him at gunpoint to give them to me?" The financial aid staff responds, "I've told you once already to lower your voice. If you keep yelling we will call the police to have you removed. I've already told you, there isn't anything we can do. You have to complete your forms. That isn't our problem." Davis storms out of the office in a huff.

## Calming the Initial Crisis

Davis is clearly upset and responding to his escalating behavior with firm limits and a lack of sympathy does little to calm the situation. While it is not OK for any student to berate and yell at staff, if our goal is to calm down the situation and handle the crisis event, responding in kind, or telling the student to calm down is not the most effective way to engage. Having the financial aid staff remain calm and attempt to discuss the matter further with Davis in a more private setting would be one way to pair with him and attempt to help solve the problem, rather than making things worse. A statement such as, "I know emails can feel impersonal. Can I talk to you a minute in our side office so we can try to figure out a plan together on what you can do next?" would go a long way in taking the wind out of Davis' sails as he blows into the office looking for a fight.

## Motivating and Inspiring Change

Once the initial crisis is calmed and everyone is talking, the financial aid staff could talk more directly with Davis about his frustration and why the paperwork is overdue. There is almost always some kind of appeal process, a request for additional loans through a personal bank or emergency fund or the opportunity to withdraw from classes for a semester while the situation is worked out. While suggesting advice here isn't the first step, these kind of "what now?" scenarios are useful for staff to practice a solution-focused problem solving approach. One approach we find helpful is encouraging the staff to view the student like a son or daughter and asking themselves what they would want someone to tell their son or daughter in a similar situation. While there may not be a way to fix the situation immediately, there is a place for a caring staff member to work with the student to figure out possible choices. Declaring himself independent from his parents, for example, may be one way to avoid having the tax form required. Perhaps a counseling referral for Davis to brainstorm ways to get his father to complete the form could be another one. The approach here is getting on the same side as Davis and trying to solve his problem with him, rather than being an obstacle in front of him.

## Managing the Ongoing Behavior

Financial aid forms not being filled out correctly is one of those continual problems departments face. Like parking problems and complaints about food service, it is to be expected that students become confused, lack initiative, or the understanding to complete these processes and forms correctly. If this is a hot spot on your campus, think about some ways to get out in front of this issue by offering assistance, case management, and advisors who help students who are entering a crisis mode in regard to their financial aid. Simply sending students multiple emails doesn't fix the problem for the student and often escalates the problem both for the student who begins to feel hassled and the financial aid staff who feel their reminders are being ignored. Simply repeating a process that doesn't work and expecting a different result won't lead to a novel solution.

## DISCUSSION QUESTIONS

1    What are some other options to de-escalate Davis when he comes into the office? What are some of the external factors that make it harder for staff to be successful in managing Davis' behavior (think culture, race, time of the year)?
2    Discuss some common problems your department has with upset students. What are some creative ways you can adjust your approach, policy, or intervention techniques to more proactively get out in front of these difficulties?
3    Based on our conversations in Chapter 4, what Prochaska et al. (1994) stage of change would you place Davis at? Discuss the disconnect between offering action-based advice to someone at a lower stage of change.

## I HAVE TO GRADUATE!

### Narrative

Sienna comes to the registrar's office upset about a form she received denying her request to drop a class late. Sienna is a senior who struggled in an advanced math class required for her major. She has taken the class three times prior and had to drop the class each time because the material was too advanced for her. This time, she missed the add/drop date and had to complete an appeal for a late withdrawal. She had the professor sign off on the late withdrawal sheet and received a notice from the registrar office that her appeal to drop the class for the fourth time was denied.

She takes the letter out of her backpack with a collection of other papers that become scattered across the front desk. Other students watch her as she sorts through the contents of her large backpack while talking to the staff at the desk. She says, "I just don't know why this happened. It's frustrating. I filled out your form correctly and brought it to the professor for his signature. I don't understand any of this and I am already running late for class. I just don't have time to be dealing with all of this." The staff waits until Sienna finds the letter and looks it over. "Yes, I see. You've already dropped this class three times. We don't allow for a fourth drop because it impacts the school's status regarding financial aid. There isn't anything else we can do. You've already reached the maximum number of drops."

Sienna becomes increasingly flustered at this. "What? No one told me that. I need this class to graduate. I already have a tutor lined up so I can take the class one more time in the spring. I must graduate. I can't do that without this class!" The staff hands her back the letter and says, "I'm sorry. There isn't anything we can do."

## Calming the Initial Crisis

A common mistake when attempting to de-escalate a crisis is jumping to an answer to the frustrated individual's question rather than listening to what they are frustrated about. This is a reasonable mistake, as the person who is frustrated is often asking very directly for an answer. The advice highlighted in Chapter 3 focuses on listening and creating a space or relationship where the student feels more at ease to have a conversation and brainstorm options. Difficult conversations rarely go well in public at a front office desk. Moving Sienna to a more private area or, better yet, appreciating that she is rushed and might do well to make an appointment and come back later to continue the conversation would be a more successful approach to manage her.

## Motivating and Inspiring Change

Once we listen to Sienna's story, we gain a deeper understanding of the larger frustration and challenge she is facing. On first glance, this seems like a problem about an appeal form and policy. When staff take the time to better understand Sienna's stress about failing to pass this class multiple times and her growing fear of not being able to graduate, then we are closer to a solution. Telling Sienna there is no solution to her problem is an insufficient response from front office staff. There are rarely no solutions to a problem, even when the solution may be a referral to another office or offering support for an emotionally upset student. Sienna may have a secondary appeal to the department chair, the registrar, or even the school president. Sienna could also be offered a chance to talk in more detail about her frustrations and brainstorm next steps with an academic advisor, counselor, or case manager.

## Managing the Ongoing Behavior

One of the concepts we teach to staff is attending to the question behind the question. This approach is based in the concept of meta-communication—the importance of attending not only to the expressed complaint but the larger question behind the question. For Sienna, she is not so concerned about the appeal form and the policy of the school, but rather the scary concept that she may not be able to graduate from school and the growing concern that she is not able to pass this difficult math class. Perhaps there is an opportunity at the institution to identify particularly difficult classes for students in certain majors that are common hurdles. When these problems can be identified up front, it allows departments to attempt to invest in some "upstream" work rather than just waiting until the crisis occurs and picking up the pieces.

## DISCUSSION QUESTIONS

1   While the staff member is technically correct about the policy around dropping a class for a fourth time, where does she make her mistakes in communicating with Sienna? What are some other ways she could have handled the crisis?

2   In Chapter 4, we discuss several techniques from Miller and Rollnick's (2002) motivational interviewing. What are some of these approaches that might have worked well with Sienna?

3   What are some common hot spots or frustrations students bring to certain offices around particular times of the year? What are some ways these departments could work to get out ahead of the crisis or better prepare to handle the problem as it manifests?

## CAN I DOWNLOAD PORN?

### Narrative

Michael has a mild form of ASD known more commonly as Asperger's. He is interested in signing a laptop out of the kiosk that is managed by the student activities front desk at the student union. He approaches the desk and gives his ID to the student worker and then engages in an odd conversation about whether there is a restriction on what kind of content can be downloaded onto these public computers.

Michael asks, "I am inquiring if there are any rules or regulations about downloading pornography or information about campus shootings?" Several students around the desk overhear this and make odd faces and are surprised by what he is asking. The desk worker looks confused and responds, "I don't think you are supposed to download anything to the computers, they are just to surf the web or work on a paper or something. You'd have to follow the university IT policy on what kind of content you view."

Michael takes the laptop and says, "The internet browser downloads all kinds of things in cookies and other programs when the user accesses the web. So, people are already downloading things. I wanted to know if you had any restriction on pornography or campus shootings. Thank you." Michael then walks away.

## Calming the Initial Crisis

Michael presents us with a different kind of crisis: a more internal or reflective one. There isn't much the staff member could have or needed to do in terms of his interaction with Michael beyond responding reasonably to his odd questions. The crisis here is ensuring this information doesn't stop with the staff member, but rather gets passed along to his supervisor or the campus BIT. While Michael may or may not be violating the conduct code or IT policy, the larger issue is one of understanding the odd nature of his question. Is the porn going to be watched somewhere publicly? Does this create a Title IX issue (it would)? Why is Michael researching campus shooters? Is this a school project? Is this potential leakage about a pending attack plan as we talked about in Chapter 6? While it is not reasonable to expect front desk staff to assess these statements for potential risk, it is very reasonable to expect them to pass the information on immediately to those who are in a better position to assess the concern and develop an intervention plan.

## Motivating and Inspiring Change

The staff could question Michael further regarding his intention about potentially viewing the pornography in a public location or why he was going to be looking at information regarding campus shootings. There could be reasonable explanations for this as both could be related to class projects. It may be that Michael's odd repetition about downloading material is related to his ASD and not further cause for concern. The only way to assess this, however, is to ask further questions and ensure a case like this gets in front of those on your campus who have more experience and training in threat and violence risk assessment.

## Managing the Ongoing Behavior

The issue for the staff here is related to training around mental health, threat assessment, and customer service. Training for front office staff should include the topics we have talked about in this book: crisis de-escalation, techniques to ask more open-ended and Socratic questions (questions that seek to help staff more thoughtfully exploring the material rather than having direct answers given to them), how to develop a safety or crisis plan, and ways to be solution focused. Additionally, for some departments, further discussion on mediation skills, problem solving, mental health awareness, suicide prevention, and threat assessment may be useful. The staff in this scenario should have been trained in a way that encourages them to ask questions and that passing information up to a supervisor is a positive thing, not an indication they can't handle problems at the front desk.

## DISCUSSION QUESTIONS

1   How might you have approached the situation with Michael? What concerns would you have? What are the pros and cons of reporting the situation up to a supervisor immediately versus engaging Michael in additional questions?

2   Based on our conversation in Chapter 2, talk about your experience with students who have ASD or Asperger's. What does it mean to have a spectrum disorder?

3   What kind of questions, based on our discussion in Chapter 6, would be useful to consider asking Michael to better assess the threat of the situation? What would be some signs from Michael that the situation was becoming more of an emergency and taking things to the next step by calling the police would be warranted?

## CUP OF COFFEE AND A CHAT

### Narrative

Alice is a client of the counseling center and often shows up hours before her appointment and hangs about the waiting room. The counseling center has a coffee and tea service and Alice stops by on the way to class to have a cup of coffee and to talk with other people in the waiting room and Julia, the office manager.

Julia is typically very understanding and when things aren't busy, she engages Alice in longer conversations about her classes and how she is doing on campus. Part of Alice's therapy is about working on developing better social connections, so her therapist finds Alice's behavior in the waiting room helpful as it provides a safe place for Alice to visit and talk with others.

Rather than dialing back on her visits, Alice starts to come by even more often. Julia's patience is tested each morning when Alice is at the locked counseling center door waiting to make herself a cup of coffee. Other counseling clients in the waiting room seem increasingly uncomfortable with Alice's conversation which often involves asking personal questions about why they are there and who their therapist is. Julia is at her wits end and while she doesn't want to be mean to Alice, in Julia's mind, something has to change.

## Calming the Initial Crisis

Following our previous advice, what not to do is setting a hard and fast limit with Alice in the semi-public space of the counseling center waiting room. This would likely cause Alice to be hurt and embarrassed and may make other students feel Julia is being overly harsh since they don't have the larger context of the behavior over time. One of the easier parts of this scenario is the lack of an acute crisis or critical time pressure to address Alice's behavior immediately. The main impetuous to talk to Alice is Julia's growing frustration, rather than an immediate health or safety concern. This buys us a little time.

## Motivating and Inspiring Change

This is one of those scenarios that really centers on an "it takes a village" philosophy. A common misstep in this scenario would be to have Julia be placed in the sole position of having to address and set limits with Alice. This behavior could be addressed in several ways with the counseling director, Julia, other office management staff, and Alice's therapist. There should be a team discussion on the best way to set limits with Alice and who would be in the ideal position to have this conversation privately with her. Alice should be praised for her pro-social behavior and the desire to connect more with others. She should be carefully shaped to take these positive behaviors to a more appropriate place such as a club or student organization.

## Managing the Ongoing Behavior

Creating community standards for waiting rooms and semi-public spaces like lounges or couches outside office spaces around campus is one way to address this problem in a more preventative way. These spaces can also be designed in a way to either limit or encourage conversation among those who are waiting, depending on the nature of the services offered in each department. It would be important to not neglect Julia's frustration here, praising her positive relationship with students like Alice and helping her build her tool set to better set limits with students who push the boundaries of the community standards.

## DISCUSSION QUESTIONS

1   What kind of problems has your front office had with students who become overly attached to staff or the environment? What kind of approaches have

worked in your office or department to set boundaries with the student about these behaviors?

2   How might you approach Alice about her behavior? What are some dos and don'ts when it comes to talking with her? In your opinion, who would be the best person in the scenario to talk with Alice?

3   Discuss how a student's mental health difficulties (outlined in Chapter 2) or Chickering's identity development (Chickering and Reisser, 1993; Robinson, 2013) mentioned in Chapter 3 apply to this scenario with Alice.

## CAN YOU READ THIS PAPER?

### Narrative

Chantel is a first generation college student who has struggled greatly with the requirements of her academic programs. She found that her high school didn't prepare her well for college and she is falling behind in her writing assignments. Her teacher told her about the academic support office and the tutoring services they provide for students on campus. Chantel saw this as a potential light at the end of the tunnel and has spent a lot of time at the center this semester.

Chantel brings papers in that are not very well fleshed out and often struggles with the tutor's request that she work more on her own before bringing a paper in for editing. There is a feeling from the tutors that Chantel does very little work at home and that she relies on the kindness of the tutors to help her write more of the content of her papers. Chantel spends a good ten hours during the week talking to tutors and other students who are available to help with editing. She jumps from tutor to tutor during the week and is known in the center as the student who eats up most of their time.

Things become worse as Thanksgiving approaches and Chantel falls further behind in her assignments. She attempts to schedule more time in the center, becoming tearful and frustrated when the appointments start to become more competitive. She sits in the waiting room for hours hoping for a cancelation and becomes borderline hysterical when the front office staff tell her about a new holiday rule where students can only schedule five appointments a week for support. She says, "I don't know what to do! I have all these papers due and you've been here to help me the whole semester and now you are saying I can't see you for help? Even if there is an open appointment?"

### Calming the Initial Crisis

Chantel does not seem to escalate to a point of threatening behavior in the center, but is more a long-term drain on the office community related to her overuse of services. Many of the tutors have avoided a conflict with Chantel, opting instead for helping and trying to move her out of their office onto the next person as quickly as possible. This creates a problem that is less acute, and more chronic in terms of it being passed from person to person.

## Motivating and Inspiring Change

Chantel is very much in need of a longer, personal connection with a staff member to assist her in finding additional resources and to help her strategize her assignments more effectively. This might include brainstorming a tutoring group that could support each other for a class or helping Chantel find some off-campus or additional peer resources to help her manage her course load. It would be useful to reframe Chantel's behavior as positive help-seeking behavior (e.g., being worried enough about her assignments that she comes into academic support to receive help) rather than having a negative view of Chantel's aggressive help seeking. A case manager or academic retention specialist could talk to Chantel in more detail about taking a more remedial class in the future or finding more effective ways to study. Additionally, it may be useful to look at a referral for Chantel to disability services for additional accommodations and/or support.

## Managing the Ongoing Behavior

The school would do well to identify students in need of additional remedial education related to courses and develop creative resources to help the students in need connect to each other and find places to locate additional help. It is a positive scenario where Chantel is seeking to be successful at school and working with tutors to better her chances at success. Supporting the tutors who are frustrated at working with Chantel through additional training and supportive, regular supervision is another way to get out in front of difficulties with students like Chantel.

## DISCUSSION QUESTIONS

1  How has your office managed a student who is overusing services and having a stress/burnout impact on your staff? What are some ways you would approach a scenario like the one described here with Chantel?

2  How does a department balance the needs of individuals versus the needs of the larger community? Given the high demand for services, should they be offered on a first come, first serve basis or restricted by quantity like in the Chantel case? Given disability law and the Office of Civil Rights (OCR), discuss the interplay between the services a student may need to be successful and the idea of providing equal services for all students.

3   What additional referrals or other departments might be useful to help Chantel with her needs on campus?

## GET YOUR HEAD OUT OF YOUR ASS!

### Narrative

Charlotte is a non-traditional college student who is part of the online program for university. She has several physical and learning disabilities and is well known to the disability center through phone calls and emails. Her complaints typically center on requests for extended time to complete assignments, complaints about instructors who are not willing to work with her, and her needs and occasional frustrations and arguments with other students in her online classes.

Charlotte has been connected to the university for eight years, slowly working her way through a liberal arts degree. She has often been argumentative with staff about her disability accommodations and disrespectful to them on the phone and over email. Staff have passed Charlotte around the office, trying their best to not get upset with her and solve her problem to get her off the phone or to stop bothering them through emails.

A new staff member started in the department who hadn't had experience with Charlotte before. Charlotte sent a harsh email to the new staff member about "their incompetence and total lack of qualifications to be doing the job they are being paid for at the college." The email ended with some veiled threats about the staff needing to "get her head out of her ass" or she would be "out on her ass" looking for a new job.

### Calming the Initial Crisis

Managing a person in an online environment is a difficult challenge given we do not have the same access to tone, body language, and other non-verbal signs to aid us in gauging the severity of the conflict. In this case, Charlotte is well known to the disability service staff and they have developed an adequate, if not perfect, way to manage Charlotte's behavior when she calls or emails. With a new staff member coming on board, Charlotte takes advantage and attempts to push buttons and get a reaction. Given the threatening nature of the exchange, it would be appropriate to try to calm Charlotte down, but also consider a referral to the student conduct process. Even though Charlotte is a known quantity to the office, it is not wise to adopt an approach that allows a student to mistreat staff and escalate toward threatening them. This is never a reasonable accommodation for mental health or physical disabilities.

## Motivating and Inspiring Change

In this case, understanding the overall context, or baseline, of the student's behavior can be a helpful mechanism to get out in front of further escalation. Staff with experience with Charlotte could share the things they have found that have worked and not worked as well. Sharing this information with new staff would be one way to get in front of this situation, though there is still the need to help Charlotte understand and comply with existing standards for behavior in the campus community. In sitting down with Charlotte, assuming this is possible given her status as a distance-learning student, it would be useful to ascertain if she behaves this way more through emails and on the phone, or if this is her typical way of interacting in person as well. A caring confrontation with Charlotte would involve supporting her sticking through her academic progress over such a long period of time and despite her physical and mental disabilities, but also setting limits about what acceptable behavior is. It might be helpful to begin a longer term intervention with Charlotte by attempting to understand why she became so upset, and encouraging some empathy for someone new to the job who felt helpless and threatened. In this case, having a staff member or manager more experienced with Charlotte would be a good starting place to better understand her motivations for treating the new staff member so poorly and how to move forward in a more respectful manner.

## Managing the Ongoing Behavior

Many offices can relate to what we call "frequent flyers" who push our buttons and challenge our ability to work effectively with others. This ongoing stress and accompanying comfort with being mistreated or mistreating others is a serious area of concern for offices and departments. Many become anesthetized to the bad behavior and threatening actions and see them as "nothing to worry about, that's just Charlotte" and expect staff to be mistreated, while losing an important opportunity to correct the behavior and potentially share with the conduct office or campus BIT to determine if this is part of a larger problem. Efforts to train staff to avoid this potential trap of accepting bad behavior as the status quo and how to appropriately intervene would be a useful investment for the office.

## DISCUSSION QUESTIONS

1   In Chapter 4, we discuss Miller and Rollnick (2002)'s motivational interviewing techniques. Talk about how some of these might be useful in conversations with Charlotte.

2   There is a bit of a conflict between just pacifying a volatile student like Charlotte and holding her accountable for her behavior. How might you approach this balance?

3   What might be some of the motivations for Charlotte's behavior? How would understanding these motivations help manage her behavior more effectively?

# Chapter 10

# Advice for Case Management Staff

People are afraid of me because I'm different.

*Edward Scissorhands*

Case managers reach out to a campus' most isolated students and provide connections for them back to the campus community. Case manager positions have expanded into colleges and universities across the nation. These roles are critical for the response to and management of disruptive and dangerous students, so we wanted to offer a chapter related to more advanced case management scenarios for staff in these positions. This chapter also helps staff to understand the role of case managers on their campus and how they can be helpful in situations involving students of concern.

Case management, at its very core, is about helping students to overcome the obstacles they encounter in their lives. This is central to the educational mission of most institutions of higher education, which seek to retain students and provide them with an environment conducive to academic success. Case management can serve as a keystone mechanism through which universities support and keep students safe.

Case management has a rich history within the fields of social work and psychology dating back to the de-institutionalization movement of the 1970s. As those struggling with mental health disorders were relocated from state run asylums back into the mainstream community, it became apparent that many struggled to successfully reintegrate. Case management programs soon arrived on the scene, not only to facilitate access to mental health treatment, but also to assist these patients in managing finances, identifying and maintaining employment, and facilitating engagement in recreational and social activities.

Despite these roots, case management today isn't limited to those struggling with mental health challenges. With the creation of BITs and TATs, colleges and universities have come to recognize the benefit of dedicating staff members to work flexibly and creatively with at-risk students, to ensure proper access to care, to help them schedule and keep their appointments, to access academic assistance (e.g., tutoring), and to effectively navigate the student conduct and other university processes, among other functions.

Case manager roles remind us of *Who Wants to Be a Millionaire?* In the game show, contestants answer trivia questions gaining money with each correct answer. With a wrong answer, they can lose it all. Contestants have "lifelines" they can use to help them along the way. They can phone a friend, narrow their choices of answers down to two, or ask the audience for help. Case managers provide lifelines to students in difficult situations. Students reach out to them in their most difficult times to ask for help with choices, seek expert advice on the college experience, or just to help figure out what options they really have. Case managers also contact students when they are struggling and remind them of the opportunities still available to them. Students working with case managers may feel like they are about to lose it all, but the case manager remains their connection or lifeline to the institution and to their goals as a college student.

Case managers exist in a variety of college and university departments. Most commonly, you will find clinical case managers in counseling centers and health departments. Non-clinical case managers have increased in departments that facilitate BITs, such as the Dean of Students. Other departments like housing, financial aid, conduct, disability services, academic advising, and Title IX are also finding benefits to hiring case manager staff to maintain cases of reoccurring student issues. Your school may not have a formal case manager, but you still may find staff playing similar roles who can benefit from the information in this chapter.

Case managers are typically focused on a special population of students, perhaps those using counseling services or those reported to a BIT, and they work in an integrated and collaborative manner to facilitate resources and referrals to assist the student in moving beyond problems occurring in their college experience. They also assess the impact of situations on other students and the campus community, thinking about secondary victims and what resources may be needed. Case managers will regularly display skills in all the phases of response outlined in this book from calming the initial crisis to managing ongoing student behaviors to understanding threat assessment. These roles require great coordination and communication among other units with an eye on the larger picture of what is occurring with a student. Table 10.1 offers the reader some review of good and bad case manager qualities.

Case management is a solution-focused approach to assisting students with a wide variety of needs. As such, case managers are concerned about *what is and what can be done*, rather than a focus on what was and what has held back the student in the past. Helping students to engage in effective problem solving by identifying solutions is the backbone of case management.

## TABLE 10.1 Good/Bad Case Manager Qualities

| Bad Qualities | Good Qualities |
| --- | --- |
| Adopts a singular approach that students need to figure out things for themselves to be at college. Offers help after the student has shown they have tried all other options. | Stresses personal responsibility as a process that develops over the college years and works best when nurtured and encouraged rather than demanded. |
| Has a distaste or frustration for working with this new generation of college students who seem lazy, unwilling to work hard and feel the world owes them something. Often drops into a rant about how "they would never have done this when I went to college." | Sees each generation as having qualities of questioning authority and a tendency to choose the easier path rather than the more challenging one. Sees the new generation as being critical consumers and more careful about commitment rather than lazy or detached. |
| Expects students to work hard to find the answers on their own. Sees their role as a last resort for help after all other alternatives are offered. | Sees their role as an advocate and mentor during the student's growth and progress. |
| Offers help through lectures, handouts or pointing the student in the direction of what they need to do. Expects students to find their own solution and adopts a "you can bring a horse to water, but can't make them drink" attitude. | Offers help through support, advocacy and guiding the student in small, progressive steps towards growth. Takes the time to build a plan with a high likelihood of success. Adopts a "teach a man to fish" attitude. |

## DOING IT WELL

> They're not gonna catch us. We're on a mission from God.
>
> Elwood Blues, *The Blues Brothers*

There are certain attributes that are essential for those who hope to do this job well. Having the right attitude and personality to encourage students to overcome obstacles is key. Working as a team player who can find creative solutions to problems is equally essential. Good case managers are also good at documentation to measure the effectiveness of interventions, reduce liability, and keep a bird's eye view of the student's progress.

## The Right Attitude

Case managers should engage students with whom they work by encouraging them with positive energy and a charismatic manner of interaction. Defining a high-energy level and charisma in a staff member is difficult to quantify, yet, these are the very qualities that seem to engage students best and encourage them to overcome their obstacles and challenges.

Successful case managers can maintain a positive outlook and willingness to work through obstacles, solve problems, and think outside of the box. Another way to describe this would be to look for a case manager with an optimistic outlook and high tolerance for frustrations and ambiguity. A quality case manager will often encounter rigid rules that make little sense, and that will require a little thought to arrive at a creative and helpful solution. They have a solution-focused and optimistic orientation. Students working with a case manager will have several challenges and obstacles in their lives. Case managers require a degree of "stretch and bounce" when it comes to helping brainstorm solutions and next steps for a student who may believe they have dug themselves too deep into a hole.

## Be a Team Player

Case managers should form collaborative relationships with key resources on and off campus. Depending on your campus, a case manager will refer students to on/off-campus counseling resources, substance abuse treatment, health/nutrition support, academic support, disability services, and counseling. They look at problems from a multi-faceted perspective that is inclusive and adopt a "it takes a village" approach to change and growth.

Practically speaking, this means that good case managers get out of the office and forge relationships with key departments around campus and the community. They anticipate the needs of the students they are working with and have referrals and solutions at the ready. When they don't have a quick recommendation, they know someone who they can reach out to find an answer. They don't solve the problems for the students, but instead help each student think critically about where they want to be and give them the tools to take the next step towards the student's goal.

## Write it Down

Accurate record keeping provides risk mitigation in the legal realm, allows for accurate tracking of cases over time, and empowers continuity of care across service providers, position, and personnel transitions. When working with students who are struggling, the behaviors the student engages in bring an element of risk and potential liability for both the student and the professionals working with them. Solid record keeping (from the initial intake document and informed consent through ongoing contact/case notes) provides documentation and a clear paper trail of the what, where, when, why, and how of the services that are offered.

The content of case management notes will depend on the department that houses the case manager. For example, case managers working out of the Student Conduct or Dean of Student's Office will likely have a different record-keeping style than case managers housed within a counseling service. Additionally, depending on where the case manager is housed, some case management notes may be considered privileged mental health records, whereas others may be considered education records and subject to FERPA. Nevertheless, once the information is shared with a BIT or otherwise outside of a counseling or health service, the information is governed by FERPA.

## PRACTICAL EXERCISES

The following five case scenarios offer some practical advice and training opportunities for case managers to better hone their skills and think about applying the concepts from this book to their everyday work. These challenging case examples relate back to the three phases of 1) calming the initial crisis, 2) motivating and inspiring change, and 3) managing the ongoing behavior as outlined in Chapters 3, 4, and 5. Discussion questions are also provided for each of the case studies to help facilitate training and discussion.

## AN ACT OF VIOLENCE

### Narrative

Curtis is excited about being in his senior year at college. He embraces the entire experience and enjoys classes, spending time with friends, and looking for internship opportunities for next semester. He spends time hanging out with friends off campus. Curtis is hanging out with his friends outside of a store and a group of local townies who notice that he is a college student start making fun of him. "Hey! Why don't you get out of here? You don't belong here."

Curtis looks down and tries to go into the store. His friends walk away and go back home. Two teenagers stop Curtis from going into the store and say, "No way. You don't belong here either. Where do you think you are going?" Curtis tries to turn around and the oldest teenager punches him as he walks away. Curtis holds his head and begins to run back home. Several of the teenagers throw bottles at him as he runs down the street.

Curtis is tearful and overwhelmed. He is shaking and has a small amount of blood from a cut on his ear. Curtis takes the next day off from class and spends it in his room, away from everyone. During the next week, he slowly returns to class and other students see him as more moody and irritable. He doesn't talk to people often and keeps mostly to himself. Curtis is particularly jumpy around loud noises and has to leave class one day after a glass breaks. He tells his friends, "I just don't want to be here anymore. Everything reminds me of that day. The sound of the bottles breaking; that thug hitting me. I just don't feel safe here anymore. I think I need to go home."

The campus BIT learns of what happens and assigns a case manager to work with Curtis.

## Calming the Initial Crisis

The case manager is well situated to contact Curtis to provide support and assistance. For case managers, the initial outreach is an art, especially when you do not have a previous history with the student. In this case, just indicating how you became aware of his distressing situation and sharing that there may be some ways you can assist should be a good way of establishing that first contact.

Once Curtis comes in to meet with the case manager, the case manager should identify ways to establish rapport and to allow Curtis to disclose what he wants about what happened to him. It's not necessary to retell what occurred; in fact, that can be traumatic as well. If Curtis seems hesitant to share, you can use a broad description to describe your understanding of what occurred while not placing labels on what he experienced:

> Curtis, your faculty member said that you had a bad situation occur off campus. You don't have to tell me everything that occurred because I know that can be difficult, but I do want to help you identify resources available for you on campus to assist with what happened. Maybe you could tell me about what you have been experiencing since the incident as a starting place, and we could focus there first.

Then, the case manager could listen, extract additional information, and determine the best resource and referral options for the student. Referrals could include medical resources for physical injuries and a police referral to report a crime.

## Motivating and Inspiring Change

The case manager would likely focus on helping Curtis through his crisis reaction first by offering support and reassurance as well as helping to normalize his crisis reactions such as being startled or jumpy. They could also discuss options that make him feel safer in the academic environment. Offering choices to victims can help them to regain a sense of power over what is occurring around them. In this stage, the case manager would want to discuss a counseling referral and other academic support resources as well as following up on the referrals for medical care and a police report. Often students do not understand the intricacies of a police investigation, and a case manager can answer some basic questions about maintaining a police report number and following up with their assigned investigator for updates. The case manager could explore more layered issues related to Curtis' friends and their reaction to the situation, if he is in contact with them, and make a determination about the need to reach out to the friends with resources. If his friend circle has changed because of this situation, discussing other social support could be helpful.

## Managing the Ongoing Behavior

Case managers may or may not have long-term interactions with Curtis depending on his recovery. Other issues that may need to be considered would be developments related to the police investigation and if it included other students. This would need to be shared with the conduct office for discussion. The case manager would also want to consider information shared by Curtis and if it indicated that he may have been targeted on the basis of race or sexual orientation, for example. These types of concerns could raise broader campus and community issues.

## DISCUSSION QUESTIONS

1   What are some of the common trauma reactions experienced by those who have been assaulted? Discuss some of the ways to assist Curtis in his recovery. How long would you expect Curtis to have this reaction?
2   Curtis is refusing therapy at this point. What are some ways he could be talked into seeing a therapist? What are some other supports that could be put in place for him short of seeing a therapist?
3   What kind of support might be available from Curtis' friends? What are the pros and cons of involving the police in this scenario?

## LIVING FAR FROM HOME

### Narrative

Mei-ling is an art major from Taiwan. She has been over in this country for a semester and feels an overwhelming sense of homesickness. She has had trouble adjusting to the food and struggles some with the language and making friends. The political climate of the school has not been very accepting of foreigners, both on campus and on the national stage and this has contributed to Mei-ling feeling further isolated and depressed.

Mei-ling's art professor notices her difficulty adjusting and shares this with the student affairs department. The department has a case manager who works with students who are struggling. The case manager reaches out to Mei-ling about how she is adjusting to college and her growing sense of depression. Mei-ling is defensive about this and resistant to the idea of going to counseling. She is willing to meet more with the case manager moving forward, however.

The case manager continues to meet with Mei-ling twice a week and her depression continues to worsen. Mei-ling has trouble getting to class and missed two of the case management meetings because she overslept. She continues to be isolated in her living environment.

## Calming the Initial Crisis

The case manager would begin by establishing rapport with Mei-ling. It may be helpful to discuss how meeting about her concerns would not have a negative impact on Mei-ling's school status. There may be some cultural aspects of her reluctance to seek help. Some of the initial discussion could focus on understanding Mei-ling's experiences with her transition to the school. The case manager would want to be attentive for signs of depression when talking with Mei-ling. Then the case manager could ask Mei-ling to participate in a counseling intake which could include a more in-depth suicide assessment.

## Motivating and Inspiring Change

Motivational interviewing and change theory could be helpful frameworks for the biweekly meetings with Mei-ling to support moving her from contemplation to preparation for action in terms of her interest in changing her interactions with her environment. These are outlined in more detail in Chapter 4. The case manager could help Mei-ling see her adjustment as a process filled with ups and downs, rather than a one time, all-or-nothing event. The case manager would do well to take a cheerleading and advocate stance with Mei-ling to assist her through the more difficult times and look more closely at a counseling referral.

## Managing the Ongoing Behavior

The case manager would want to be attentive to any critical moments that might negatively impact Mei-ling and derail her progress, such as a sudden academic failure or an interpersonal crisis. This scenario also raises broader issues about the services offered to international students on campus through student organizations, orientations, and other academic and co-curricular support services. In terms of systems issues, the case manager could assist with encouraging parental involvement and/or connection to clubs or organizations on campus that may be supportive to the student.

## DISCUSSION QUESTIONS

1   How would you proceed if Mei-ling refused to participate in a counseling intake?
2   How can your campus support international students in their transitions to the institution and with navigating the new culture?
3   What resources and departments would the case manager need to coordinate with to assist Mei-ling?

# CHIP ON HIS SHOULDER

## Narrative

Chip is a second semester sophomore who has a long history of minor conduct and academic disruptions in the classroom. He served in Iraq and had a traumatic brain injury because of his service. Chip is a commuter student who lives off campus and gets into frequent arguments with financial aid and registrar staff about his status on campus and what classes he can register for on campus. Early in his time at the college, he came to the attention of the BIT and was assigned a case manager as part of his sanctioning and probation.

Chip's case manager meets with him weekly to help him better manage his impulse control and build frustration tolerance for times when he gets upset. The case manager often feels challenged and frustrated working with Chip as he continues to get into arguments with fellow classmates, faculty, and staff around campus. Nothing the case manager does seems to "stick."

Chip's behavior continues to escalate and he gets into an altercation with another student who he thinks cut in front of him in a line at the student café. Chip pushes him down and threatens to "kick his ass" if he tries to mess with him again. Chip has a pending conduct hearing for the incident that will likely result in his separation from the college.

## Calming the Initial Crisis

Case managers really have to master staying calm in these ongoing moments of escalation and crisis with students. Chip is described as someone who is easily angered and frustrated. As we discussed in Chapter 3, if our response is to engage with him in a similar manner, he is likely to continue to escalate and opportunities for productive conversation will decrease. There is a desire to want to express frustration to Chip and say "I told you so" about his ongoing behaviors, but case managers instead have to focus first on calming the storm in order to continue constructive discussions around behavior change.

## Motivating and Inspiring Change

While Chip has not responded favorably up to this point with strategies related to shifting his attitudes and behaviors, case managers should stay committed to good research-based techniques such as motivational interviewing. When these behaviors reoccur, we can forget to engage in active listening about what has happened from the student's point of view. Give Chip an opportunity to express what he experienced, remain empathetic with him, and you are still poised to discuss his actions in the situation. Knowing the potential outcomes of a conduct hearing, the case manager can begin to talk with Chip about his options if he is suspended, and staff can make additional referrals to counseling and perhaps veteran services. Case managers should be knowledgeable of threat assessment techniques as well (Chapter 6), so they would be continuing to gather information to gauge Chip's risk factors for violence and aggression.

## Managing the Ongoing Behavior

The case manager should continue to work in coordination with the campus BIT and the conduct office as Chip's case is considered. These times of potential separation create additional stress and concern for the student. Case managers should be knowledgeable of community resources available to students. Identifying resources that are options for Chip even if he is not enrolled in school becomes important as well as helping him transition from on-campus to off-campus providers as necessary.

## DISCUSSION QUESTIONS

1   When students have pending conduct violations, how does communication and coordination with the conduct office work?
2   What other support and resources could assist veterans in educational environments and specifically those with traumatic brain injury?
3   If Chip was suspended for one year, how would the case manager be involved with Chip upon his return?

## WRITING BINGES

### Narrative

Billy has always struggled with bipolar disorder. He is a creative writing major and feels his manic phase swings are positive and good for his creative spirit. During these intense writing binges, he disappears from campus, misses classes, and isn't seen for days. He returns exhausted and often has over-spent his credit cards on hotels and alcohol to fuel his Hemingway-esque binges. His work during these times is powerful and moving, and professors tend to forgive his absences as his work is of such a high quality.

When he doesn't feel as inspired, he tends towards being broody and withdrawn. He has had a few times where he has dropped into an existential crisis and seriously considered suicide. Billy attends counseling on campus but is inconsistent with appointments and rarely takes his medication as prescribed. Billy is assigned a case manager who works with the BIT and counseling department.

Billy's case manager works with him and forms a positive relationship. The case manager is impressed with Billy's writing, but not very successful at helping Billy appreciate concepts such as moderation, balance, and planning. The case manager worries that Billy might move to suicide during one of his depressive periods but feels frustrated at how hard it is to predict Billy's mood swings.

## Calming the Initial Crisis

Case managers should be skilled in basic suicide protocols, such as suicide gatekeeper training. Billy is a student who may challenge the limits of a case manager. His situation tempts us to move beyond our role and responsibilities as it relates to predicting his suicidal ideation and other moods. Case managers should stay committed to their training on suicide protocols and partner with other mental health professionals to assist in this case.

Billy's writing is a challenging element to this case. On one hand, case managers want to encourage educational activities that the student enjoys and in which he excels, but part of our role is helping Billy to see the impact of how he is currently pursuing his passion on other aspects of his life.

## Motivating and Inspiring Change

Case managers communicate not only to the student involved in a situation, but they consider other individuals and groups influencing the student's behavior or impacted by the student's behavior. In this case, the case manager could discuss with professors Billy's academic performance and the importance of setting and upholding consistent standards related to deadlines and class attendance. The case manager could consider the impact of discussing with Billy's family the school's concerns. Billy may be willing to talk with them alongside the case manager, or the case manager may determine a safety need to bring Billy's parents into discussions. In addition to family, the case manager would work with Billy to determine what support structures are in place to help him when things are difficult for him.

## Managing the Ongoing Behavior

With continued concerns around Billy's suicidality, the case manager may have to work with the campus BIT to require a mandated assessment for Billy with the counseling center or other designated party to consider his suicide risk and other interventions. This is an advanced case manager referral, not discussed in detail in this book, but we mention it here to highlight other tools available when students continue to present with the same high-risk attitudes and behaviors.

## DISCUSSION QUESTIONS

1   What role were faculty attitudes and behaviors toward Billy playing in this scenario? How could the case manager handle conversations with faculty about Billy?
2   What are the pros and cons of involving parents or family members? How could their involvement serve to improve or worsen the situation?
3   What processes are available at your institution for mandated assessments? How would those processes work in Billy's situation?

## GIVE ME YOUR ANSWER TRUE

### Narrative

Daisy is a junior and has struggled with Asperger's disorder and social problems during her time on campus. She has met with a counselor once a week for her entire time at college and was part of the early intervention program during her first year. This program was designed to provide extra support to those students who need it to be successful on campus. Daisy continues to meet with her case manager as part of this program well into her junior year.

Daisy struggles with being overweight and this contributes some to teasing on campus by her peers, has a negative impact on her self-esteem and health and presents a barrier to connecting to social outings as she often gets tired and overwhelmed with the stress and worry of being far from campus. Daisy is undecided in her major, despite numerous meetings between her and her parents and her case manager and academic advisor.

Daisy has some issues with depression, but not suicidal thoughts or actions. Recently, she has talked more in therapy about her parents pressuring her to choose a major and how she feels like everyone around her is dating someone and she has never kissed anyone. Daisy comes across as childish to other students, sitting in the waiting room playing with several toy trolls on her keyring. This makes it more difficult for her to connect socially with others.

### Calming the Initial Crisis

Daisy experiences an almost daily sense of low-grade crisis that leaves the therapy and case management staff at the university well utilized. Daisy is liked by these staff, despite her "frequent flyer" status in these departments; she is easy to work with, despite her lack of change and growth. When she does have a crisis, or becomes more intense in her frustration, Daisy often shows up in the counseling center waiting room and uses those services appropriately, although loudly, and with some disruption to other students waiting for services.

**171**

## Motivating and Inspiring Change

As the saying goes, "College is a marathon, not a sprint." With a student like Daisy, the main challenge here is the ongoing nature of her service needs. Some universities and colleges pride themselves on offering specialized care and accommodations to students who require more than most to be successful at college. Daisy has been well connected with disability accommodation staff to address her learning differences. Another referral or connection for Daisy might be working more closely with health services, a nutritionist, or the fitness center staff to address her weight problem. Ongoing case management meetings would be useful to keep her parents connected to her progress and keep everyone working together to ensure Daisy's success on campus.

## Managing the Ongoing Behavior

Case management programs exist differently across the country. Some schools pride themselves on offering these services to students to ensure retention and successful navigation of existing services. Other campuses reserve case management services in a more emergent manner. Daisy finds herself with increased support for her college years, which is helpful given that her needs during this transition time are more pressing than other similarly aged students might experience.

## DISCUSSION QUESTIONS

1   How does case management operate at your campus? Do you allow students to opt in, pay for services, or is it more limited to those in crisis?
2   What are some of the challenges in working with a student like Daisy? How would a case manager balance the different expectations of Daisy and her parents related to her academic progress?
3   What are some ways to engage Daisy in a more holistic approach to her health and social connection? As her case manager, what are some ways you could assist her in connecting to resources on campus?

# Chapter 11

# Advice for Student Activities Staff

So, what would you little maniacs like to do first?

Lisa, *Weird Science*

This chapter is directed primarily at student activities staff, a broad term we use to encompass student affairs professionals working with students in a number of capacities related to involvement, transition, and engagement experiences. Staff may be working with student organizations, fraternities and sororities, campus programming boards, athletic teams, multicultural and diversity programs, orientation programs, or recreational sports as some examples.

This work predominantly occurs outside the classroom, in extracurricular activities, and in many cases after regular campus office hours. At their best, these experiences help students develop leadership skills, apply theory and knowledge they have learned in the classroom, practice their capabilities, and establish lasting connections with other students and their campus communities. At their worst, students find that these experiences can overwhelm, corrupt, and even traumatize.

It's important for student activities staff to acknowledge some of the inherent challenges and opportunities associated with their work. In these settings, the role of group dynamics becomes an important element to consider in our response to a student in crisis. Other students are more likely to be impacted by the disruptive behavior of a student in a group setting, and groups may influence the behaviors and attitudes of members, triggering crises or influencing our treatment of others.

The work of student activities staff is further complicated by the location where these activities occur. Programs may be held off campus, and teams and organizations may travel to out of town locations. Student activities are also designed, in many cases, to be planned and organized by students, so student officers or team captains have an important role to play in the identification of student concerns and a managed group response. Also, how could we not mention the common presence of alcohol or other substances in social settings associated with student activities or groups?

Yet, student activities staff are also in key positions to help with the prevention of student concerns and with interventions for individuals. When it comes to educating students about wellness issues, utilization of campus resources, or other risk factors related to student crisis, student activities staff know the ins and outs of campus programming and gaining access to audiences of students. Student organizations also offer a good venue for training students on bystander intervention skills and techniques which work well for identifying situations of concern where a student is in harm's way.

They also know students really well. Student activities staff are front and center to most aspects of student life and the college experience. When dealing with student concerns, if they involve a student participating in some aspect of student activities, the staff associated with that area are important to understanding the perspective of the student, interactions with the group, and their experiences at the school. Student activities staff must be part of a coordinated response when student concerns arise involving a student involved in a group or activity. Otherwise, a crucial piece of the response puzzle is missing and the intervention is incomplete.

## RULES OF ENGAGEMENT

First of all, keep him out of the light, he hates bright light, especially sunlight, it'll kill him. Second, don't give him any water, not even to drink. But the most important rule, the rule you can never forget, no matter how much he cries, no matter how much he begs, never feed him after midnight.

Chinese Boy, Gremlins

When talking to faculty about managing disruptive and dangerous behavior, one of the first discussions is around classroom management. For student activities staff, especially those working with groups of students, a first consideration needs to be about organizational management. Consider some of the items below to help create "rules of engagement" for how you work with your student populations. These expectations and boundaries are increasingly important during times of crisis within groups.

- What behavioral expectations and standards exist related to the program or organization? At the college level? At the organizational level? When do students communicate about these expectations? Do student leaders and staff role model these standards?
- How would you define the organization's or activity's relationship with the college or university? Is there a formal relationship statement in a student handbook or policy?

- What staff job responsibilities include elements of helping skills, crisis response, or reporting on student behaviors?
- Are volunteers or part-time advisors part of your work with students? What outlines their roles and responsibilities related to these situations?
- Where can you incorporate wellness programming and activities into the organization or program? What topics would be important for your group of students (alcohol, stress, nutrition, depression, suicide, violence, etc.)?
- What training do student leaders in the organization or activity receive on these topics? Review Chapter 12 for train-the-trainer ideas.
- How is civility integrated into the organization or activity? How does the group handle discussions around contrasting viewpoints? Are meetings organized in order to value all viewpoints?
- What emergency contact information does the activity or organization have on its members? How is this accessed and when?

While each of these student activity areas has its own specializations, staff will find a great deal of overlap in the types of situations they may confront related to disruptive and dangerous behavior. Being proactive about organizational management will help during these times of difficulty. Below we provide scenarios for student activities staff related to advisor scenarios, online group behaviors, sexual assault, civility and diversity, mental health concerns, and complex encounters in a student organization.

## PRACTICAL EXERCISES

Student activities staff have a unique perspective with students who are struggling. They often have more informal and trusting relationships with students that provide a unique opportunity to form a connection. This chapter is designed to highlight some more challenging case examples and offer advice related to the three phases of 1) calming the initial crisis, 2) motivating and inspiring change, and 3) managing the ongoing behavior as outlined in Chapters 3, 4, and 5. Discussion questions are also provided for each of the case studies to help facilitate training and discussion.

## STUDENT ORGANIZATION ADVISORS

### Narrative

Ms. Benson is a staff member in biology and an advisor to a student organization. She is approached by a student officer who is concerned about the recent behaviors in the organization of Jeff, another student. He has been falling asleep in meetings and looks increasingly disheveled.

## Calming the Crisis

In these initial conversations with the student officer about Jeff, Ms. Benson can encourage the peer to express their concerns to Jeff directly and encourage Jeff to talk with Ms. Benson or to consider a resource like the counseling center. It is OK to teach other students to know how to help and offer resources to their peers if they are comfortable doing so. The staff member could give the student officer tips related to talking with Jeff in private and using direct, nonjudgmental statements (e.g., I've noticed that you seem tired and that your participation is not what it has been. I'm concerned about you). Ms. Benson could also use this approach with Jeff if the student officer was not comfortable in this role and ensure that referrals are made for Jeff. Notice that these initial interactions are not about holding Jeff accountable for falling asleep in the meeting. Instead, these discussions are about showing care and concern while helping him with good resource referrals.

## Motivating and Inspiring Change

Ms. Benson later receives an email from Jeff disclosing that he has been struggling with sadness and depression following the loss of a close friend. Staff should know that they are not expected to provide all of the professional support that a student needs. Staff can consider themselves facilitators in these processes rather than feeling as though they have to address all of the personal issues of the student. Upon receiving Jeff's email, Ms. Benson could acknowledge what Jeff has shared with her and use phrases like "I'm glad you told me. I had noticed that you did not seem yourself. Perhaps you would consider letting me connect you with someone you can talk with," and following with a referral to the counseling center. Ms. Benson should also follow up with the officer who initially reported concerns about Jeff to see how the conversation with Jeff went and provide encouragement to the officer for trying to help a peer. Bystander intervention is a skill that can be taught to students to help get ahead of concerning behavior.

## Managing the Ongoing Behavior

This type of outreach to a student, as offered by both Ms. Benson and the student officer, should lead to productive and engaging interactions with Jeff moving forward. They should remain supportive of him and encourage his use of resources to discuss his grief. It can help to be attentive to Jeff's demeanor around the time of the anniversary of his friend's death as well as watching for signs of declining emotional stability.

## DISCUSSION QUESTIONS

1 Would you report this issue to a campus BIT? Why or why not?

2    What if Jeff was not open to going to counseling? How would the staff member's interactions change?

3    If Jeff continues to sleep through organization meetings, how could the staff member address this behaviorally while still being supportive of the grief he is experiencing?

## CYBER-BULLYING CLUB

### Narrative

Carol Anne is the president of a student organization, the Student Organization for Service (SOS), a group of about twenty members providing community service assistance to local and campus agencies. After a number of member transitions left the organization struggling for student leadership, Carol Anne moved into the role of president after one year of membership.

Dana is a freshman member of the organization. She emails Carol Anne that she is going to drop out of the organization. Dana's email reads, "I cannot continue as a member of SOS. The other members are hypocrites, and it's not healthy for me to be part of an organization that is not supportive of its members." Carol Anne runs into Dana on campus the same day and tries to talk to her about the email. Dana quickly says, "Why don't you just look at the SOS GroupMe account? It is pretty clear why I feel the way I do!" Dana storms away from Carol Anne without explaining.

When Carol Anne logs onto the SOS GroupMe account, she sees that a senior member named Steve has been posting about Dana. His posts include a picture of Dana passed out at an SOS party and what appears to be her pants with a urine stain on them. Other members have been making comments on the photo. Carol Anne comes to discuss the situation with the student activities staff.

### Calming the Crisis

Those who work with student activities are probably familiar with issues related to social media or other private online group accounts. Organizations use these accounts to coordinate communications among members, but if left unmonitored, they can quickly take a turn to a chain of inappropriate and harassing comments. Upon notification from Carol Anne about this concern, the staff member needs to immediately begin reviewing and addressing the situation. The first step should be contacting Dana to offer support and resources. The staff member could seek assistance from the conduct office related to how to approach the situation and what resources to offer Dana. The staff member would want to quickly assess who the account managers are and ask them about the content and how it can be pulled down. They should document the posts with a print screen or save function in case they are needed by a conduct officer later.

## Motivating and Inspiring Change

Once the online behavior has stopped, the staff member can help Dana with options to move forward. Dana may be more comfortable talking with a staff member not associated with the student organization, and this is OK. More than likely, a conduct officer would take the lead in reviewing the concern, determining if there were Title IX implications or university discipline implications.

This allows the student activities staff member to focus on the student organization aspect of the concern. In many cases, there may be other student organization advisors to update on the concern. The student activities staff would want to work with the student leader, Carol Anne, and other officers on options for internal discipline related to the behavior. As with any written or verbal comments, an analysis must be done about the severity of the behavior and if it crosses the threshold to harassing behavior, and there may be other organizational standards that have been broken with what occurred. Staff would also want to offer options to help Dana feel more comfortable continuing her involvement in the group and keeping her updated on the discipline processes in the organization and other steps that are being taken that may help. The student activities staff should also determine what other students were impacted by the online behaviors and contact them as appropriate.

## Managing the Ongoing Behavior

The staff member should work with other advisors and student leaders to discuss educational opportunities to prevent this type of behavior in the future. These issues may be trending in other organizations as well and require campus-based solutions.

## DISCUSSION QUESTIONS

1 What other issues are arising in online and social media environments for organizations? What prevention and education initiatives are available or could be implemented in the future?
2 What training should student officers and organization advisors receive related to situations like this?
3 Do you think this behavior crosses the threshold to harassment? Why or why not?

# IT HAPPENED ONE NIGHT

## Narrative

Victoria, a member of the women's club sport soccer team, reports to the recreational sports staff member that she was sexually assaulted by a member of the men's club sport soccer team during a recent trip.

## Calming the Crisis

As a starting place, staff members should be aware of their college or university's Title IX-related trainings and requirements. These trainings often include tips and processes for when a student discloses a sexual assault or other form of sexual violence. In most cases, staff should thank the student for talking to them and trusting them. Depending on when this occurred, ask the student if they are injured and need medical attention. If it is within about ninety-six hours of the incident, a sexual assault nurse exam (SANE exam) at an emergency room can collect evidence and offer a number of options should the student at some point decide to report the assault to the police.

The staff member wants to stay focused on broad helping skills. While they do not want to stop the student from talking, they should realize if the student makes the decision to report this to the police and/or the institution, then she will have to discuss what happened as part of those investigation processes. By not asking them to tell what occurred and prioritizing initial help and assistance, the staff keep the student from an additional accounting of what occurred.

Most importantly, the institution probably requires that staff report this incident to a Title IX coordinator. This is a staff member who can help the student know all of the resources and options available to them. Staff can say, "I want to help get you in contact with someone who can help us know all of your resources and options. They won't take any action without talking to you first." Then, pick up the phone and call together, schedule a meeting, or walk over together.

## Motivating and Inspiring Change

This scenario will vary depending on the course of action chosen by Victoria as well as how much information the school has about what occurred. It is likely that the Title IX Coordinator will ask you questions related to how much interaction is required between the men's and women's teams. Are there upcoming trips where they will travel together? Are practices held together? Essentially, the Title IX Coordinator will be looking to provide ways to allow students to continue their participation while an investigation occurs and to ensure that students are not at an additional risk. Information about these processes and thinking through associated risks will be helpful.

The recreational sports staff will probably not be involved in the specific aspects of Victoria's report and investigation. When this staff member sees Victoria again, they can continue to offer general support and assistance, asking how she is doing and if there is anything she needs, and encouraging her to utilize counseling and other support services available. Also, the staff should offer opportunities to reengage with her soccer team if she wants to participate.

## Managing the Ongoing Behavior

Upon completion of an investigation into this incident, it will be important to consider the broader scope of club sport policies and processes. These types of incidents can bring to light concerns related to club travel, team relationships, substance use, bystander responsibilities, and other team leadership concerns. Staff would want to take an honest assessment of the club sport program to determine if this was an isolated incident or if there were other factors across the sports contributing to this type of incident.

## DISCUSSION QUESTIONS

1    What type of education and prevention programs related to sexual violence are available to student organizations, club sports, athletes, and other groups on your campus? Do they include content related to bystander intervention, consent, and healthy relationships?
2    What are your institution's policies and processes related to reporting incidents of sexual harassment and sexual violence?
3    In what ways can the staff member build trust and rapport with Victoria? What are some ways the staff member can help Victoria stay involved with her club sport following this incident?

## DEPRESSED DEFENSE

### Narrative

Julius is a freshman member of the football team. His first semester was difficult. He struggled adjusting to the demands of college—both on the field and off. An incident occurs following a tough spring practice, when Julius is seen slamming his helmet into his locker and driving away from the practice facility at a high speed. The athletic department is notified later that evening that Julius was found passed out in his car in a nearby parking lot. He was taken to a local hospital because of the amount of drugs and alcohol in his system.

## Calming the Crisis

Since Julius is currently hospitalized and his family has been notified, the initial crisis has calmed. Coaching staff would likely be involved in a hospital visit if appropriate and contact with Julius' family about what occurred. The Athletic Department would want to coordinate with a campus BIT on this situation to help in talking with parents, coordinating resources for Julius' release from the hospital, and addressing any conduct issues related to what occurred.

## Motivating and Inspiring Change

Upon Julius' release from the hospital, staff are told that Julius intentionally took a large number of prescription pain relievers and drank alcohol to help him pass out and forget about everything that was going on in his life. This information should be shared with a campus BIT and is an indication of more severe concerns related to suicidal ideation. The coaching staff can help encourage Julius' use of resources identified for him at the hospital or by the campus BIT. Coaching staff can make sure that Julius has time outside of practice and classes to devote to his own wellness by participating in counseling or other programs. Sports teams are small communities, so coaches would want to identify any teammates impacted by Julius' incident. The staff would want to create a good balance of expectations for Julius' continued involvement on the team while also supporting an opportunity for him to shift some of his patterns of behavior related to academics, sports, and his own wellness.

## Managing the Ongoing Behavior

Julius' incident points to the need for good mental health resources and discussion across organizations and teams. Men's athletic teams can be particularly vulnerable to discouraging help-seeking behaviors by members experiencing stress, depression, or suicidal ideation.

## DISCUSSION QUESTIONS

1   How could staff have intervened with Julius before his incident? What warning signs might have been visible?
2   What are some ways staff could assist and support Julius upon his release from the hospital? Should team disciplinary actions also occur? How do you balance accountability and support?
3   How can organizations and teams support the mental health of their members?

## COMPLEX ENCOUNTERS IN A STUDENT ORGANIZATION

### Narrative

John is a member of an academic student organization and running for an officer position. Following the night of elections, John begins sending numerous emails to members, officers, advisors, and student activities staff about the unfair process and discrimination by current officers and advisors. The same day, Shelby, one of the current officers, meets with student activities staff to discuss concerns about a member in the organization and his behaviors. The member is John. Shelby says that John has been misrepresenting the organization to community agencies and that he lies to the members about his experiences in the field.

### Calming the Crisis

Student organizations can be leadership laboratories for students, but student activities staff have to be ready to unwind complicated interpersonal conflicts within the group and assist the students in finding ways to address organizational concerns. This can be complicated when the office is hearing from multiple parties in the organization, and it is increasingly complicated when a student may also exhibit some mental health concerns.

In these situations, student activities staff first want to focus on the concerns of each student separately. During these moments of crisis, we can have a tendency to want to jump in and solve the entire problem for the organization. This can be counterproductive in the long term with unresolved issues cropping back up for the organization. Instead, listening carefully to John and Shelby's concerns and identifying resources and options for both is often a better course of action. For John, there are likely clear processes available for him to dispute an election on the bases of discrimination at both the institutional level and the organizational level. Establishing trust with John that you will listen to his concerns and assist him in options to address them is a good first step. For Shelby, she is expressing some conduct concerns about John. In a similar manner, gathering more context about what is occurring in the group and discussing some possible courses of action is where staff should begin.

### Motivating and Inspiring Change

For both students, staff should maintain a goal-oriented approach as they work through the complexities of the situation. For John, he may just be looking for involvement opportunities and connections, but his approaches are not effective and are having the opposite impact on his reputation at the school. Staff should start by helping John to utilize appropriate grievance processes and explaining why his mass emails could be counterproductive to his goals. For Shelby, exploring what has been occurring in the organization and why there seems to be concerns with John would be starting points. It would also be important to ask about the involvement of other officers and advisors, and their intentions as it relates to John's involvement in the organization.

## Managing the Ongoing Behavior

At the organizational level, the student organization constitution really drives how membership selection or officer elections occur. From a long-term perspective, it could be important to work with the organization to clarify their operational processes. At the institutional level, a student handbook or operating policy will outline the processes required and the institution's relationship in the oversight of student organizations. Ongoing training for students, advisors, and staff on these aspects of organizational involvement and leadership can help to clarify how to approach these situations when they arise.

## DISCUSSION QUESTIONS

1   Would you discuss this situation with a campus BIT? What if they had additional concerns about John related to delusional and paranoid behaviors in the classroom and residence halls? How does it change how you would approach this situation with John?
2   What is your institution's relationship with student organizations? When disruptive behavior occurs within the organization, what options are available for addressing it?
3   What role could mediation play in a scenario like this? Could it be effective to offer mediation between John and the organization? What are the pros and cons of this approach?

## RADICAL PERSPECTIVES AND CIVILITY

### Narrative

Students for America is a new student organization created around the time of the most recent presidential election. They have been disseminating flyers around campus with subtle white supremacist themes. The Black Student Association President comes into the student activities advisor to discuss concerns from his members about the activities of the group. A faculty member has also expressed concerns about some of the statements made in class by Noah, the President of Students for America. Some of his statements and writings outline his thoughts about the inability of government structures to address the needs of Americans and how the people must take matters into their own hands in order to bring about change. He references actions of extremist leaders, some of which were violent. The student activities advisor is aware of this because the campus BIT called to ask for information about the status of Students for America.

## Calming the Crisis

In this scenario, the student activities staff member should be working in coordination with the campus BIT related to concerns about Noah. The staff member would want to focus on supporting and assisting the officers of the Black Student Association with their concerns. Consulting with the conduct office about the nature of behaviors described by the Black Student Association will help to determine if there is a course of action related to formal conduct. Regardless, there is a student group of members in distress over civility and diversity issues on campus. The initial layer of the crisis is reassuring the group president that there are resources available to his organization and his members. The staff member should also be on the lookout for any immediate issues of harassment being experienced by specific individuals in the group.

## Motivating and Inspiring Change

In this scenario, the student activities staff member not only needs to build rapport and trust with the individual officer seeking assistance, but it is likely there is a need to attend a Black Student Association organization meeting and actively listen to concerns and provide resources to assist the members. In group settings, rapport building is more difficult, but showing empathy and being open to hear the students' experiences should go a long way.

In coordination with the campus BIT, the student activities staff may also be tasked with talking with Noah about his actions related to the Students for America organization. This might include gathering more information about his efforts, discussing appropriate resources related to his organization, and reminding him about college policies. Information should be actively shared with the campus BIT because of the additional concerns about violence and extremism.

## Managing the Ongoing Behavior

It is likely that the Black Student Association is not the only organization on campus feeling upset about the messaging from Students for America. This situation would require additional strategy and coordination with other units on campus to address civility and diversity concerns across the community. These issues require a delicate balance between individual rights, free speech, and community safety. With this, it can become frustrating for students expecting immediate responses from the institution. Transparency in decision making and open communication can help students to understand the college processes and still feel an institutional commitment for their individual needs.

## DISCUSSION QUESTIONS

1   What other forms of radical and extreme ideologies are present on your campus among groups? Where do the perspectives raise concern?
2   How could you structure a conversation with Noah, especially knowing he is likely to have a hardened perspective about his organization's mission?
3   What community efforts should be employed related to civility and diversity in this scenario?

# Chapter 12

# Campus-Wide Staff Training and Processes

Always pass on what you have learned.

Yoda, *Return of the Jedi*

Staff in all corners of campus can find themselves confronted with how to respond to concerning behaviors. Ideally, all members of a campus community will be trained to be on the lookout for concerning behaviors and will understand the resources available to help with distressing, disruptive, and dangerous situations. This chapter offers a framework for thinking comprehensively about training staff on the management of student concerns by identifying some often overlooked aspects of staff responses to disruption on a campus and providing a train-the-trainer outline that can be easily adapted for use in specific campus communities.

In this chapter, we approach the practical exercises a little bit differently. Given the numerous departments covered in this chapter, we will offer a brief introduction to the challenges facing staff in these departments and follow with a practical case scenario for discussion and training. The chapter ends with a look at how best to teach the concepts in the book to staff in these miscellaneous departments.

## STAFF WORKING WITH PROSPECTIVE AND ADMITTED STUDENTS

Just because a student has not enrolled in classes does not mean that we can ignore strange or disruptive behaviors that occur. Staff in admissions, visitor centers, housing, financial aid, registrar, orientation, and numerous other offices interact with students and families prior to admission to the college. They may observe behaviors during this time period that raise concern about the student. They also have access to records with high school information, previous college enrollment, and other disclosures.

In coordination with the conduct office or campus BIT, staff in these positions should have clear processes in their departments for how they handle some of these more common situations:

- disclosures on admission or financial aid forms of criminal history and background;
- notification of sex offender status;
- conduct violations occurring during the admission and enrollment process;
- disclosures of previous mental health hospitalizations, suicide attempts, or other related concerns;
- comments or discussion about conditions that may qualify for disability accommodations; or
- disruptive or dangerous behaviors occurring during campus visits.

Staff working with prospective and admitted students can help the institution be proactive about student behaviors and student success. What we do not want to happen is for incidents to occur during the enrollment process that are not confronted or reported as they would be if they occurred once in classes. This does not mean that students with histories of concerns or problems should not be admitted to the school. Instead, this reporting allows campus BIT staff, conduct staff, or other departments to have discussions about campus policies and resources that can assist the student during their enrollment so that additional concerns do not arise on campus. In addition, some of the examples listed above require that the institution provide certain resources or make certain notifications, so by having clear reporting processes related to these types of incidents, the institution is also remaining in compliance with various legal requirements and maintaining consistency in how they handle these types of situations.

## WANDERING AND LOST

### Narrative

During new student orientation, an Orientation staff member notices a new transfer student, Patrick, looking very disheveled, and he appears confused about what he is doing during the event. The staff member tries to talk to him, gets his name, and he says, "No man, I'm great! Just heading to see my advisor," and the student heads off quickly out the door. During no show reporting for advising appointments, the staff member notices that the student did not make it to his advising meeting that morning.

Later toward the end of the day, the Orientation front office receives a phone call from the same student; he is panicked. He says he left campus to go to drive to his advising appointment and had a flat tire. He says he needs directions back to campus. The location he gives is almost thirty minutes from campus. Nothing he is saying on the phone makes sense, and he seems irrational. The staff member is able to walk him through getting back to campus and suggests that he come in and talk to someone about what has happened.

The front office staff member reports this to Orientation staff, and they are able to piece it together with the student from the morning. Patrick does not come to the office as requested, and staff remain concerned. They check his emergency contact information for participating in orientation activities, and he has only provided his own cell phone number. Staff leave a message on his phone and report the concern to the campus BIT.

The next day Patrick comes to the office as though nothing has happened and asks about registering for classes.

## Calming the Crisis

Instead of being frustrated about his behavior the previous day, staff should try to engage with Patrick about what occurred, express concern, and learn more about him. The Orientation staff have an opportunity to gather more information from Patrick to share with the campus BIT. The staff should ask him directly about what occurred the day before and gauge how he responds. It's possible he was just confused, it could be a more severe medical or mental health concern, or it could be that he was using some kind of substance that resulted in the confusion. It's OK to ask Patrick what he thinks happened as well. This information can be shared back to a campus BIT to assist in recommendations and referrals for Patrick as needed. If he appears to be able to handle the tasks, the staff could identify some steps for Patrick to take in order to continue pursuing enrollment at the institution and see how he does.

## Motivating and Inspiring Change

Assuming Patrick is able to negotiate the tasks to enroll at the school, this is a student that could use some follow-up during the first weeks of classes to see how he is doing. Does he appear to be navigating the various tasks associated with school? Have other incidents occurred similar to what happened at Orientation? Did he follow up with recommendations made during the last interaction? Staff could see how techniques related to motivational interviewing could be appropriate with this student, especially developing discrepancy between some of his behaviors and how that impacts his goals.

## Managing the Ongoing Behavior

Patrick could be a student who continues to raise concern on campus if his confusion and irrational behavior continues. This is a student where consistency of communication across units is important in order to reinforce success messages to him. It may also be necessary to make referrals to a mental health provider for a more advanced assessment of what may be creating some of his confusion.

## DISCUSSION QUESTIONS

1 How does Patrick's status as an incoming/prospective student change the nature of the staff's response? What resources are available to prospective students at your institution?

2 How would you approach the initial conversation with Patrick about what happened during Orientation? What if he continued to be irrational? How would it change your discussion?

3 Think about a motivational interviewing-based conversation with Patrick. What elements would it include? What about the WDEP system of planning? How could it work for Patrick?

## MARKETING, PUBLIC RELATIONS, AND ONLINE ACTIVITIES

Many of our interactions with students and the campus community now occur through a college's online presence, whether it be on a college website or social media tool such as Twitter or Facebook. While traditional forms of marketing still occur through press releases and media interviews, college marketing, and communication staff now use advanced analytics to deploy marketing messages across the internet. These marketing staff may exist in centralized units and provide marketing services for the entire college or university, or they may be in specific units such as athletics, housing, campus life, alumni relations, or development. Other staff may not be specifically responsible for marketing, but they may be engaged in extensive online interactions with students through campus activities or online communities for students.

Staff in these positions should have an understanding of red flag behaviors they may observe in these online settings. Students interact with the institution and members of the campus community through comments on websites or with social media posts directed toward or about the institution. During these online interactions, students may make disturbing comments, post concerning content, or even target specific members of the campus community through bullying, threats, or intimidation.

Moreover, marketing and public relations staff often have protocols for data mining and real-time "listening" or monitoring of online activity related to the institution. For example, they may use tools that provide alerts when someone's post contains the institution's name. For better management of disruptive and dangerous behaviors in the campus community, these staff can employ these same listening and analytical tools to monitor for potential threats. While many posts and tweets may be false positives and not require a response, Van Brunt and Langman (2016) provide a complete list of keywords to pair with an institution's name to identify potential threats from online behaviors. The list includes words and phrases related to weapons, past attacks, general threat action verbs and phrases, and other words that can indicate a concern. Staff responsible for these online activities should coordinate with the campus BIT or conduct office on a list of alerts to create for the institution.

## SOCIAL MEDIA CHALLENGES

### Narrative

University communication staff, coordinating the institution's social media tools, notice a post shared by a student to one of the university department's Facebook accounts. The post is a Snapchat of one student, Erik, making a racial slur against other students in a class and threatening the Hispanic students in the class.

### Calming the Initial Crisis

This situation requires immediate notification to the campus police because the content of the post contained threats against individuals and/or the campus community. Communication staff should coordinate with law enforcement on the removal of the post from the site and ensure that it is documented appropriately. They could issue a statement either on the site or to the broader community, as appropriate, about an ongoing investigation and the inappropriate nature of the behaviors. Outside of managing the public relations aspect of this incident, any interactions with the student in the video should be left to law enforcement or the campus conduct office.

### Motivating and Inspiring Change

While the communication staff are unlikely to have direct contact with Erik, they can be involved in prevention and education activities related to digital identity and responsible online conduct for students and employees. By helping individuals understand that behavior on the internet and social media has consequences similar to face-to-face incidents, communication and marketing staff are meeting an important development need that relates to the prominence of technology in our lives. By getting ahead of issues related to civility, bullying, and harassment that occur online, the campus community better understands the impact of these concerns and are able to respond quickly and effectively when issues arise.

## Managing the Ongoing Behavior

When considering this scenario from a broader, long-term perspective, communication staff may want to look for patterns of concerning online activity as well as trends of campus internet and website usage. For example, are certain topics more likely to be controversial on campus? Are certain departments or organizations often targeted for comments on their website or social media accounts? While staff should not look to stifle speech and expression related to these topics, they can prepare for increased activity and have appropriate communications prepared related to resources for community members. By monitoring high-use websites and search analytics, communication staff can help make identifying helpful resources such as the counseling center or BIT easier for those needing assistance and are prepared when online activity becomes concerning.

## DISCUSSION QUESTIONS

1   Who on the campus has responsibilities related to active "listening" or monitoring of college social media and websites? What processes are in place when concerning posts or activity are identified?

2   What strategies could be used to address public relations concerns related to the post described?

3   What if the post did not include a direct threat to others? How would your interaction with law enforcement, conduct office, or campus BIT change?

## THE STAFF WHO SEE IT ALL—CUSTODIANS, FOOD SERVICE, PARKING, GROUNDS STAFF

The campus experience would not be the same without support and operation staff providing custodial services, food service, building maintenance, traffic and parking activities, and grounds maintenance. These staff also have a unique perspective on student life and may become aware of disruptive or distressing behavior from students in ways only accessible because of the nature of their duties and positions.

Let's consider a few examples:

- Housing custodial staff regularly find vomit in the same bathroom area.
- Building maintenance staff see a student in a construction area off limits to the public.
- Parking staff notice an unregistered vehicle circling campus daily near the campus recreation center.
- Food service staff see a student purchasing food and throwing it away uneaten regularly.

- Grounds maintenance staff see a student leave a box unattended near a building.
- Housekeeper notices a student appears increasingly disheveled and sad.

On a college campus, support and operation staff in positions like those listed here really have a bird's eye view of student behaviors that should not be overlooked. Many campus training programs on disruptive and dangerous behaviors forget to include staff in these areas, or the training offered is not accessible to staff because of how it is offered or when it is offered. These staff, who truly seem to see it all, should also have adequate training on how to identify behaviors of concern and how to report them.

## THREATENING TRASH

### Narrative

A custodial staff regularly providing cleaning services to a campus academic building finds flyers left in several classrooms with images of a gun and various words including "change will come," "it is time," and "look out." Because the staff member had received training in identifying and reporting concerns, he notified his supervisor about what he had found.

### Calming the Initial Crisis

Staff members should immediately report these flyers to law enforcement and the campus BIT. This scenario illustrates the importance of staff members reporting concerns, but not investigating them or stepping beyond their duties and roles. They may be asked questions related to where they found them, when they first noticed them, and if they saw anyone disseminating the flyers.

### Motivating and Inspiring Change

Since it is likely staff would not be involved directly with anyone specifically related to the flyers outside of the police or conduct office, staff could instead remain observant for other flyers or patterns of communications that may be related to the incident already reported. They should continue to report any suspicious behavior that might assist with the investigation into this concern.

### Managing the Ongoing Behavior

Staff in charge of academic buildings should consult with other appropriate administrators and consider carefully the policies related to dissemination of printed materials as well as freedom of expression policies and solicitation policies. Even littering policies may be relevant to this discussion. When trying to better enforce policies related to distribution of printed materials, it is best to address concerns consistently, regardless of the content of the materials. Staff should coordinate these discussions and processes with the conduct office who can help with legal interpretations and distinctions.

## DISCUSSION QUESTIONS

1   What obstacles exist to providing training to operations staff like those identified here?
2   How would training for supervisors and directors in these areas differ from the training received by their staff?
3   How can you make reporting easier for staff in these positions?

## CAMPUS ADMINISTRATORS

We also want to spend a moment talking to campus administrators, those staff in positions at the director level or higher, about their unique role in the management of disruptive and dangerous student concerns. Campus administrators may have some training on emergency response for their departments and how to manage crisis situations, but there are some distinctions when dealing with disruptive and dangerous student behaviors.

Campus administrators have the responsibility of ensuring that staff in their areas are trained on these matters and are encouraged to use the train-the-trainer outline at the end of this chapter as a guide. At the administrative level, it is also possible to consider opportunities to address systemic concerns that may factor into student issues. During much of our discussion around managing the ongoing behavior of students (Chapter 5 and the various scenarios in the later chapters), we share initial ideas on how campus processes, programs, and initiatives can also serve to prevent some of the behaviors described.

In addition, the nature of a position in campus administration makes it possible that you will be contacted directly by a student of concern, particularly those with grievances and hardened points of view. These students may be looking to be heard, may be attempting to change the narrative related to their behaviors up to that point, or may be attempting to find other ways to disrupt the daily activities of the institution. Because of a campus administrator's position of power, the response to a student of concern needs to be thoughtful and intentional as well as coordinated with other campus BIT or conduct activities.

## THE STUDENT WHO DIDN'T DO IT

### Narrative

The President's Office receives a phone call from a student insisting that he be immediately reinstated to the institution and that he has been treated unfairly by staff in the conduct office. He is agitated on the phone and is unable to calm down enough for the secretary to gather information from him. He insists on talking to someone in charge.

### Calming the Initial Crisis

Sounds familiar, doesn't it? Now, it is possible that there has been a staff or procedural error involving this student that deserves attention, but in that case, there are typically institutional appeal processes available to the student. It's also likely that some type of behaviors have occurred that resulted in concern from the conduct office, even if the suspension was not a fair outcome. It may also be possible that this is a student who has already exhibited some concerning behaviors, is now even more grieved than when processes started, and may be escalating in terms of the likelihood of future disruptive and dangerous behaviors in the campus community.

The campus administrator who receives contact from this student needs to consider carefully the most appropriate response. We would suggest the administrator should remain calm and give the student an opportunity to tell their story. Use active listening and try to paraphrase or repeat back to the student what they have indicated is a concern. Show empathy without committing to a change in regard to the decision. Use phrases such as, "It sounds like this has been a frustrating process for you" or "I can understand being angry or scared about being suspended from school."

The goal in the conversation is to calm the student in order to redirect them to the institutional processes available to them related to grievances or appeals. In most situations, administrators should be able to do so with patience and empathetic listening. As the administrator, it would be important to clarify the limitations of your role in any processes, but if your position is one that provides some broad oversight to units that they are working with, you could assure them that you would continue to monitor the status and outcome of the student's case. If you have no oversight, you would want to be clear about that and work to get them directed to more appropriate staff.

In more escalated situations, the student may not calm down and may be unable to discuss rationally his concerns. This is a more difficult situation and an indicator of more elevated issues. It may be possible to ask the student directly for ways to proceed to see if he is able to offer rational solutions (more than just being reinstated in school), or ask the student questions about why the suggested processes will not work in the student's mind. The ability to answer these questions reasonably will provide an indicator to the administrator of the student's state of mind. In some cases, if the student is unable to calm down, it may be necessary to end the meeting or communication until the student is able to gather himself.

Responses that are not suggested are agreeing that the student should be reinstated or stepping into appeal or grievance processes that the administrator does not officially play a role in according to policy. Instead, it is suggested that the administrator make quick contact with the conduct office or campus BIT to discuss the communications and coordinate on how to best proceed with the student. BIT and conduct professionals know that these moments of transition when a student is being separated from the institution can be catalysts for students who were already considering violence or other disruptive behaviors. The role of the administrator in this situation is to assist with deescalating the situation while not straying from campus processes that are in place related to student conduct or grievances.

## Motivating and Inspiring Change

Let's consider what would happen if, after this first conversation, the student proceeded with the conduct appeal process available to them. In this case, the appeal office finds that no errors occurred in the process and upholds the decision for a suspension. The student makes contact again to express concern over the same decision. It would be important for a conduct office to give the President's Office an update on this decision in advance in anticipation of additional contact from the student. This is an opportunity for the President's Office to listen, but also to begin confirming the decision that has been made. It may be possible to look for win—win solutions related to the student's return to the institution in the future if that is a possibility, or even the student's transfer to another institution if that may occur. Helping the student to be forward-thinking to see that this decision does not have to be the end of opportunities for him is also important. If the student is expressing distress over talking with his parents, it may be possible to allow the student to talk with a counselor as part of his transition out of the institution. This resource would need to be coordinated with the conduct office.

## Managing the Ongoing Behavior

What about the student who does not accept the decision and continues to escalate communications via email and phone? It is likely that at a certain point the conduct office or BIT would issue an indication to the student that he could no longer be on campus property, or they would coordinate with the campus police to ban the student from campus with a no trespass order. There is a fine line to walk here. On one hand, communication with the student increases the opportunities to engage with them about their concerns and to monitor possible threats or escalation. On the other hand, these communications can be exhausting, concerning, and disruptive. The President's Office would want to discuss and coordinate with the campus BIT and campus police/security around these ongoing communications with the student. These entities will coordinate a broader threat assessment and help determine the benefit of continuing communication or limiting it in other ways.

## DISCUSSION QUESTIONS

1   How can campus administrators support comprehensive staff training on issues of identifying and responding to disruptive and dangerous concerns?
2   Are front line staff in administrative units trained for scenarios like this? What processes are in place to help them manage a grieved student presenting on the phone or in person?
3   What other approaches could work in de-escalating this situation and upholding the decision of another unit?

## TEACHING ADDITIONAL STAFF ON CAMPUS

This book does not include a complete list of every type of staff member working at a college or university, but it highlights some of the most common groups to be trained in these issues. A few additional staff groups not mentioned but important to efforts include information technology staff, alumni relations, career centers, and other student affairs staff not previously mentioned. Ultimately, this is a community effort in which everyone should be exposed to information on identifying and reporting disruptive and dangerous behaviors.

## LEADING CAMPUS TRAININGS ON DISRUPTIVE AND DANGEROUS BEHAVIORS

For staff in positions of training other staff on the skills and information outlined throughout this book, we wanted to provide some guidance to help with those efforts. Most campus BITs or conduct offices have a "road show" training similar to what is outlined below. Contact them to present to your areas or work in coordination with them to plan a training for your staff. Table 12.1 contains train-the-trainer tips to get you started as well as thoughts on how to incorporate this book into your training efforts.

This book can be used as part of departmental and campus training efforts on addressing student concerns and keeping campus safe. It is not necessary for staff to read the entire book. Advisor staff could read the introductory material in

## TABLE 12.1 Train-the-Trainer Tips

| Concept | Examples |
| --- | --- |
| Program Overview | Programs are best when they are tailored for the needs of the department or unit as well as branded for the college or university. Trainings should be a mix of information on recognizing student behaviors of concern, skills for responding, resources for assistance, and scenarios for practice. |
| Program Content | Depending on the amount of time available and the nature of the audience, content may include:<br>• information on today's college students (Chapter 2);<br>• difference in disruptive and dangerous behavior, how to recognize, and examples of each (Chapter 1);<br>• reporting and referral information, clear direction on how to report concerns to law enforcement, conduct, campus BIT (online, phone, in-person);<br>• skills training on crisis de-escalation or other techniques (Chapters 3–6); and/or<br>• scenarios or case studies (Chapters 7–12). |
| Program Delivery | Options include in-person, online, or hybrid versions. |
| Length of Program | Consider allocating 60–90 minutes for in-person trainings. Online trainings can be 15–20 minutes, but they will not include the depth of content and interactive features. |
| Attendance | By working with individual departments and units, department leaders can host this training in conjunction with regularly occurring department meetings. This increases the number of trainings, but it also increases the likelihood of attendance and ability to address scenarios specific to each area. Campus-wide sessions can be hosted as part of centralized professional development days or campus training requirements. Online trainings can be required for staff or offered as supplemental information. |
| Supplemental Materials | Handout or promotional items that staff can easily access with quick reminders about how to report concerns, and websites to access information when they need it. |
| Other Training Ideas | After this basic training, staff may be interested in more extensive education on certain topics. Options could include a panel discussion with campus police, conduct, counseling and student affairs, specialized speakers on identifying threat and preventing harm to others; or scenario-based training with role play and discussion. |

Chapter 1, skills training in Chapters 3–5, and the scenario training in Chapter 8. They could review materials in Chapter 2 on today's college students and Chapter 6 based on need and interest.

The student experience does not begin and end when they walk in and out of the classroom. Instead, this chapter highlights the many aspects of the college experience and how even passive interactions with the campus community can result in incidents that should be addressed by a conduct office or campus BIT. Staff can utilize concepts in this chapter to share their learning and experiences related to managing student concerns. By developing a collaborative community of staff committed to positive and fair behavioral management, students will also experience a difference in their interactions with staff across campus.

# Chapter 13

# Conclusion

Bastian: Why is it so dark?

The Childlike Empress: In the beginning, it is always dark.

*The NeverEnding Story*

Writing a book with a close friend and colleague is an amazing experience. There's a sharing of ideas, a remarkable collaboration and blending of experience, perspective, and, hopefully, a little bit of wisdom. While we could have written a traditional conclusion to this book, we thought it would be more useful (and fun) to offer the reader a bit of an unscripted interaction with the authors. You've read a carefully crafted book that has been well researched and full of practical case examples. We wanted to find a creative way to bring together some of the ideas outlined so far.

So, here's what we've done. As we approached the conclusion of the writing and editing, we each began to toss questions back and forth to dig a bit deeper into our experience managing difficult student behavior. A new question was created and sent once the author completed their response to the previous one. For added fun, each author is also required to work in one eighties' music reference, lyrics, or song title hidden in their response.

We hope you enjoy this format and that it survived the editing process. If not, our editor likely made us write this in a more traditional format and these words will only be read in the director's cut of the book. If you are reading these words— then hooray! Our editor liked the idea and we sincerely hope you do as well.

## QUESTION 1

### Brian to Amy

You were the Dean of Students at a Big 12 school for five years and worked there for almost two decades (this question is not designed to make you feel old, I promise). You now teach and train faculty as well as students. You've coached, mentored, and supervised hundreds of faculty, staff, and graduate students during your career. If you were asked to give a ten-minute talk to staff on how to address disruptive students, what three points would you make?

## Amy Response

Well, as Blondie said, "Call Me!" First, I want staff to know that they are not alone in these situations and that help is available to them from a campus BIT or conduct office. We want them to report their concerns. Second, I'd want to build confidence that they have the right stuff to work with students exhibiting a wide array of behaviors. How we respond to disruption does not have to be complicated. Simple steps like listening and being empathetic go a long way. Last, you really shouldn't put Baby in a corner, and by Baby, I mean any student. We have a tendency to disengage with odd or difficult behavior, and what we really need is staff that are making connections to those students who are the most isolated.

## QUESTION 2

### Amy to Brian

Alright, this question *is* designed to make you feel old. In college, you were a registered white water rafting guide. I'm pretty scared of water (not a great swimmer). In this book, we talk a great deal about building rapport and trust with students. What would you do to help me feel comfortable getting into that raft and heading through some white water rapids with you and how can we apply that to our work with students?

### Brian Response

Well, I suppose I could take you to the bridge, throw you overboard, see if you could swim, and then get you back up to the shore, but I don't think that would work. For me, I think the analogy of road signs is important for students. While we can't make their decisions for them, we can help them read the road signs when they are traveling down a highway of bad choices, letting them know when they are moving into territory that will have a negative impact on their future.

I also think back to my rafting days (far, far back), and I remember teaching people who were about to get on the boat that the real dangers, the important things to pay attention to, weren't the rapids you saw or the rocks in the middle of the river or the other boats splashing around, but instead the things underneath. There were recirculating holes that could hold you down, branches that created foot entrapments, and large sharks (OK, I made up that last one). Sometimes we need to focus on what is underneath and not just what is visible to us. When a student comes in yelling and upset, our tendency is to respond in kind to their aggression. A better approach is to respond to the underneath message, which is almost always a sense of worry, fear, or panic about the future. When we respond that way, it's as if we have mastered some kind of Jedi mind trick, helping them feel calmer and more understood.

## QUESTION 3

### Brian to Amy

OK, I'm bringing Izzy and Maree into this, your two epic Dobermans. As the alpha female in the house, and with the clear caveat that our college students are not dogs, can you talk a little bit about lessons from dog raising that may apply to managing disruptive behavior with students? Also, that Baha Men classic "Who Let the Dogs Out" was released in 1999, just in case you were tempted.

### Amy Response

I just wish I was the alpha female in my house! Like students, my dogs are both very distinct, so I'll share a tip related to each of them that reflects my thoughts on managing disruptive behavior with students. Izzy is an eater—hungry like a wolf all the time. When there is food present or it's meal time, she cannot focus on anything else. I share this to remind staff that students who are not able to meet their most basic needs (think Maslow's hierarchy) are often unable to focus on other issues. If a student has not eaten or slept in the past couple of days, they are probably not able to focus on your instructions related to a campus process or make good decisions about their class schedule. Similarly, if they are not feeling safe on campus, they are less likely to be involved and engaged. It's a reminder to help students deal with their most basic needs first before advancing to more complex issues of student development. Also, remember students may appear difficult but actually be dealing with more basic issues related to their health and safety.

Now, Maree on the other hand, she just loves to play all the time. Her favorite game is ball. Drop the ball in your lap, wait for you to throw it, retrieve the ball, and repeat. It is fun at first but pretty annoying when you are trying to work on your laptop, watch TV, or do any other task that does not involve Maree and her toy. It reminds me a little of how I feel sometimes when you have been working with a student, and they continue to require the same assistance, ask the same question, or display the same poor conduct over and over again.

I'm sure every staff member reading this book can think of the student that when they walk into the office there is almost a collective moan from all of the staff. The student spins you right round, like a record. My suggestion is that when

**201**

you find yourself in that place of rolling your eyes, sighing with your colleagues, or reaching a breaking point with a student, this is an indicator that it's time to try to hit the reset button. Take a deep breath and try a new approach. Reinvest in the student instead of withdrawing. I can't guarantee that like Maree they won't just keep throwing the ball back in your lap, but at least you know that the way you are responding is not contributing to the repetitive behavior of the student.

## QUESTION 4

### Amy to Brian

Before you were a college counselor you worked in emergency services where you coordinated involuntary psychiatric commitments. You've also been an Emergency Medical Technician (EMT-R) and a member of Ski Patrol. You had to make quick decisions and help people at their most vulnerable. Can we learn anything from how you managed those high-pressure situations and how you took care of yourself at the same time?

### Brian Response

I think for me, what helped deal with all that pressure was a sense of being prepared before the crisis event occurred. While the calls I received were random and chaotic (chainsaw injury to the head, skier hit a tree and broke their leg, arriving first on the scene to a minivan that had careened off the road), having the training to know what to do helped me move out of the flight/fight/freeze place and feel more prepared to act. Pressure is all around us… pressure pushing down on me, pushing down on you… But what we can control is our preparedness to respond. In many ways, I think that was one of the central ideas for us writing this book. Giving staff a chance to think a bit more about these crisis situations and the tools they should bring to address the conflict moving forward.

As for self-care, I think for me it was more about making sure I carved out some alone time after a crisis. I used to swim laps a lot when I was stressed, and found the exercise and water a soothing way to reorient myself when I became stuck. It also helped to remind myself that it would not always feel this way for me and that I was reacting to a temporary situation. Having a drink or two after work also helped. Which sometimes raises an eyebrow when mentioned in a professional text. The concern here is when the drinking goes from one or two and turns into five or six, or *every* time you are stressed you turn to drinking.

Another approach could be running just as fast as we can, holding onto one another's hands, trying to get away… into the night… And yes, I worked in two eighties' songs here. Tiffany was my spirit animal.

## QUESTION 5

### Brian to Amy

Let me ask you a similar question about self-care. I know things have not always been easy with your work previously as a Dean of Students and currently managing faculty, staff, and students at San Angelo. You've been involved notifying parents their child has been hurt or hospitalized, hearing some pretty horrific Title IX cases, and have been the target of aggression, insults, and anger from students unhappy with the conduct process, a bad grade or general frustrations. What are some of the ways you take care of yourself when you are feeling those signs of stress or burnout? How would you talk to staff who are new in the field or on the front lines about ways they can keep their wits about them when they aren't feeling great about the components of their job or the way they are being treated?

### Amy Response

This is a tough topic for me because I hope staff can learn from what I did not do instead of some of the things that I did. I loved my work and enjoyed my interactions with students, faculty, staff, and even parents. Some of my most rewarding moments were when I helped students through the difficult situations you mention in your question. But, every rose really does have thorns. I let the thorns poke at me and did not make the adjustments that I needed to stay in my position longer. I created patterns of work that were not healthy for me and probably impacted my ability to serve students.

With that, staff need to take seriously concerns related to burnout and compassion fatigue. I think I thought those were issues someone else had and that I was too strong to need to worry about them. Asking for help is not a weakness. We need to be able to talk to our supervisors about our limits and ensure that our position responsibilities are realistic. Being busy is OK, and there are always times that staff need to step in and help out with other responsibilities. When we are overextended for long periods, this becomes problematic for you and the school. Consider what aspects of the job are not essential and find ways to eliminate them. Create and rely on teams to handle the most difficult tasks in your department. And, it's important to work for the weekend occasionally and make sure that you are able to entirely disconnect from your job (no cell phone, no email). Those times help you to be able to fully engage when you are on the job.

## QUESTION 6

### Amy to Brian

Let's shift gears a bit. You travel around the nation training schools on BITs and managing student concerns. Pull out your magic 8 ball. Are there any emerging trends related to student characteristics or student behaviors that you are noticing? Do you foresee new competency areas evolving for staff related to the knowledge and skills needed to respond to student concerns?

### Brian Response

I have been all around the country talking about this... walkin' the streets at night, just trying to get it right. During this time, I've noticed there is a tendency to see this new generation of college students as presenting with more problems than those in the past. They are seen as lazy, feeling as if the world owes them something, lacking respect, and questioning authority. I'd argue that this is a trait many generations share, certainly something I had said about myself as a Gen Xer growing up and going to college. Perhaps today's traditional aged students are a bit more critical in what they consume. They are hesitant to sign a mortgage, buy a car, or commit to a long-term career. But some of that comes from the age in which they grew up.

Helping students through a crisis remains a pretty direct task. Stay calm and don't respond in kind to their escalation. Attempt to understand why they are upset and what is motivating their anger and frustration. Build rapport and connection with them through questioning. Avoid embarrassing or shaming the student. And partner with them to find solutions and help them make critical choices moving forward. The most common challenge I find with faculty and staff is they get stuck way up front. They react to the crisis without proactively choosing the best way to respond. And this is very human. It's our nature to treat someone with the same disrespect they treat us with when confronting an angry person. But if we truly want to shape and change behavior, staff and faculty must take the high road here and teach and demonstrate concepts like grace, patience, and kindness in our interactions.

In the end, all we need is just a little patience... mm, yeah... gotta have a little patience.

## QUESTION 7

### Brian to Amy

We talk a good deal about hope and inspiration in this book. How to manage behavior and help students be successful academically. I'd imagine you would agree that there is a point and time where we switch from trying to give support and make things work on our campus to a point where we shift gears to discussing having the student move along to another institution or take a break from college for a while. Can you talk some about where that tipping point is, based on your experience? How do staff know to move from a helping stance to one where they need to set firmer limits and perhaps escalate the intervention to the police?

## Amy Response

You make a good point here. Throughout the book, we focus so much on engaging with students, but I would never want a staff member to put themselves in a situation where they risk their own safety or the safety of others. There are certainly immediate threat and emergency situations that without delay should result in a police notification. (Janie's got a gun. We are going to call the police.) It can get a little tougher from there. You may find yourself thinking "Do you really want to hurt me?" or "Do you really want to hurt someone else?" If the student is threatening to hurt you, themselves, or someone else, you need to request assistance from the police. There are a variety of ways that police can respond and assist. Not every police response requires them to roll up with lights and sirens blaring. Be clear when you call about what assistance you need. Last, this is a situation where it's OK to listen to your gut. If you are feeling weary and concerned about the situation you are in, do not ignore that feeling and ask for help. The tips in Chapter 3 related to having a plan for these situations are really helpful.

But, your question also touches on the idea of how do you determine that now is the time to consider processes to separate a student from the institution or suggest a withdrawal to the student. Ultimately, if the student is continuously not successful in the university environment, it is not helpful to them or the campus community to allow them to continue. Academic and disciplinary requirements exist to benefit both the individual and the collective, although it may not feel that way to the individual required to leave the community for a period of time. I like to think about encouraging short-term stop-outs in order to preserve the opportunity for long-term persistence and success. I truly hope students can take these broken wings and learn to fly again.

## QUESTION 8

## Amy to Brian

Brian, you have a pretty amazing family—four really creative and cool kids as well as your awesome wife (not to mention the herd of cats currently). I think readers could learn something here related to diversity. How do you stay open and responsive to your kids' diverse interests and needs? Have you had to help them deal with microaggressions or reactions from others? Moreover, do you ever find bias creeping into your responses to situations, and how do you handle that?

## Brian Response

I think we've been successful fostering an Ally Sheedy, *Breakfast Club* level of snark with my girls as they interact with the world. That seems to help. Seriously, though, overall I think it's encouraging a sense of openness and willingness to see things from other points of view beyond your own. The term "cultural humility" comes to play for me. Taking a moment and seeing things from another person's perspective without trying to make your own points or even relate your cultural experience or challenges. As I mentioned in Chapter 2 about the cookies and brownies, sometimes it isn't about what you are saying, but it becomes that you are trying to say something when the other person is trying to talk or express something. There is this lost art to listening empathically to another person's viewpoint, culture, or perspective that we try to nurture in our family.

As you know, we all have bias from our experience. The key is to understand these biases and how they shade or influence our interactions. The problem occurs when a bias develops a blind spot that keeps us from hearing another person's perspective. Though, even in writing this, you see my bias for humanism, respect, connection, and understanding, which may be different from other's priorities of success, achievement, ambition, and competition. This, in some ways, creates a potential for division and conflict when these underlying morals and goals in life are out of step with those you are attempting to de-escalate or change. For me, I hope my bias towards love, acceptance, equality, patience, tolerance, and helping those who have been marginalized by society would be a positive in my interactions with others. Of course, loving would be easy if your colors were like my dreams... Red, gold, and green... red, gold, and green.

## QUESTION 9

### Brian to Amy

I think people tend to learn best from our missteps rather than our greatest accomplishments. Assuming you have a situation or two in your past that you would want to hit a cosmic do-over on, let me ask you that tough time machine question. If you could go back in time and change one interaction you had with a student, what would it be and what would you do differently?

### Amy Response

How many times have I wanted to be Doc Brown in his DeLorean time machine? I think anyone who does this work can probably think of missteps they have made during interactions with students. The situations I regret are the ones where I reacted to the student's anger, aggression, and disrespect in similar fashion. I lost my cool. Instead of listening, I found myself interrupting and arguing with the student. I've even shared with you the story of having to walk out of a meeting with a student because I was so upset with their behavior.

In Chapter 3, we discussed concepts of crisis de-escalation, specifically elements of finding a calm and balanced stance in the face of a difficult situation. Brian, you know that for a period of time I was skeptical about the value of cycle breathing as a technique for dealing with crisis. You also know that I have changed my perspective and now believe this is one of the more valuable tools for maintaining a calm and thoughtful mindset. Recently, I've reintegrated yoga practice into my routine. Part of why I like it so much is the focus on your breath and its impact on your mind and body. When I replayed the situations where I was most out of control and ultimately ineffective, I realized that I allowed other aspects of my day, my own biases, and my own emotional response to guide my time with the student instead of focusing on listening and identifying a more useful approach for the situation. So just remember, cool it now, watch out, you're going to lose control.

One other thing, after some of my worst moments, I have found that it really helps to have another staff member or group of staff members to talk with about what occurred. Vanilla Ice got it right when he said, "Stop, collaborate, and listen." For me, I need to laugh at myself a bit. This is serious work we do, but we can't take ourselves too seriously. By sharing and reflecting with other staff, I am able to find the courage to jump back into the next situation or even find the strength to try again with the same student where things did not go well before. We don't have time machines, but do have another student waiting for us.

## QUESTION 10

### Amy to Brian

Much of your expertise is in threat assessment. You have written books on campus violence and harm to others. What are the behaviors that concern you most when you see them present in a situation? Also, this book is about students, but what if a faculty or staff member is the one being disruptive and dangerous?

### Brian Response

Oh Amy, so many to choose from, right? What worries me most would be a direct threat with a time and location mentioned along with objectified and depersonalized language. An example would be: "Listen, asshole. I'm going to show up at your office at 3 p.m. on Friday and if you haven't fixed this I'm going to make your worthless excuse for a life a living hell like you have made mine." The specificity of that threat shows forethought and conditional ultimatum that would require immediate assessment and intervention. And while most direct, communicated threats are not acted upon, they always require assessment and intervention. Readers can learn more about these concepts in Chapter 6 on BIT and threat assessment.

About half the BITs in the country also monitor faculty and staff behavior. If a school does not use the BIT to monitor this behavior, they would use someone in human resources. Whether the threat or concerning behavior is coming from a student, faculty, or staff member, there is a requirement to share that information with human resources or the BIT for further assessment and intervention. I've given the example of a package left unattended in an airport. We teach those traveling to report the package (the behavior) regardless of who may have left the package unattended. We wouldn't want someone to ignore a potentially dangerous unattended package because it was left by someone wearing an airport employee uniform or by a pilot. The same applies to schools: we want to focus on the assessment and intervention of the behaviors, regardless of whether it comes from a student, faculty, or staff member.

Remember, with every breath you take, every move you make… I'll be watching you.

## MOVING FORWARD

We hope you have enjoyed this chapter and our, shall we say, creative approach at a conclusion. Our goal was for it to be informative as well as entertaining. In fact, that is our hope for the book, too. We have found that in addition to grounding our advice in theory and teaching through practical examples, it is helpful to have a more conversational style to our writing. If you happen to be teaching some of these concepts to those you supervise or colleagues you work with, perhaps there is something you can borrow in terms of our style, by including some personal information (perhaps pop culture references from your own childhood) that help connect the reader or participants more to the topic.

When people are scared, afraid, or worried about managing an out of control situation, we have found that our help is more effective when the person receiving the information is more relaxed and comfortable. Before we share our solid advice and practical suggestions, the first task we have is to engage and calm the reader or participants so they understand that things are going to be OK. Then, we can share some tried and true guidance that will make situations better. We hope our way of writing this book, as well as the content and counsel we shared, help you in your journey.

We will end the same way we started, by thanking each of you for the work you do on college campuses. By reading about the other staff roles and scenarios described throughout the book, roles different from your own, hopefully you are feeling part of a larger staff community who also struggle to manage difficult situations just like you. One of our favorite eighties songs when we are feeling tired or drained is Journey's "Don't Stop Believing." Next time you reach the end of a tough and trying day, remember—don't stop believing in the work you do, your ability to positively impact a student's college experience, and the opportunity to find the hope in challenging and difficult situations.

# Afterword

## A Little Dignity Please...

Joseph Allen[1]

> First of all you can never go too far. Second of all, if I'm going to be caught,
> it's not gonna be by a guy like that!
>
> Ferris, *Ferris Bueller's Day Off*

My mother taught me at an early age, "Life is about relationships!" I have observed this proclamation over and over in how teams are formed, work is completed, problems get solved, and students achieve success. In situations where I've mitigated disruptive and dangerous situations, I have found success most often when I show respect and uphold the dignity of those I confront.

As higher education administrators, I think we often overlook what we perceive as obvious about higher education: exactly how many hoops our students need to jump through to navigate the system of higher education. We might need to rethink our relationships with our students. We, as administrators, may know that there are twelve hoops and yet by hoop nine or ten our students are over it, or flat out rude or disrespectful, or threatening. Perhaps we need to take a step back. It might not be our hoops alone that are frustrating our students. Maybe we haven't done the best job of informing them what they should expect. Most likely though, we need to learn the whole context of their world. What are the stressors that have contributed to where they are and how they are feeling in that moment? It's time to pause and remember our mission. We are educators, no matter our title. Are we here for our students? If we aren't, then why are we here? It's time to do some deep introspection. If you haven't asked yourself or your employees why are you doing the work you are doing, you're missing an opportunity to have passionate employees who want to go above and beyond.

I have always believed in the golden rule: "Treat others how you want to be treated." Recently, however, I discovered the platinum rule. The platinum rule goes above and beyond. It turns a platitude of kindness and compassion on its head. It makes the true focus others, through unselfish service.

The platinum rule follows: "Treat others the way *they* want to be treated."

To put it plainly, the platinum rule treats everyone with dignity. I find merit in self-reflection, empathy, and adjustment on the part of administrators, as it is necessary in treating others how they want to be treated. With that said, in this chapter, I want to challenge you to examine your motives. Explore what adjustments you can make to meet your students where they are, and to help them get to where they need to be. What changes can you make to treat your students with dignity? Are you treating them as honored, worthy, and esteemed?

While overseeing residential life and housing for several years in my career, I learned many lessons. The first and most important is open communication. One of the funniest, though saddest, demonstrations of passive-aggressive communication was a sticky note in a dorm apartment refrigerator. It read, "Which one of you B$#^%@$ ate my cheese?" To respond and mediate the obvious breakdown in communication, I was forced to ask everyone involved not "How did the note get here?", but "Why did the note get here?" In our minds, it's clear that the sticky note isn't the most common approach to communicating a simple question. In the minds of stressed and socially anxious young adults, the sticky note seems like an easy way to solve the problem. My interest in resolving this matter pushed me to investigate the earliest interaction among roommates and the dynamics around the relationship in this dorm. I was required to dig into their communication styles and to understand where each one of the girls was in her journey. Communication works best as an intervention tactic, in the early stages of a conflict, before it reaches a boiling point where parties will not listen openly, or default to sticky notes. Had the girls reached out to someone early on in their relationships, this situation may have been avoided. Our responses must be formulated specifically to each party, so they can then learn to respond empathetically to others. We teach these students to put themselves in someone else's shoes, and to then walk a mile in those shoes. When we guide others into serious self-reflection, we can give them tools to treat others with respect and dignity. It turns the focus from an inward, self-centered perspective to one of an outward, humble, and compassionate view.

I find many of the same challenges exist in situations I respond to in my role overseeing online student conduct. Referrals made to my office include statements like:

- Your day is coming, and it's coming soon!
- You spit in my face and kicked dirt on me when I was down for weeks.
- The student made fun of my pictures of my cats and information they found out about me online.
- This is a warning.
- Thanks for no help!
- I will be in your office in a couple of hours to handle this.
- If you email me one more time, I'm going to kill myself.

How many of us, as Student Affairs professionals, are thankful for diagnostic tools such as The National Behavioral Intervention Team Association (NaBITA), the Violence Risk Assessment of the Written Word (VRAW$^2$), and the Structured Interview for Violence Risk Assessment (SIVRA-35)? It's through these lenses that I'm able to find a level of consistency in rating and responding appropriately with my colleagues. I don't know about you, but for me, each and every one of those referrals bulleted above causes me to want to know more. Perhaps that is where we should start.

## CONTEXT AND PERSPECTIVE OF THE STUDENT'S REALITY

Never make assumptions! There are always two sides to every coin and rarely have I seen a coin stand on its side. If I am, however, to get that coin to stand up on end, I must first pick it up and apply the right pressure to both sides. I use this analogy because the students I have worked with have often felt that the support is only on the side of the instructor or institution. It is important to lift the student up, get on their side, and collect the context and perspective of their world in order to understand their reality. There is a country music song I love which talks about a homeless man; that is all that people see. It goes on to point out what they don't see, which is the recent loss of his wife and child in an unfortunate automobile accident. We never know what is going on in a student's life until we ask. Until we put in the effort to get to know students, who some deem disruptive and dangerous, we won't be able to figure out how best to assist them.

I've formed some of the strongest and most supportive relationships with students I have evicted and expelled because I've done it in a way that supports them and treats them with dignity no matter the altercation. Perhaps through self-reflection and listening to our students, we may discover it is our processes or employees who set our students off. We will never know until we listen and seek to understand. Do the student's personal life stressors factor into your conversation when you are seeking to understand? Is the student struggling to articulate their frustration? Are we, as an institution, quoting policy and academic catalog language that even we, at times, don't read and fully understand? The first step from my perspective in responding and resolving disruptive and dangerous behavior is seeking to understand the context and perspective of the student's reality. I may be the first person who has ever actually listened to them, and that alone has been calming to a raging temper. People want to be heard and to be understood. It is our responsibility to listen.

## FACTORS CONTRIBUTING TO THE FRUSTRATION

We have all experienced someone "passing the buck" when we are seeking assistance. All we were looking for was a straight answer, and then we get the runaround? Are our students experiencing an environment that doesn't walk them down the hall or pass the phone call over with someone on the line? Are departments and administrators all business? Don't get me wrong, we work in higher education, but there is a lot of "business" to be done to complete the administrative requirements for simply enrolling, registering, paying, passing, and graduating our students. Pack those administrative stressors with human beings and *bam!* you've got tension. Given the size of our institutions, we must become efficient with our processes. These efficiencies can often leave outlying situations and unique student scenarios outside of our box and comfort zone. If we are designing an environment solely focused on efficiency, does that assume that it is effective? Perhaps effectiveness for all students is measured by the equity our students experience within our environment.

Recently, I went to get my cap and gown at Gradfest in preparation for my upcoming graduation. Walking into the conference room, I noticed it was well lined with stations, clear signage, and was serving thousands of students. Photos were being taken, tickets were being distributed, frames were being sold, and caps and gowns were being handed out. That all works well for the masses but as one of less than a couple dozen doctoral students, it was clear that the employees, who thought they had their jobs down pat, weren't quite sure what to do with me. It was clear that they knew a few of us doctoral students were coming but it was also clear they hadn't put those instructions to memory. After awkwardly communicating with a few different employees who weren't sure what to do with me, I was whisked away to a back room with no signage for a private measurement. It's easy for our environment to consume our focus, and when we run into these unique and non-cookie cutter scenarios, it rattles both the student and the staff who know their job well.

As a thirty-seven-year-old father of two about to graduate with my Ed.D., you would think going to college to get my graduation package wouldn't make me uneasy or uncomfortable. What you wouldn't have seen in that scenario was that I drove across town, tracked down a parking spot, paid my parking fee, hiked across campus only to find myself surrounded with twenty-two-year-old graduates and found nobody really knew what to do with me when I got there. Time was against me as I was on my lunch break and my expectations weren't being met. I was sweating, stressing about the cost of a diploma frame, and was texting my wife to see if we had enough in savings to purchase the "nice cap and gown."

Have you ever gone anywhere where you felt alone, isolated, like you didn't fit in, and perhaps socially uncomfortable based on how you looked, your age, race, gender, clothing, piercings, or tattoos? Until I had that one individual help me with my needs, I felt alone, isolated, I didn't fit in, and was socially awkward based on my business attire. I could feel frustration, disappointment, and annoyance creep up inside of me. Perhaps this is just a taste of what our students feel. We are all human. We all have feelings, insecurities, doubts, and anxieties.

Is our environment designed in a way that meets our students' reality? Are our processes and procedures designed to meet the unique situations our students face? Are we navigating homelessness, those struggling with food insecurities, parenting, substance abuse, military deployments, traumatic brain injuries, non-traditional student adjustments, students with disabilities, arrogant and dismissive staff, etc.? Are we honestly attempting to understand what our students feel when navigating our campuses? Perhaps our environments and institutional structures are contributing factors to our students' frustrations, rather than being the resolutions we feel they ought to be?

## THE CONTEXT AND PERSPECTIVE OF STAFF

Before working in higher education, I began my management career in hospitality at four-star hotels. I learned quickly that not only must we understand our customers and the environment; we must also understand the context and perspective of the staff on our teams. Does your staff want to help, or do they want to pass it off to someone to "fix" the problem? You can teach the functions of the job, but it's hard to teach team members to care. Having managed many people in my career, I seek to understand why my staff wants to do the tasks associated with the work we do. It's important to understand their motivation. A staff member who cares will answer that phone call or open the office door at 4.59 p.m. on a Friday afternoon for the student in need. They will recognize the signs in a student's tone, their words, or even their actions. The caring staff members, who treat people with dignity, will understand the unspoken need.

To get to that place, administrators need to understand the context and perspective of their staff. Are they burnt-out? Are they underappreciated? Are they passing the buck? If we are tasking our staff with the heavy lifting of supporting students who are disruptive or perceived as dangerous, we must understand the frame of mind those employees are in. It's hard to support someone if your head, and more importantly, your heart, aren't in it. There are several ways to get your team in the ready status, like a firefighter on deck.

- *Review your job descriptions.* All roads lead back to the job description. Key job elements rarely include customer service and compassion as key job requirements. Over the years, I have said I could administratively hire candidates with Masters in Business Administration (MBAs) or marketing degrees to do the work we do in Student Affairs. The reason is this: administratively, the majority of the work we do is behind the scenes, on a computer somewhere. Here is the key difference between hiring an MBA and someone with a higher degree in Student Affairs or Education: the skill set of an MBA may not align with the skill set of someone who pursued a counseling or social work degree. From my experience, there has been a clear difference in the motivation and drive between candidates who seek out degrees in higher education. They understand "why!" These colleagues understand the impact that extra phone call or that walk across campus will make for their students.

- *Coach / train your employees.* If you don't have systematic coaching and training on compassion, self-reflection and success stories, these priorities aren't being communicated to your teams. What gets measured gets done. Are your employee reviews and coaching feedback focused on frequency and volume or are they focused on holistic student outcomes? Some of the best trainings I've been a part of educate me on new ways to see the students for who they are, what they need, and creative ways I can serve those unique needs.

- *Manage or manage out!* The hard work of mediating student to student, roommate to roommate, student to instructor, or student to staff isn't for the faint of heart. Institutional leadership is not doing anyone favors by allowing an employee to fill a role where all they want to do is come in and check a box. This may very well fill a seat but you could have a passionate and caring individual, supporting students holistically. It's hard work to manage our employees. If done correctly, administrative leaders can assist and support employees in finding his or her next career opportunity, while not sacrificing the needs of your students and department. This is managing out an employee. It is one of the hardest changes, so I recommend steps one and two early on, before this becomes necessary.

## EFFORT SPEAKS VOLUMES

This work isn't easy, but it's necessary. It's not often that a student goes from zero to disruptive and dangerous in one conversation or situation alone. Granted, there are situations we as administrators face where there are mental health challenges in play, and those situations often don't follow the same escalation pathways. That is why it's so important we, as administrators, seek to understand our student's reality, our environments, and the perspectives of our staff. Like any relationship, this work takes time and effort. My staff often hear me say, "effort speaks volumes." To respond and support our community in these situations, we need self-reflection and a reminder of what our mission is. Are we here to serve all students? Some of the most concerning and threatening students I've worked with are students of principle, and somewhere along life, their dignity has been compromised or disregarded. Whether they have initiated a disagreement or misinterpreted something, it's my responsibility to understand who they are and what they need. This doesn't mean we aren't all accountable for our behaviors, and there may be consequences for our actions. At times, situations call for tough decisions to stop behavior, prevent it from reoccurring, and mitigating the impact on our community. If done well, by the right people, with the right goals, our mission, as educators, can be felt by our students, their families, and the communities that they serve.

## NOTE

1   A close friend of the authors, Joseph Allen, served as the Director of Student Development & Engagement for over five years, and Adjunct faculty member for over two years, at Ashford University, a predominantly on-line University serving over approximately 45,000 students. He currently works as an affiliated consultant for the NCHERM Group. We asked him to share some of his insights related to customer services and about his passion to improve people's lives through education as a way to bring together some of concepts in this book by focusing on the perspectives of the students we are trying to help.

# Scenario-Based RA Training

The following are a series of scenario-based training examples that may be helpful for schools looking at training residential life staff in the behind closed doors fashion. This approach typically has two or more students acting out a scenario in a residence hall room and a newly trained RA entering to act out how they would handle the scenario.

There are five scenarios for each of the following categories:

- Drinking and Substance Abuse
- Homesick/Over-Involved Parents
- General Rule Enforcement
- Suicide, Depression, and Self-Injury
- Anxiety and Panic Attacks
- Academic Support and Study Habits
- Roommate Conflicts
- Eating Disorders
- Aggression and Violence

Each scenario is described in a brief paragraph and three examples of responses are given that fall into a poor (0-point score), moderate (1-point score) and good (2-point score) range. Creative residential life staff could use these scenarios in a game-like fashion and award prizes for those new RAs who received the highest scores in their responses. Resident Directors could be used as judges to determine how to score each RA's attempt at addressing the scenario.

There are likely more scenarios than a team would need for a training. Multiple examples for each category are listed to allow for multi-year training exercises.

# DRINKING AND SUBSTANCE ABUSE #1

An RA is doing their rounds on a busy Friday night. They walk past an open door and see several beers on a table in a room. There are two students sitting on the bed, each holding a beer. When they see the RA walk by, they tuck their beers behind their backs and one of them quickly throws a towel over the beers on the table. The RA sees this happen. The RA also knows that each of the students is underage, since this is a first-year hall.

## 0-Point Response

Since there was not much beer involved and the students showed some willingness to admit their policy infraction (e.g., hiding the beers), the RA makes a mental note to hold the students accountable if they see a future infraction. The RA does not report the behavior to the RD.

## 1-Point Response

The RA talks to the students and confronts them about their policy violation. The RA has them dump out the beer and agrees to let each of them off with a warning if they promise to not do something like this again. The students are appreciative and agree to not do this again.

## 2-Point Response

The RA confronts the students in a caring but firm manner. The RA disposes of the beer in the manner outlined in housing policy, checks the student's IDs and writes them up for policy infractions. The RA consults with their RD and makes a basic assessment of the intoxication level of the students. The RA calls police and back-up as needed.

# DRINKING AND SUBSTANCE ABUSE #2

An underage student comes into an RA's room to talk. The student is worried and concerned. They tell the RA that they have been "drinking more than I want to be... and have tried to stop or cut back several times, but it hasn't worked." They share that they have been drinking since they were thirteen and drink now mostly with friends at off-campus parties. The student tells the RA that they have been missing class and last weekend had a period of time they couldn't remember. The student wants to know if this was a "blackout."

## 0-Point Response

The RA reports the student's alcohol problem and violation of the school alcohol policy to the RD in order to enforce policy and suggests the RD refer the student to alcohol treatment.

## 1-Point Response

The RA tells the student that they are clearly an alcoholic and that they need to take this situation seriously. The RA makes an appointment for the student at the counseling center and to have treatment and the RA tells the student they will need to meet with the RA and RD tomorrow.

## 2-Point Response

The RA talks to the student about their drinking problem. Without labeling the behavior "alcoholism," the RA encourages the student to get some additional help at the counseling center. The RA offers to walk the student over to see a counselor. The RA also lets their RD know about the situation to seek support and direction.

## DRINKING AND SUBSTANCE ABUSE #3

An international student has been caught twice for underage drinking. The student reports a frustration since "I have been drinking for years! This is not fair that I cannot drink here. It is only the United States' drinking laws." The RA comes by to talk to the student, who is clearly upset after the last time they were confronted about their alcohol use. The student has a judicial hearing tomorrow and is frustrated with the school, the US alcohol policy, and the conduct office.

## 0-Point Response

The RA takes a firm stance on the school's alcohol policy and shares "I know you don't like it, but that's how things are done over here." They explain to the student that these are the rules that everyone has to follow, and that if they don't like it they should have looked at attending another school overseas that had a more lax alcohol policy.

## 1-Point Response

The RA explains there is nothing that they can do since this is the school's policy. The RA expresses sympathy for the student but explains that they have to follow the college's rules like other students on campus. The RA explains that the student

**219**

is in danger of being suspended or asked to leave school if they continue to drink on campus.

## 2-Point Response

The RA lets the student to talk freely to vent their frustrations. The RA realizes that the student is worried about their status in the country and is far from home and their support group. The RA encourages the student to talk and offers to help them better understand the conduct process and how the meeting will be organized.

## DRINKING AND SUBSTANCE ABUSE #4

Several students have talked to an RA throughout the semester about the pervasive smell of "weed" in the hallway. The RA has not witnessed any use of marijuana, but several students have reported that the smell seems to come from a certain room. There is an intense smell of pot coming from the room. The RA knocks on the door and hears the window being slammed shut.

## 0-Point Response

The RA tells the student that everyone knows they are smoking pot and that it needs to stop. The RA threatens to call campus safety the next time they smell anything coming from the room. The RA also tells the student they will be reported to the hall director or campus safety if this happens again.

## 1-Point Response

The RA leaves the room and calls an "all-floor" meeting to address the problem. The RA says, "We need to work through this as a group. Consider this a chance to talk about the elephant in the room—the smell of pot in the hall." The RA encourages all the students to talk about their concerns. The RA also restates the student handbook policy on illegal substance use.

## 2-Point Response

The RA talks to the student about their concerns around the smell of marijuana coming from the room. The RA is clear they have not seen anything and don't want to assume, but also knows part of their job is to confront potential problems. The RA listens to the student's concerns and continues to talk to their RD in supervision about the best course of action.

## DRINKING AND SUBSTANCE ABUSE #5

One RA visits a fellow RA across campus during their weekly assigned rounds. The RA knocks on the door of their friend and then opens the door. The RA finds their friend with a beer in hand. The friend says "I'm so sorry... I just have been trying to relax more lately. You know how crazy it has been with our housing staff lately. Don't tell anyone." The RA who has the beer is underage.

### 0-Point Response

The RA who found their friend with a beer agrees to keep it between them as long as something like this never happens again. The RA lectures their friend about the importance of being smart about their drinking and not doing it on campus.

### 1-Point Response

The RA tells their friend they are going to report them. The RA tells the student that, "We are both held to a higher standard on campus as student leaders. How can you break this rule and be able to enforce any other rules?" The RA reports their friend to the RD immediately and complains about their friend's lack of dedication to the school and their job.

### 2-Point Response

The RA sits down and talks to their friend about the situation. The RA listens to the reasons and problems the fellow RA had that led up to the drinking. The RA stresses that, while one beer does not make a drinking problem, RAs can't drink underage and then enforce these rules. The RA suggests their friend talk directly to their RD about what happened. If not, the RA will talk to their RD about the situation.

## HOMESICK/OVER-INVOLVED PARENTS #6

A new first-year student is withdrawn from others in the residence hall and isolates themselves. The student often talks about missing home and appears tearful and upset, rarely enjoying college or going to dinner with others on the floor. The RA has been watching this behavior get worse and has tried talking to the student several times and involving them in group activities.

### 0-Point Response

The RA tells the student that this behavior is getting in the way of their success at college. Unless they can let go of home, they will continue to have problems. The RA tells the student they are isolating themselves and everyone on the floor is worried about them.

## 1-Point Response

The RA talks to the student about their homesickness and their feelings about being away from home. The two brainstorm some ideas that help make the homesickness better (e.g., calling parents, visiting over a break) and the RA gets the student to agree to attend dinner with them later that week.

## 2-Point Response

The RA listens to the student about their homesickness. They discuss ways the student can reduce their homesickness. The RA explains that things don't seem to be getting better. They offer to take the student to counseling. The student is worried about being labeled "crazy," so the RA agrees to come with them for the first session.

## HOMESICK/OVER-INVOLVED PARENTS #7

A new student's mother has been visiting them several times a week over the fall semester. Other students on the floor laugh that the student's mother still does their laundry in the residence hall laundry room on Saturdays. The student doesn't seem to be aware that this is a growing joke around campus.

## 0-Point Response

The RA tells the student, "You need to cut the apron strings and get away from your mom. She's destroying your reputation on campus." The RA makes the point that college is a time to separate firmly from parents, and if the student can't do that, then maybe they need to go back home.

## 1-Point Response

The RA has a firm but caring talk with the student about their mother's involvement in their lives and how this is having a negative impact on their reputation at school. The RA explains that they should still stay connected to their mom—but maybe try to cut things back a bit.

## 2-Point Response

The RA realizes that it may not be the student's preference to have their mother at school so often. They talk about the student's goals for college and how this situation is preventing them from growing. The RA and student brainstorm ways to talk to the student's mother about her visits. The RA seeks supervision before having the meeting to make sure to approach it well.

## HOMESICK/OVER-INVOLVED PARENTS #8

An international student has been having difficulty with their adjustment to college and life in the United States. They have been having stomach problems with the food on campus and have had trouble balancing the course work. The student is often alone in their room and has few things in common with other students in the hall.

### 0-Point Response

The RA reports the problem to the RD and suggests someone from international services address the problem with the student. The RA has invited the student to floor events, often with pizza and soda, and is frustrated they haven't showed up at any of the events.

### 1-Point Response

The RA continues to invite the student to floor events and looks for ways to connect the student to the rest of the floor. The RA talks to their RD about the situation to try to find other ways they can connect the international student to the rest of the students on campus.

### 2-Point Response

The RA meets often with the international student, spends time with them, and tries to connect them to other students. The RA hosts an international food night and helps the student cook some of their favorite foods. The RA helps the student meet with the international student association and reviews the situation with their RD to brainstorm other ideas.

## HOMESICK/OVER-INVOLVED PARENTS #9

Parents of a student are very over-involved and protective. This is a first-year student, and their parents often call the front desk asking the housing staff to "check on my child because I haven't heard back from them after I called an hour ago." The student has also voiced concern that their parents have been monitoring text messages—calling the cell company and tracking the time text messages were going out and then calling the student because they sent a text during class time or after 1 a.m. Other students on the floor are expressing concern.

## 0-Point Response

The RA tells the student to ignore their parent's phone calls and pestering. The RA says, "The only way your parents are going to learn is to teach them a lesson." The RA suggests the student just be out of touch for a few days and that should solve their problem, suggesting "that's what a normal college student would do."

## 1-Point Response

The RA tells the student to confront their parents about the behavior and ask them to stop pestering the front desk staff. Explain to the student that they need to take care of this problem or they are going to be called into the housing office because their parents are mistreating the front office staff.

## 2-Point Response

The RA helps the student understand that their parents are calling too often and perhaps a meeting with the student, their parents, and a member of the housing staff (RD or director) would be helpful to address the problem. The RA suggests the student visit counseling to find ways to talk more directly to their parents in the future.

## HOMESICK/OVER-INVOLVED PARENTS #10

An RA begins a conversation with a student who has been having trouble feeling comfortable at college. They have been somewhat withdrawn, trying to make friends but having trouble connecting socially with others. The student says "I'm not sure college is for me. There is so much work and I'm thinking I should have gone to a school closer to home."

## 0-Point Response

The RA tells the student that these feelings are all normal and if they are not happy with this college, they should talk to their advisor about switching majors or look at transferring to another school. The RA tells the student if they keep isolating themselves from other people they are going to end up alone and more depressed.

## 1-Point Response

The RA talks to the student and recommends that they speak with a counselor immediately. The RA explains that these early warning signs are clear indications of depression and, left unchecked, could lead to suicidal thoughts. The RA takes the student over to counseling the next morning.

## 2-Point Response

The RA talks openly with the student about their fears and worries about college life. The RA offers little advice, but listens and helps the student identify what they are concerned about. The RA suggests that talking to someone in the counseling center may be helpful to clarify their future plans, but this doesn't mean they are "crazy."

## GENERAL RULE ENFORCEMENT #11

A student chronically forgets their ID card and gets into arguments at the front desk. The most recent argument happened as the RA walked by. The student yelled, "It's not like you don't know who I am! Why is this always such a problem? Just let me go up to my room and I'll get my ID and show it to you." The front desk worker responded, "My boss said not to let you up without your ID. I don't have a choice."

## 0-Point Response

The RA ignores the problem and walks by because it isn't their problem to address. The RA isn't sure what the front desk staff instructions are and they don't want to get in the middle of this argument since it doesn't directly involve the RA's responsibility.

## 1-Point Response

The RA sides with the front desk student worker and tells the student without their ID, "This is your fault. If you had your ID, you wouldn't be having this problem." They argue some more and the RA once again is clear that the student cannot come into the building without their ID. This has been a frequent problem and the only way the student will learn is if there are clear consequences.

## 2-Point Response

The RA tells the student they need to bring their ID. The RA offers to fetch the student's ID from their room. The RA then has a discussion with the student about the importance of building security and why coming into the building isn't just about whether the staff know who you are or not. The RA also tells the student next time they will have to fill out an incident report.

## GENERAL RULE ENFORCEMENT #12

A student is in their room smoking a cigarette out of an open window. The RA walks by the outside of the building and sees this going on. The RA walks up to the room and finds the student still smoking by their window, music turned up loud (it is past quiet hours) and with a candle lit on the table to cover the odor of the cigarettes.

### 0-Point Response

The RA tells the student to stop smoking out the window, turn down the music after hours, and put out the candle. The RA is firm but caring, and tells the student "don't let any of this happen again or I'll have to report you and I don't feel like having to fill out all that paperwork."

### 1-Point Response

The RA immediately confronts the multiple violations for smoking in the room, an open flame, and loud music after quiet hours. The RA is strict and upset at the student's flagrant disregard for the policy. The RA reports the student for the policy violations and keeps a close eye on them for the remainder of the semester.

### 2-Point Response

The RA asks the student to turn down the music and talks to them about the problems with their rule-breaking behavior. The RA is firm but caring in the confrontation, and aware that the three rules require some kind of documentation with their RD. The RA talks about this with the student and the two make a plan to address the behavior in the future.

## GENERAL RULE ENFORCEMENT #13

Several students have set up a dart board at the end of the long hallway in the residence hall and are having a tournament. One student is wearing a green banker's cap and is holding a notepad and some cash. Other students are throwing darts. There are a number of doorways open between where the dartboard is set up and where the students are throwing the darts from.

### 0-Point Response

The RA laughs and tells the students to find a better place to do this. The RA talks privately to the student in the banker's cap and reminds them of the campus policy about gambling on campus.

## 1-Point Response

The RA yells at the students about "being dangerous and reckless. There are safety issues that are being violated." The RA tells the students they will be reported for putting the floor at risk because of their unsafe behavior throwing darts around. The RA also reports all the students for violating the gambling policy (pointing out to two involved students that they will probably lose their National Collegiate Athletic Association (NCAA) scholarships).

## 2-Point Response

The RA asks the students to stop the dart game and redirects them to play in another room. The RA explains that a student running through the hall could be hit with a dart and it isn't safe. The RA also talks to the students about the gambling and talks to their supervising RD about planning an in-service training for the students on the school's gambling policy.

## GENERAL RULE ENFORCEMENT #14

An RA sees a student throwing trash out of a fourth-floor window into the dumpster beside the building. The RA has talked to the student several times about this and when the student sees the RA witness the trash throwing, they quickly close the window and turn out the lights in the room. The RA returns to the floor and knocks on the student's door.

## 0-Point Response

The RA bangs against the student's door yelling "I know you are in there! Open the door or I will call campus safety." When the student opens the door, the RA tells them, "This is the third time I've caught you doing this. You will be lucky if you are allowed to stay in the residence hall after this."

## 1-Point Response

The RA talks to the student about their violation of policy. The RA is frustrated and clearly lets the student know that they cannot continually break the rules on campus. The RA tells the student they will be reported to the housing office and likely end up with a serious sanction since this is their third offense.

## 2-Point Response

The RA takes a minute or two to gather their patience before confronting the student. The RA calmly explains the policy once again about throwing trash out the window and then reports the student in an incident report to the RD the next day. The RA lets housing and the conduct office address the problem.

## GENERAL RULE ENFORCEMENT #15

An RA is doing rounds one evening and comes across a student who has some odd squeaking noises coming from their room. The RA knocks on the door (which isn't completely shut) and it swings open. The student is covering a hamster cage by the bottom of their bed. The student is clearly upset that the RA saw their hamster. This is the middle of the semester and it is likely Mr. Cuddles has been here the entire year.

### 0-Point Response

The RA tells the student they need to have the hamster gone that evening and that they are being reported to residential life and housing. The RA threatens the student that they will be "kicked out of housing by tomorrow and they had better find a new place to live."

### 1-Point Response

The RA tells the student they need to have the hamster gone by the next day when they come back and check. They explain that animals aren't allowed in the halls and even something as small as a hamster is a violation of the housing contract and could lead to them having to leave the residence hall.

### 2-Point Response

The RA talks to the student about having animals in the hall. The RA explains that while animals are good companions, they aren't allowed in the halls. The RA also explains that they have to write up an incident report and someone from the housing office will need to have a meeting with them to discuss what happens next.

## SUICIDE, DEPRESSION, AND SELF-INJURY #16

A non-traditional student recently returned from serving in Iraq has been having some trouble with depression and isolation from others. The RA has talked to the student once before about their difficulty related to other students, keeping up with coursework, and generally adapting to life back in the United States. The student tells the RA, "I just can't relate to all of this. My friends are a bunch of kids. They haven't seen what I've seen. I just feel so... I don't know... I don't know what's going to happen to me."

## 0-Point Response

The RA listens to the student and then encourages them to work harder to connect more with other students on campus. The RA says, "Part of the problem is you are always by yourself. If you just got out of your room once in a while, you'd be less depressed." The RA makes a plan to check in on the student next week.

## 1-Point Response

The RA talks to the student about their time in Iraq and questions them about their frustration coming back to school. The RA asks the student if they have ever felt suicidal. The RA is worried because they are not trained for working with suicidal students. The RA calls campus safety and the counseling center.

## 2-Point Response

The RA talks to the student about Iraq and questions them about their depression. The RA asks about suicidal feelings and refers the student to the counseling center (offering to walk them over for the first session). The RA talks to the RD or housing staff on duty after the conversation for additional supervision.

## SUICIDE, DEPRESSION, AND SELF-INJURY #17

Several students approach an RA worried that a student has locked themselves in their room and has a razor. The friends confide in the RA that their friend has cut themself before and they are worried "something more serious might happen." The RA knocks on the door of the student and the student opens it. The RA notices a small, superficial cut and a razor.

## 0-Point Response

Once the RA sees a razor and a small cut on the student's arm, they leave the room and call an ambulance and campus safety to come take the student into custody. The RA feels they aren't trained to deal with these kinds of things and that the student needs to be locked up somewhere off campus.

## 1-Point Response

The RA talks to the student and the student shares their thoughts about hurting themselves with a razor. The RA gets the student to agree to talk to the counseling center the next day. The student agrees to get up before their 8 a.m. class and go to the counseling center to make an appointment. The RA agrees to this plan and tells the student they will check on them later in the week.

## 2-Point Response

The RA talks to the student about their cutting behavior. The student denies feeling suicidal, but says "I just cut myself when I feel depressed." The RA explains to the student that they need to check in with the on-call housing staff (or counseling) to get some guidance. The student agrees to go to counseling the next day and the RA calls to check in with their RD and counseling staff.

## SUICIDE, DEPRESSION, AND SELF-INJURY #18

A senior biology major (who is also an international student) has been under a lot of stress lately. In the past few days, they have been withdrawn, missed several important classes due to oversleeping, and appear disheveled. The RA learns the student has been giving away several of her favorite pictures, clothes, and laptop because "I won't need them anymore." The RA knocks on the student's door.

## 0-Point Response

The RA decides that this is important enough to report to their RD the next time they meet in supervision later in the week. They share the information and the RD immediately calls the counseling center. The student is then assessed at the counseling center for suicidal feelings.

## 1-Point Response

The RA talks directly to the student about how they have been feeling lately. The RA expresses concern about the apparent suicidal behaviors and the student denies any of these problems. They instead say, "I'm just going through a rough time." The RA tells the student they are available to talk in the future if needed.

## 2-Point Response

Before talking to the student, the RA talks to their RD for advice. The RA talks to the student, who denies having any suicidal thoughts. The RA is able to convince the student to go to a meeting with the counseling staff. The RA follows up with the RD and continues to check in on the student throughout the semester.

## SUICIDE, DEPRESSION, AND SELF-INJURY #19

A student comes rushing to find the RA. They say "my friend just posted on Facebook that they are taking pills to commit suicide! You have to help me." The RA finds out who the student is and knocks on their door to talk with them. When the student opens the door, the RA sees a bottle of pills next to the computer. The pills are all lined up with a glass of water. There must be over a hundred pills.

## 0-Point Response

The RA runs from the room to call campus safety. They report a suicidal student in their building that needs immediate help and transport to the hospital.

## 1-Point Response

The RA talks calmly to the student about their concern. The student admits they have been upset lately and they thought of taking pills. The student assures the RA, "I feel better now—several of my friends said I shouldn't do it. So I feel cared about." The RA gets the student to agree to go to counseling the next day. The RA talks about the case later in the week with their RD.

## 2-Point Response

The RA talks to the student about their suicidal feelings. The student reports they no longer feel suicidal since their friends care about them. The RA tells the student they still have to call an on-call counselor and their RD to have them review what happened. The RA gets the student to come with them to the lobby (leaving the pills) while the RA makes a phone call for back-up.

## SUICIDE, DEPRESSION, AND SELF-INJURY #20

A student seems sad and withdrawn after their partner broke up with them. The student is typically happy and outgoing, but lately has been isolating from friends, crying, and listening to sad music in their room. Some friends approach the RA and request they check on their friend.

## 0-Point Response

The RA is worried the student is suicidal and calls the counseling center to bring the student over. The RA tells the student, "You are depressed and need help. If you don't go with me to the counseling center, I'm going to have to report you to campus safety."

## 1-Point Response

The RA talks to the student and tells them that "everyone has been through something like this before; it's nothing to worry about." The RA explains that college is about finding lots of relationships and that the student "shouldn't let one bad relationship get you down. There are plenty of other fish in the sea." The RA offers to try to fix the student up on a date with a friend.

## 2-Point Response

The RA lets the student talk about their loss. The RA is aware that sadness is normal after the break-up of a relationship and doesn't try to force the student into counseling. The RA continues to check in with the student and offers a referral to counseling if the sadness and withdrawal lingers for more than a week or two. The RA discusses the case with their RD in supervision.

## ANXIETY AND PANIC ATTACKS #21

A student is worried all the time about their classes. They talk to other students about failing out of school, not having enough time to study everything they are supposed to be studying, and generally feeling overwhelmed with college. The student has panic attacks several times a week where they lock themselves in their room and don't come out for several hours.

## 0-Point Response

The RA confronts the student about their behavior and explains that this is exactly the kind of stuff that gets other students talking about them behind their back. The RA shares stories of how other students are worried about them and think they are "the crazy kid on the floor." The RA suggests the student changes their behavior quickly if they are going to stay in college.

## 1-Point Response

The RA listens to the student about their frustrations and worries about college life. The RA offers some advice to better deal with stress and encourages the student to talk more openly with others about what is bothering them. The RA makes an appointment with academic advising to help the student better prepare for their classes and balance their workload.

## 2-Point Response

The RA talks to their RD about their concerns around this student to better brainstorm an approach. The RA then approaches the student and listens to their concerns and frustrations. The RA explains to the student that their anxiety seems pretty serious and it might be helpful if they talked to someone over at the counseling center. The RA walks the student over for an appointment later in the week.

## ANXIETY AND PANIC ATTACKS #22

An international student approaches an RA about feeling overwhelmed in their classes. The student is specifically concerned about an upcoming presentation in class and tells the RA, "I've never had to give a speech like this in front of so many people. I get so upset I think I may pass out."

### 0-Point Response

The RA explains this is a common experience and the student should just try to imagine all the other students in class naked. The RA says everyone gets stage fright now and again and the student just has to get through it on their own. The RA explains, "That's just how it is in our country. You have to step up and achieve your goals. You can't stop when something gets hard."

### 1-Point Response

The RA listens to the student's concerns and talks openly about some of the problems they have had in their own speech classes. The RA tells the student that it is all in the preparation. If the student can just prepare and be ready, the anxiety will go away—or at least become manageable.

### 2-Point Response

The RA listens to the student and brainstorms some ideas for how the student could better deal with their anxiety of speaking in front of others for the class. The RA tries to normalize the student's fears and offers several suggestions of people they could talk to (e.g., academic tutoring or counseling) that might be helpful for the student. The RA follows up the next day to see how the student is managing.

## ANXIETY AND PANIC ATTACKS #23

A student has been feeling isolated from others in the hall. The student is overweight and is often teased by others. The student rarely talks to other people on the floor and their roommate recently requested a transfer to another room. The RA talks to the student who is crying and upset. The student says, "No one will ever like me! I try everything I can and nothing works. I worry I will always be alone." The student is so upset they start to hyperventilate.

## 0-Point Response

The RA rushes from the room and calls campus safety to have an ambulance take the student to the hospital. If the student can't breathe, they could die. The RA sees this as a medical emergency.

## 1-Point Response

The RA tells the student firmly to calm down. The RA then explains that there is nothing for the student to worry about. The RA assures the student that other people on the floor like them. The RA tries to invite the student out more often and suggests they go to the gym together so the student can lose some weight.

## 2-Point Response

The RA talks calmly and slowly to the student to help them calm down and catch their breath. The RA then listens to the student's frustrations and worries and tries to offer some normalizing thoughts (it can be hard to make friends; many students struggle to make friends). The RA suggests a meeting with a counselor to talk further about the student's concerns.

## ANXIETY AND PANIC ATTACKS #24

An RA is doing homework when a senior student who lives on their floor tentatively knocks at the door to talk. The student floods the RA with worries about their choices while at college, fear about finding a job after college, and worries that they are disappointing their parents.

## 0-Point Response

The RA tells the student that these are normal fears and they should go talk to someone in career services about them. The RA tells the student this isn't the best time for them to talk and offers the student the number for the career service to help with their problems.

## 1-Point Response

The RA listens to the student and then gives the student advice about how to better prepare for their future, the job market, and how to go about switching majors. The RA says, "It's up to you to take charge of your life. You can talk to career services about all of this and they will help you get a better handle on things."

## 2-Point Response

The RA listens to the student's concerns in a relaxed and unrushed way. The RA shares some of their own concerns about the future and talks about how career services and counseling may be helpful for the student to have some extra guidance. The RA brainstorms with their RD around other ways to help the student with their anxiety.

## ANXIETY AND PANIC ATTACKS #25

An Iraq war veteran student recently moved into the hall and other students are telling the RA they are "freaked out." They explain to the RA that the student is jumpy and jittery all the time, talks in weird militaristic language (like calling 10 p.m. 2200 hours) and jumps through the roof anytime there is a loud noise. The RA goes to check in on the student.

## 0-Point Response

The RA is concerned that the student is a potential violence threat to the other students and has the military knowledge to kill other students. The RA gathers information while talking to the student and then reports back their RD.

## 1-Point Response

The RA talks to the student and explains to them that other students on the floor are starting to see them as "weird and strange." The RA encourages the student to "lose the military language" and try to find ways to better fit in with other college students. The RA tells the student they should "get some help at the counseling center before things get any worse."

## 2-Point Response

The RA talks to the student in a calm and relaxed manner. The RA encourages the student to talk about their adjustment from Iraq to being in college. The RA offers referrals to counseling to help with the adjustment, but assures the student "that going to counseling doesn't mean they are crazy." The RA shares some positive stories about counseling and offers to accompany the student on the first visit.

## ACADEMIC SUPPORT AND STUDY HABITS #26

An RA checks in on an overwhelmed first-year student on their floor. The student has been having trouble balancing their coursework and other students on the floor have been concerned because the student has been yelling at them and seems "frustrated and freaking out."

## 0-Point Response

The RA meets with the student and explains to them that stress and anxiety are part of the college experience and they need to "pull it together" because the other students in the hall are worried about them.

## 1-Point Response

The RA talks to the student about their stress load and then tells them that they need to take better care of themselves and find ways to relax. The RA offers to take the student off campus a few times during the week to relax and then helps the student better organize the work they have due in their classes.

## 2-Point Response

The RA listens to the student's concerns and offers some suggestions on how they can better organize their workload. The RA reassures the student that stress is a normal part of college, especially the first year. The RA offers a referral to academic support and tutoring. The RA talks to their RD to review how they handled this and find other ideas to help the student.

## ACADEMIC SUPPORT AND STUDY HABITS #27

An international student has been having trouble adjusting to their move to college and the United States. The student is having trouble with the language and has been falling behind in classes. The RA talks to the student.

## 0-Point Response

The RA explains that "things are harder in the United States compared to their country" and that they need to "work harder and apply themselves in order to succeed." The RA tells the student to spend more time with other students from their country who might have some advice to help them.

## 1-Point Response

The RA talks to the student and offers some suggestions on how to better manage their academic course load. The RA tells the student they need to work on their English more and that this will help them be more successful at college. The RA suggests they find some more time to study during the week in order to get ahead in their class work.

## 2-Point Response

The RA talks to the student about their difficulty and offers several referrals to the offices of international students, academic advising, and the counseling center. The RA tells the student "things will get better" and offers to help them get to these appointments for the first time. The RA assures the student that they are doing well adjusting and moving to a new country and that starting college isn't easy.

## ACADEMIC SUPPORT AND STUDY HABITS #28

A student comes back from class very upset. The student kicks his door and yells, "This is bull, man! This is total bull! I hate this place!" The student had been caught plagiarizing a paper in one of his classes and is now worried they are going to be kicked out of school. The student was told they couldn't come back to class again until they could "learn how to be a college student, not a cheater."

## 0-Point Response

The RA agrees that the student should learn how to be a student and not cheat. The RA has little tolerance for the student and thinks it is now time for the student to "pay their dues."

## 1-Point Response

The RA listens to the student's complaints and then says, "That's ridiculous. Professors can't talk to you that way." The RA helps the student write a letter of appeal to the department head and tells the student to calm down and talk to the department head before doing anything drastic.

## 2-Point Response

The RA explains to the student that they need to calm down. The RA lets the student talk and then offers some suggestions for some next steps. The RA tells the student to talk to their advisor, academic support, or the professor. The RA reassures the student and encourages them to calmly discuss the matter with the professor or department head.

## ACADEMIC SUPPORT AND STUDY HABITS #29

A student who normally has a 4.0 GPA comes to the RA to talk about a problem in their class. They explain that they haven't been to class for over three weeks, after they had been embarrassed about doing a lab incorrectly. The student reports "freaking out" and walking to class several times, but then just turning around and coming back to their room. The student is worried they are going to fail the class.

### 0-Point Response

The RA agrees the student is likely going to fail the class. The RA reassures the student that they can fail a class and then retake it the next semester and replace the grade from the new class with the failed one. The RA tells the student that "this happens all the time and you shouldn't worry about it."

### 1-Point Response

The RA talks to the student about a similar situation that had happened to them in class. The RA tells the student, "You just need to call the professor. They will probably work something out with you." The RA encourages the student to talk to the professor and agrees to check in on them the next day to see how it went.

### 2-Point Response

The RA listens to the student talk about their worries. The RA reassures the student that there is a solution and praises them for talking about the problem. The RA offers to walk the student over to counseling or academic support to have some help in taking a next step. The RA explains the student could take an incomplete or could talk with the professor to make up the work.

## ACADEMIC SUPPORT AND STUDY HABITS #30

A student is worried about how they are doing in their classes. They tell the RA that they used to have a learning disorder when they were in high school but wanted to "have a fresh start at college and try to do it on my own." The student is worried they are failing all their classes and isn't sure what to do.

### 0-Point Response

The RA says that academic issues like these aren't something that they can talk about with students. The RA suggests the student talks to a counselor or someone in the ADA office.

## 1-Point Response

The RA talks to the student about their difficulty in class. The RA offers some suggestions in terms of study habits, class attendance, taking better notes, and organizing information before a test. The RA checks in with the student later in the week to make sure they are following the advice.

## 2-Point Response

The RA listens to the student's concerns and offers suggestions on how the student can address the problem. The RA praises the student for talking about their learning disability issues and suggests a meeting with one of the counseling staff or someone in the campus disability (ADA) office. The RA offers to accompany the student to the first appointment. The RA checks in with their RD for other ideas.

## ROOMMATE CONFLICTS #31

An RA walks past two roommates fighting over a video game. They begin yelling at each other and complaining about everything from what time the alarm is set to how messy the room is. The argument escalates in volume and begins to spill over into the hall. This is the fourth or fifth argument like this the two of them have gotten into this semester (and it's just the second week of classes!)

## 0-Point Response

The RA jumps in and firmly yells back at both students, "This isn't second grade! You two need to calm down and treat each other like people." The RA explains the yelling needs to stop or both of them are going to be looking for a new place to live.

## 1-Point Response

The RA tells them both that this yelling isn't appropriate and they need to stop. The RA has a long sit down with them to talk out the problems and address the differences in their level of room neatness, time they get up in the morning, and how they both need to argue less and spend more time enjoying each other's company.

## 2-Point Response

The RA listens to each of them in turn and calms down the current situation. The RA expresses concern that things are not getting better between the two of them and sets up a meeting later in the week for both of them to meet with the RA and the RD to discuss their living arrangements. The RA asks them each to write down their concerns and bring them to the meeting.

## ROOMMATE CONFLICTS #32

A student approaches an RA with concerns about their roommate. The student is worried that the roommate is "super-religious" and odd. The student thinks their roommate is unstable mentally and is worried about sleeping in the same room with them. The student reports that their roommate gets up at 5 a.m. every morning, prays out loud in the shower, and calls any music that isn't Christian music "the devil's music."

### 0-Point Response

The RA tells the two roommates they need to work it out. The RA clearly says they don't want to hear any more of these problems going on and asks the two to "go to counseling if you can't work it out together." The RA then keeps a close eye on each of them over the next few weeks and writes an incident report for any infraction that occurs.

### 1-Point Response

The RA talks to the religious roommate. The RA expresses concern about the odd behavior and praying and how the student criticizes other students' "secular, non-Christian music." The RA makes it clear that discrimination and this odd behavior needs to stop and recommends the student to see a counselor.

### 2-Point Response

The RA talks to their RD and the counseling staff for some advice. The RA talks to the students about what it means to live together as roommates and how they should be handling each other's differences. The RA recommends that if the tension continues, they each may want to consider switching rooms or talking with the RD or school counselor to reduce the conflict.

## ROOMMATE CONFLICTS #33

An RA is called into a roommate argument between an international student and a student from the United States. The American student complains about their roommate's odor, odd behavior (like getting up early to pray, not eating certain foods like bacon, and dressing in an overly conservative manner). The international student is concerned their roommate is a "dirty pig, has no values, and doesn't take their studies seriously."

## 0-Point Response

The RA talks to both of them and then firmly tells them that this is part of college and they both need to work harder to get along with each other. The RA tells them that if they don't, each will be looking for a new place to live. The RA also takes the side of the American student and tells the international student to "shower more often."

## 1-Point Response

The RA encourages each student to listen to the other's concerns and to find ways to live together in peace and harmony. The RA has each of them write down some things they like about each other and then encourages them to share their feelings. The RA checks in with them throughout the semester to make sure they are getting along better.

## 2-Point Response

The RA meets with them and encourages them to talk openly about their concerns and expectations about rooming together. The RA mediates this discussion, looks for common ground, and tries to improve their communication with each other. The RA tells them the next step is to either have mediation with an RD or look for new roommates.

## ROOMMATE CONFLICTS #34

A student tells their RA they are at "the end of their rope." The student complains that their roommate is always having their "friend with benefits" in the room late at night and the two of them are having sex. The roommate tells the RA that "this needs to stop" and they have tried to be civil about it, but "I can't handle this anymore. It feels like I'm on a porn set."

## 0-Point Response

The RA tells the student that they need to relax and realize that this is college and people are going to have sex. The RA explains that this wouldn't be such an issue if the student also had someone to have sex with and maybe they should just work on finding their own "friend with benefits" and stop being so uptight.

## 1-Point Response

The RA tells the student that they need to confront their roommate about this behavior and that if it happens again the RA will fill out an incident report and will meet with the student to address the behavior. The RA thanks the student for bringing this to their attention and assures the student that if it happens again there will be clear consequences.

## 2-Point Response

The RA meets with both students and talks about both of their concerns in the given situation. The RA makes clear the housing policy on having overnight guests and the two roommates are encouraged to try to work out some kind of compromise where both feel as if they are getting their needs met. The RA encourages them to meet again and offers to meet with both of them and the RD if needed.

## ROOMMATE CONFLICTS #35

A student approaches their RA concerned about their roommate's drinking behavior. The student reports that their roommate is "out to all hours of the night, drinks like a fish, and often vomits or pees the bed." The student tells the RA they don't want to be a tattletale and get their roommate in trouble, but they are really worried their roommate might have a more serious problem.

## 0-Point Response

The RA reports the roommate's drinking behavior to the student conduct office. The RA tells the student "not to worry, the judicial affairs people will handle this" and to report any further problems with their roommate's drinking immediately it occurs.

## 1-Point Response

The RA talks to the roommate with the drinking problem and expresses concern. They require the student to go to the counseling center to get an alcohol assessment and tells them, "If you don't, I'm going to report you and you won't be able to live here anymore." The RA offers to go with the student to counseling for the first session.

## 2-Point Response

The RA talks to their RD and the counseling staff to get some guidance and access to resources. The RA confronts the student about their drinking behavior in a caring and supportive way. They offer to go with the student to counseling to have an assessment and keep a close eye on the student over the next few weeks to ensure their drinking is being addressed.

## EATING DISORDERS #36

An RA is worried about a student on their floor who has not been eating well over the course of the semester and seems to have a serious eating disorder. The student is very thin, exercises four to five hours a day, and has not been to the dining hall. The RA talks to the student and they admit to a long-term eating disorder.

### 0-Point Response

The RA tells the student that this is something serious and they probably shouldn't be going to school while dealing with something like this. The RA calls the student's parents to express concern and reports the student to the counseling office.

### 1-Point Response

The RA talks to the student and offers advice about how to deal with an eating disorder. The RA pledges to help the student, encourages them to go to dinner with the rest of the floor, and helps the student to exercise only two to three hours a day. The RA keeps a close eye on the student throughout the rest of the semester.

### 2-Point Response

The RA talks to their RD and some of the counseling staff, as they realize this is a serious eating disorder. The RA talks to the student and encourages them to consider going to the counseling center on campus to receive some assistance. The RA offers to take the student over to the office if they are worried about making that first appointment.

## EATING DISORDERS #37

Several students approach the RA concerned about bags of vomit that were found in the bathroom trash. The students have some idea who has been vomiting in the bags and then leaving them in the bathroom. They want to approach the student and confront them.

## 0-Point Response

The RA encourages the students to talk to the student in question who may be vomiting in the bags. The RA tells the students to do this calmly and with the understanding that the student may have a serious eating disorder. The RA gives the students a pamphlet from the health center on "helping a friend with an eating disorder" to assist with the intervention.

## 1-Point Response

The RA calls an all-floor meeting to discuss the issue of finding bags of vomit in the bathroom. The RA avoids accusing anyone directly, but says that this behavior "has to stop—it is not sanitary and is having a negative impact on this community." The RA encourages any students struggling with an eating disorder to talk to them or a member of the counseling staff on campus.

## 2-Point Response

The RA talks to the counseling staff and their RD to solicit advice on how to handle this problem. The RA realizes that many people with eating disorders who purge have difficulty doing this in a public bathroom and the bags of vomit may be them purging in their room and then getting rid of it in the trash. The RA talks to the student in question, without accusation, and offers help and referral.

## EATING DISORDERS #38

A group of students approach the RA about their friend who lives on the hall who "clearly has an eating disorder." The students report their friend "never eats, is really thin, and needs someone to help them."

## 0-Point Response

The RA meets with the student and explains to them the signs and symptoms of eating disorders and shows them on a pamphlet from health services. The RA points out where the student seems to be meeting all the essential criteria. The RA refers the student to counseling and asks them to seek help for their problem.

## 1-Point Response

The RA encourages the students to talk to their friend about going to counseling. The RA tells the students their friend "may or may not have an eating disorder" and that they should be careful confronting their friend about this because they could get really defensive or angry. The RA gives the students some pamphlets from the counseling center.

## 2-Point Response

The RA understands the student in question may or may not have an eating disorder and approaches the student cautiously saying, "I'm worried about you. It looks as if you aren't eating enough and are really thin." The RA has a referral to counseling ready, but also understands the student may just have a fast metabolism or is under stress adjusting to college.

## EATING DISORDERS #39

An RA is concerned about a student athlete who has been wearing a skin-tight suit under their clothes in order to "make weight" for an upcoming event. The RA is concerned that the student is not eating or drinking, exercising almost non-stop and developing some unhealthy habits.

## 0-Point Response

The RA calls the student's coach and reports the concerning behavior. The RA also calls the counseling department and reports that they have a student on their floor who is engaged in an eating disorder and that they need some advice on how to talk to the student about their problem.

## 1-Point Response

The RA talks to the student and outlines the signs and symptoms of an eating disorder and shows the student how they seem to meet all the criteria to have an eating disorder. The RA refers the student to counseling and suggests that if they keep doing what they are doing, the RA may need to tell their coach.

## 2-Point Response

The RA talks to the counseling department and their supervisor for some assistance on how best to approach the student athlete. The RA talks openly to the student about their concerns and encourages the student to be aware that their behavior is likely putting them at risk for future eating disorder problems. The RA offers a referral to counseling and offers to go with the student to the first session if needed.

## EATING DISORDERS #40

A student comes to their RA to talk about some recent weight they have gained since being on campus. The student says "I can't believe I've gained 25 pounds since I've been here. I have to change this now!" The student does appear slightly overweight, but nothing too extreme. The student is upset and feels overwhelmed.

### 0-Point Response

The RA offers the student some advice on how to do a quick diet to lose some weight fast. The RA helps the student stay on their diet over the next few weeks in order to drop the weight they gained. The RA also is firm and yells at the student any time they see them eating unhealthy foods or getting off track.

### 1-Point Response

The RA tells the student that there isn't anything wrong and that they are probably worried for nothing. The RA encourages the student to "like themselves for who they are" and that they shouldn't be so concerned with their weight and physical appearance.

### 2-Point Response

The RA listens to the student's concerns and talks with them openly about how to work on exercising more and eating healthier. The RA offers to connect the student with a trainer from the campus gym, a nutritionist from health services, and a counselor to help them stay on track.

## AGGRESSION AND VIOLENCE #41

An RA comes across two roommates arguing over a PS3 video game they are playing. One student stands up, throws the controller on the ground, and yells, "This is over. I'm going to kill you for that. What are you thinking!?!" The roommate looks down and the other student continues to yell, "Well! Stand up. I'm going to finish you for doing that!" The students have been in frequent arguments throughout the semester, but this one seems much more intense. The RA steps inside the room.

### 0-Point Response

The RA tells both students to "take it outside" if they are going to have a fight. The RA is clear that there is no fighting in the residence halls and if the roommates can't work out their problems, then they need to take it somewhere else.

## 1-Point Response

The RA backs slowly out of the room and calls campus safety and their RD for backup. The RA then tries to calm the students down until the police arrive and the RA lets the police handle the potentially violent situation.

## 2-Point Response

The RA tries to calm down the students by asking to talk to one of them in the hallway alone. The RA explains that the roommates can't have these kinds of arguments in the hall and if things continue, they may be jeopardizing their ability to live in the hall. The RA reports the case to their RD supervisor and calls campus safety if they feel at risk.

## AGGRESSION AND VIOLENCE #42

A group of students seems to take pleasure out of mercilessly teasing another student on the hall. The students pick on the other student, making fun of their clothes, physical appearance, and amount of time the student spends studying. The teasing gets so bad that the student often locks themselves in their room to calm down.

## 0-Point Response

The RA talks to the student who is being teased and encourages them to be assertive in arguing back with the students who are teasing them. The RA encourages the student to file a conduct report if the teasing continues. The RA keeps an eye on the situation.

## 1-Point Response

The RA talks to the group of students and reprimands them for teasing the student. The RA is firm, but caring about how they approach the confrontation. The RA gets the other students to agree to stop teasing the student for being different. The RA continues to monitor the situation.

## 2-Point Response

The RA talks directly to the student who is being teased to support them. The RA discusses their options (filing a conduct report, having a hall meeting to discuss respectful behavior, and meeting with the RD). The RA assures the student that they are concerned about the teasing and brainstorms ways to address the behavior on the floor. The RA continues to consult with their RD about the case.

## AGGRESSION AND VIOLENCE #43

A student is known for collecting pictures of weapons and strange, militaristic knives. The student has had several knives confiscated by campus safety (the larger swords that violated the conduct code), but still has several weapons in their room. They talk casually about recent school shootings and, while they never make any direct threats, convey to others that they admire the shooters for taking the initiative to follow through on their beliefs.

### 0-Point Response

The RA confronts the situation with the student and expresses their concerns about the weapons and talk about the school shootings. The RA looks for any violation that would require the student to meet with the conduct officer. The RA makes their frustration about the student's behavior clearly known.

### 1-Point Response

The RA keeps a careful eye on the situation and reports any additional concerning behavior to campus safety and their RD. The RA realizes the student isn't breaking any campus rules right now but they need to stay vigilant in case this changes. The RA also talks to other students to better assess any other danger or potential threats.

### 2-Point Response

The RA forms a connection with the student and finds ways to seek common ground and a relationship. The RA talks to the student with respect and shares that all the talk about weapons and school shooters makes the RA uneasy. The RA keeps the RD informed of any policy violations and suggests the case be reviewed by the campus BIT.

## AGGRESSION AND VIOLENCE #44

One student has been dating another student for several months and the two of them have been getting into very loud arguments and occasional physical shoving fights late in the evening. The RA has talked to the student who lives in the hall about their behavior and told them that if the fights keep occurring the RA will call campus safety. Another loud fight erupts in their room behind a closed door.

## 0-Point Response

The RA bangs on the door and yells at both of them, "I told you two to knock this off!" The RA has a strict and firm stance, telling the students "to stop this right now or the next person you will be talking to will be the campus police!"

## 1-Point Response

The RA keeps their promise and immediately calls campus safety. The RA shares with the officer that these two students often get involved in these kinds of fights and that this one seems to be escalating. The RA calls their RD to let them know what is going on and seek additional guidance.

## 2-Point Response

The RA knocks on the door and attempts to calm the situation down between the students, reminding them that if they can't calm down the campus police will be called. The RA calls the campus police if needed and makes the RD aware of the situation. The RA documents the argument in an incident report.

## AGGRESSION AND VIOLENCE #45

An RA has been watching a student get into increasingly disturbing arguments with some student athletes who live at the other end of the hallway. The student in question often challenges the athletes about leaving their equipment in the hallway, tells them "you are all just a waste of space... why don't you study instead of throwing a ball around campus?" The athletes have little tolerance for the student and often yell back. The student mumbles to themselves one night when leaving the public bathroom "they are going to get what's coming to them... just wait."

## 0-Point Response

The RA confronts the student directly and tells them that these kinds of statements are exactly the kind that campus shooters make before going on a rampage. The RA says, "You either need to get to counseling to deal with your anger problems or find another way to stop saying threatening things like this."

## 1-Point Response

The RA reports the student's behavior to their supervising RD and then calls campus safety to report the threat. The RA knows they need to take any threats like this seriously and that reporting threats like these—even if they are unsure of their seriousness—is essential to keep the campus safe.

## 2-Point Response

The RA talks to the student. The RA brainstorms with the student ways to make the situation better (e.g., the RA talking to the athletes about their equipment in the hallway.) The RA shares with the RD and lets them make a decision about passing this on to campus safety and/or the BIT.

# Reality Therapy
# WDEP Worksheet

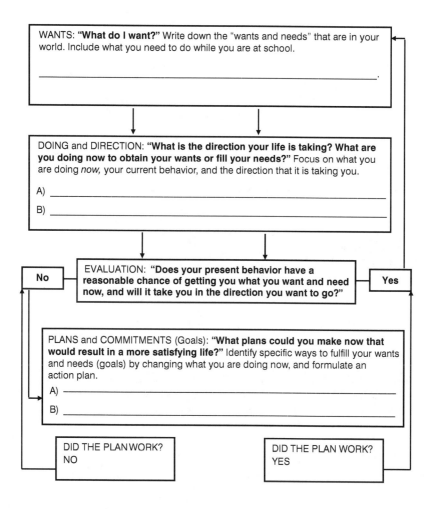

WANTS: **"What do I want?"** Write down the "wants and needs" that are in your world. Include what you need to do while you are at school.

_____ .

DOING and DIRECTION: **"What is the direction your life is taking? What are you doing now to obtain your wants or fill your needs?"** Focus on what you are doing *now,* your current behavior, and the direction that it is taking you.

A) _____

B) _____

**No**

EVALUATION: **"Does your present behavior have a reasonable chance of getting you what you want and need now, and will it take you in the direction you want to go?"**

**Yes**

PLANS and COMMITMENTS (Goals): **"What plans could you make now that would result in a more satisfying life?"** Identify specific ways to fulfill your wants and needs (goals) by changing what you are doing now, and formulate an action plan.

A) _____

B) _____

DID THE PLAN WORK?
NO

DID THE PLAN WORK?
YES

Goals: S-Simple, A-Attainable, M-Measurable, I-Immediate, C-Consistent, C-Controlled by the Client, committed to by the Client, T-Timely. (Francis & Van Brunt, 2010; Glasser, 1975; 2001).

# References

Albrecht, S. (2010). Threat assessment teams: Workplace and school violence prevention. *FBI Law Enforcement Bulletin, 21*, 15–21.

Alvarez, S. & Schneider, J. (2008). One college campus's need for a safe zone: A case study. *Journal of Gender Studies, 17*(1), 71–74.

Ancis, J. R., Sedlacek, W. E., & Mohr, J. J. (2000). Student perceptions of campus cultural climate by race. *Journal of Counseling and Development, 78*, 180–185.

ASME-ITI. (2010). *A risk analysis standard for natural and man-made hazards to higher education institutions.* Washington, D.C.: Association Society of Mechanical Engineers (ASME) Innovative Technologies Institute (ITI).

Association for University and College Counseling Center Directors (2016). *Survey of counseling center directors.* Retrieved from www.aucccd.org/assets/documents/aucccd%202016%20monograph%20-%20public.pdf

Banks-Santilli, L. (2015, June 3). Guilt is one of the biggest struggles first-generation college students face. *The Washington Post.* Retrieved from www.washingtonpost.com/posteverything/wp/2015/06/03/guilt-is-one-of-the-biggest-struggles-first-generation-college-students-face/

Barker, E. (2014, May 13). Building rapport with anyone. *Time.* Retrieved from http://time.com/98473/top-10-fbi-behavioral-unit-techniques-for-building-rapport-with-anyone/

Ben-Ari, A. (1998). An experimental attitude change: Social work students and homosexuality. *Journal of Homosexuality, 36*, 59–71.

Blair, C. (2008). Better test performance the Navy SEALs way. Retrieved from http://studyprof.com/blog/2008/11/25/better-test-performance-the-navy-seals-way/

Byrnes, J. (2002). *Before conflict: Preventing aggressive behavior.* Lanham, MD: Scarecrow Education.

Chao, R. & Good, G. (2004). Nontraditional students' perspectives on college education: A qualitative study. *Journal of College Counseling, 7*, 5–12.

Chickering, A. W. & Reisser, L. (1993). *Education and identity* (2nd ed.). San Francisco, CA: Jossey-Bass.

Chonody, J., Rutledge, S., & Siebert, D. (2009). College student's attitudes toward gays and lesbians. *Journal of Social Work Education, 45*(3), 499–512.

Crain, W. (1985). *Theories of development.* New York: Prentice-Hall.

Csíkszentmihályi, M. (1990). *Flow: The psychology of optimal experience.* New York: Harper & Row.

Deisinger, G., Randazzo, M., O'Neill, D., & Savage, J. (2008). *The handbook of campus threat assessment and management teams.* Stoneham, MA: Applied Risk Management, LLC.

Dill, P. & Henley, T. (1998). Stressor of college: A comparison of traditional and nontraditional. *Journal of Psychology, 132*, 25–32.

Drysdale, D., Modzeleski, W., & Simons, A. (2010). *Campus attacks: Targeted violence affecting institutions of higher education.* Washington, D.C.: United States Secret Service, United States Department of Education and Federal Bureau of Investigation.

Dweck, C. S. (2010, September). Even geniuses work hard. *Educational Leadership, 68*(1), 16–20.

Eells, G. & Rockland-Miller, H. (2011). Assessing and responding to disturbed and disturbing students: Understanding the role of administrative teams in institutions of Higher Education. *Journal of College Student Psychotherapy, 25*(1), 8–23.

Ellis, A. (2007). *The practice of rational emotive behavior therapy.* New York: W. W. Norton.

Emmons, R. A. & Crumpler, C. A. (2000). Gratitude as a human strength: Appraising the evidence. *Journal of Social & Clinical Psychology, 19*, 56–69.

Figley, C. R. (Ed.) (1995). *Compassion fatigue: Secondary traumatic stress.* New York: Brunner/Mazel.

Francis, P. & Van Brunt, B. (2010). Classroom management 102: Working with difficult students. *Magna Communications Online Training.* Retrieved from www.magnapubs.com/online-seminars/ classroom-management-102-working-with-difficult-students-3030-1.html

Fry, R. (2015). Millennials surpass Gen Xers as the largest generation in U.S. labor force. *Fact Tank: News in the Numbers. Pew Research Center.* Retrieved from www.pewresearch.org/fact-tank/2015/05/11/millennials-surpass-gen-xers-as-the-largest-generation-in-u-s-labor-force

Gearon, C. (2008). Back to school days for adults. *US News and World Report, 144*(10), 46–48.

Glasser, W. (1975). *Reality Therapy: A new approach to psychiatry.* New York: Colophon Books.

Glasser, W. (2001). *Counseling with choice theory: The new Reality Therapy.* New York: HarperCollins.

Gossett, B., Cuyjet, M., & Cockriel, I. (1998). African Americans' perception of marginality in the campus culture. *College Student Journal, 32*, 22–32.

Greenhaus, J. & Beutell, N. (1985). Sources of conflict between work and family roles. *Academy of Management Review, 10*, 76–88.

Grossman, D. & Siddle, B. (1999). Psychological Effects of Combat. In L. Curtis & J. Turpin (Eds.), *Academic Press Encyclopedia of Violence, Peace, and Conflict* (pp. 144–145). San Diego, CA: Academic Press.

Haidt, J. (2000). The positive emotion of elevation. *Prevention & Treatment, 3*(1), 3c.

Haiken, M. (2013). Suicide rate among vets and active duty military jumps – now 22 a day. Retrieved from www.forbes.com/sites/melaniehaiken/2013/02/05/22-the-number-of-veterans-who-now-commit-suicide-every-day/

Hart, A. (1995). *Adrenaline and stress, the exciting new breakthrough that helps you overcome stress damage.* Nashville, TN: Thomas Nelson Publishers.

Heggins W. & Jackson J. (2003). Understanding the collegiate experience for Asian international students at a Midwestern research university. *College Student Journal, 237*, 379–391.

Howard, P. (1999). *The owner's manual for the brain: Everyday applications from mind-brain research* (2nd ed.). Austin, TX: Bard Press.

Hyun, J., Quinn, B., Madon, T., & Lustig, S. (2007). Mental health need, awareness, and use of counseling services among international graduate students. *Journal of American College Health, 56*(2), 109–118.

Keith, P. (2007). Barriers and nontraditional students' use of academic and social services. *Journal of College Student Development, 41*(4), 1123–1127.

Kohlberg, L. (1973). The claim to moral adequacy of a highest stage of moral judgment. *Journal of Philosophy, 70*(18), 630–646.

Kohler-Giancola, J., Grawitch, M., & Borchert, D. (2009). Dealing with the stress of college: A model for adult students. *Adult Education Quarterly, 59*(3), 246–263.

**253**

Laur, D. (2002). The anatomy of fear and how it relates to survival skills training, integrated street combatives. Retrieved from www.personalprotectionsystems.ca/books/articles/the_anatomy_of_fear.pdf

Lopez, Shane J. (2014). *Making hope happen: Create the future you want for yourself and others*. New York: Simon & Schuster.

Luck, L., Jackson, D., & Usher, K. (2007). STAMP. Components of observable behaviour that indicate potential for patient violence in emergency departments. *Journal of Advanced Nursing, 59*(1), 11–19.

Meloy, J. R. (2000). *Violence risk and threat assessment: A practical guide for mental health and criminal justice professionals*. San Diego, CA: Specialized Training Services.

Meloy, J. R. (2006). The empirical basis and forensic application of affective and predatory violence. *Australian and New Zealand Journal of Psychiatry, 40*, 539–547.

Meloy, J. R., Hoffmann, J., Guldimann, A., & James, D. (2011). The role of warning behaviors in threat assessment: An exploration and suggested typology. *Behavioral Sciences and the Law, 30*(3), 256–279, doi: 10.1002/bsl.999

Meloy, J. R. & O'Toole, M. E. (2011). The concept of leakage in threat assessment. *Behavioral Sciences and the Law, 29*(4), 513–27, doi: 10.1002/bsl.986.

Meloy, J. R., Hart, S., & Hoffmann, J. (2014). Threat assessment and management. In J. R. Meloy & J. Hoffmann (Eds.), *The international handbook of threat assessment* (pp. 3–17). New York: Oxford University Press.

Meloy, J. R. & Mohandie, K. (2014). Assessing threats by direct interview of the violent true believer. In J. R. Meloy & J. Hoffmann (Eds.), *The international handbook of threat assessment* (pp. 388–398). New York: Oxford University Press.

Miller, W. & Rollnick, S. (2002). *Motivational interviewing: Preparing people for change* (2nd ed.). New York: The Guilford Press.

Nay, R. (2004). *Taking Charge of Anger.* New York: The Guilford Press.

O'Toole, M. E. (2000). *The school shooter: A threat assessment perspective*. Quantico, VA: National Center for the Analysis of Violent Crime, Federal Bureau of Investigation.

O'Toole, M. E. & Bowman, A. (2011). *Dangerous instincts: How gut feelings betray*. New York: Hudson Street Press.

Office of Violence Against Women (2013). Building cultures of care: A guide for sexual assault services and programs. *United States Department of Justice.* Retrieved from www.nsvrc.org/sites/default/files/publications_nsvrc_guides_building-cultures-of-care.pdf

Poyrazli, S. & Lopez, M. (2007). An exploratory study of perceived discrimination and homesickness: A comparison of international students and American students. *Journal of Psychology, 14*(3), 263–280.

Prochaska, J., Norcross, J., & DiClemente, C. (1994). *Changing for good*. New York: Harper Collins.

Rai, G. (2002). Meeting the educational needs of international students. *Journal of International Social Work, 45*, 21–33.

Randazzo, M. & Plummer, E. (2009). Implementing behavioral threat assessment on campus. Virginia Polytechnic Institute and State University. White paper. Retrieved from http://rems.ed.gov/docs/VT_ThreatAssessment09.pdf

Robinson, M. (2013). Chickering's seven vectors of identity development. Retrieved from https://studentdevelopmenttheory.wordpress.com/chickerings-seven-vectors/

Rothstein, W. & Rajapaksa, S. (2004). Health beliefs of college students born in the United States, China, and India. *Journal of American College Health, 51*, 189–194.

Sanford, N. (1966). *Self and society*. New York: Atherton Press.

Schafer, J. (2015). *The like switch: An ex-FBI agent's guide to influencing, attracting, and winning people over*. New York: Simon and Schuster.

Seemiller, C. & Grace, M. (2016). *Generation Z goes to college*. San Francisco, CA: Jossey-Bass.

Seligman, M. E. (2006). *Learned optimism: How to change your mind and your life*. New York: Vintage.

Selye H. (1936). A syndrome produced by diverse nocuous agents. *Nature, 138*(3479, July 4), 32.

Smith, A. A. (2015, November 10). Who's in first (generation)? *Inside Higher Ed*. Retrieved from www.insidehighered.com/news/2015/11/10/who-are-first-generation-students-and-how-do-they-fare

Strauss, W. & Howe, N. (1997). *The fourth turning: An American prophesy*. New York: Broadway Books.

Strauss, W. & Howe, N. (2003). *Millennials go to college*. Washington, D.C.: American Association of Collegiate Registrars and Admissions Officers.

Stringer, E. (1999). *Action research*. Thousand Oaks, CA: Sage.

Sue, D. (2010). *Microaggressions in everyday life: Race, gender, and sexual orientation*. Hoboken, NJ: John Wiley & Sons.

Toossi, M. (2012). Employment outlook: 2010–2020. *Bureau of Labor Statistics*. Retrieved from www.bls.gov/opub/mlr/2012/01/art3full.pdf

Tseng, W. & Newton, F. (2002). International students' strategies for well-being. *College Student Journal, 36*, 591–597.

Turner, J. & Gelles, M. (2003). *Threat assessment: A risk management approach*. New York: Routledge.

United States Postal Service. (2015). Threat assessment team guide. Retrieved from www.nalc.org/workplace-issues/resources/manuals/pub108.pdf

Van Brunt, B. (2012). *Ending campus violence: New approaches to prevention*. New York: Routledge.

Van Brunt, B. & Lewis, W. (2014). *A faculty guide to disruptive and dangerous behavior in the classroom*. New York: Routledge.

Van Brunt, B. & Langman, P. (2016). Website and social media search terms. *The Journal of Campus Behavioral Intervention, 4*, 46–48.

Vossekuil, B., Fein, R., Reddy, M., Borum, R., & Modzeleski, W. (2002). The final report and findings of the safe school initiative: Implications for the prevention of school attacks in the United States. Retrieved from www2.ed.gov/admins/lead/safety/preventingattacksreport.pdf

Wallis, D. (2012). Coming home from war to hit the books. *New York Times*. Retrieved from www.nytimes.com/2012/03/01/education/soldiers-come-home-to-hit-the-books.html

Woodford, M., Howell, M., Silverschanz, P., & Yu, L. (2012). "That's so gay!": Examining the covariates of hearing this expression among gay, lesbian and bisexual college students. *Journal of College Health, 60*(6), 429–434.

# Index

Page numbers followed by *n* indicate note numbers.

**259**